AF361569

A HERMENEUTICS OF VIOLENCE

A Four-Dimensional Conception

A Hermeneutics of Violence

A Four-Dimensional Conception

MARK M. AYYASH

UNIVERSITY OF TORONTO PRESS
Toronto Buffalo London

© University of Toronto Press 2019
Toronto Buffalo London
utorontopress.com
Printed in Canada

ISBN 978-1-4875-0586-8

∞ Printed on acid-free, 100% post-consumer recycled paper with vegetable-based inks.

Library and Archives Canada Cataloguing in Publication

Title: A hermeneutics of violence : a four-dimensional conception / Mark M.
   Ayyash.
Names: Ayyash, Mark Muhannad, author.
Description: Includes bibliographical references and index.
Identifiers: Canadiana 20190134542 | ISBN 9781487505868 (hardcover)
Subjects: LCSH: Violence—Political aspects.
Classification: LCC HM1116 .A98 2019 | DDC 303.6—dc23

This book has been published with the help of a grant from the Federation
for the Humanities and Social Sciences, through the Awards to Scholarly
Publications Program, using funds provided by the Social Sciences and
Humanities Research Council of Canada.

University of Toronto Press acknowledges the financial assistance to its
publishing program of the Canada Council for the Arts and the Ontario Arts
Council, an agency of the Government of Ontario.

Funded by the Financé par le
Government gouvernement
of Canada du Canada | Canadä

Contents

Acknowledgments

Writing this book was a very long journey. It began with an article I published in 2010 about "violent dialogue" in Palestine/Israel, followed by a substantial development, elaboration, and refinement of my arguments in this book. There are many obstacles to writing a book: time, resources, a scholarly field's receptivity to one's ideas, and so on. But as countless others have indicated before me, *doubt* is the book author's most formidable nemesis. Throughout the writing process, the force of doubt was ever present. I managed to keep it in the background for the most part, but when it came to the fore, there was little I could do beyond taking some time off from the manuscript, gathering myself, building up my defences, and then re-engaging with the material once more, until doubt came back to the fore, and on it went. Doubt can be made to retreat, but it never leaves once and for all. My greatest inspiration for moving forward in the face of doubt was the prospect of "doing something" about the suffering endured by so many people around the world, but especially in Palestine/Israel. It was the prospect of shedding new light on the problem of political violence that inspired me to carry on. I don't know how much new light this book has managed to shed, and most troubling for me, I'm not sure that it will make even a very small difference for those who suffer political violence. But I simply felt that it was my duty to try to write something meaningful and impactful. And if and when this particular effort fails, I will simply continue to carry on with my duty to try to do something.

Going back to the beginning of this journey, I wish to thank Dr. Brian Singer, as well as Dr. Michael Nijhawan and Dr. Radhika Mongia, for their many comments, questions, and criticisms. Without their careful and thorough reading of many drafts, and their critical and constructive dialogue, the initial foray into the subject matter would not have been possible. I also wish to thank Dr. David Mutimer, Dr. Olivier Clain,

Dr. Malcolm Blincow, and Dr. Ratiba Hadj-Moussa for their insightful and engaging discussions, questions, and suggestions over my years of study at York University. Thanks also to Dr. Shane Gannon for reading through a draft of the book manuscript and offering his comments and questions. Finally, without the input, criticisms, and comments of the three UTP reviewers, this work would've been lacking in important ways. Thank you for your constructive critiques. I am thankful to Douglas Hildebrand, Jodi Lewchuk, Breanna Muir, and Leah Connor for their professionalism, patience, and support for the book throughout the review and production process. Finally, I wish to thank Rebecca Russell for her excellent copyediting and careful reading of the manuscript, and Jonathan Adjemian for his excellent work in proofreading and indexing the book. Whatever mistakes remain in this book are of course my own.

The writing of some of the initial material was supported by the Social Sciences and Humanities Research Council of Canada. This book has been published with the help of a grant from the Federation for the Humanities and Social Sciences, through the Awards to Scholarly Publications Program, using funds provided by the Social Sciences and Humanities Research Council of Canada. Funding support for the indexing of the book was provided by the Internal Research Grant Fund, Office of Research, Scholarship and Community Engagement, Mount Royal University.

Finally, and most of all, I wish to thank my grandmother, Nafisa, my brothers, Mike and Matt, and my parents in particular for their endless support. My mother, Samia, you taught me how to learn. My father, Said, you taught me how to see things beyond their simple appearances. Ultimately, I can never know all of what you have all taught me.

A HERMENEUTICS OF VIOLENCE

A Four-Dimensional Conception

Introduction

During the late morning of 8 October 1990, we heard the bell ring midway through our lesson. There was a collective, almost palatable, feeling that this was not a prank or an accidental ringing of the bell, but a sign that something was wrong. Our feelings of concern and unease were soon confirmed by the rushed words of the school's principal to our teacher ordering him to evacuate us quickly but in an orderly fashion. Even at our young age, we were aware of the increasing tensions surrounding the planned visit of an extremist Jewish group to Haram al-Sharif, which the Israelis called the Temple Mount. The unusual ringing of the bell, we intuitively knew, was related to this tension. And we were right. The whole school, which was located just inside the walls of the Old City, was evacuated. Outside of the New Gate, in a large concourse, we all gathered and waited. Some waited for their parents, others waited for further instructions from our teachers; some formed small groups to walk home, while some of the older students began to form a large group that would heed the calls of the Palestinian resistance movements and march down to defend Haram al-Sharif. But for most, fear about the uncertainty of the situation became mixed with the joy of not having to go to school for the rest of the day – after all, we were kids who enjoyed playing with each other free of the constraints of schoolwork! And soon enough, the normalcy of play inserted normality into the situation we were in, and we almost forgot why we were thrust out of our classrooms so suddenly in the first place. We carried on with our play until the moment came – one that I remember as if it happened yesterday. I can still sense, feel, and see it. Everyone, simultaneously, began screaming and running down the hill and away from the New Gate. I didn't run. I am not sure why. I know it wasn't bravery – despite what everyone said after the event, it most certainly was not bravery or courage. I was simply frozen in my place, the only student left in the concourse, standing just a few short feet away from the actors who descended on the scene. To my left, coming from inside the New Gate, were a handful of young Palestinian men, masked with keffiyehs, holding rocks and slingshots in their hands. To my right, coming from the main road that led up to West Jerusalem, were a handful of Israeli forces, also young men, "masked" in their own sort of way with uniforms, armed with guns. The two sides stared at each other for what felt to me as an eternity. They were sizing up one another. Not one of them looked at me, or perhaps they did, but I did not notice because I was absolutely fixated on the tension I saw and felt between them. It was in the air, it was as present as anything could be present, yet it was not really visible. Regardless, I was caught in its mix, and I could not move. It was a thing I could not exactly see, certainly was unable to express, and it was obvious to me from the very first moment that I would never fully know or understand it. The next thing I remember is my father's arm yanking me out of the scene to the safety of the car that took me far away from the violent events that unfolded that day, both at the New Gate but to a much greater extent at Haram al-Sharif itself, where twenty-one Palestinians were killed and many, including students from my school, were injured.

For weeks after the event, I became somewhat of a known personality with my fellow students and teachers. The narrative that took hold told a story of a brave eleven-year-old who stood strong while others ran. Everyone had this idea that I was willing and ready to face armed Israeli forces with my frail, unarmed, and not yet developed body. My teachers, parents, and school principal were all worried sick that I would become a resistance fighter, or worse, a martyr. They all sat me down, explained to me that the best path for struggle went through education, not through violence. I found all of this amusing – what eleven-year-old wouldn't like this kind of attention! But I knew and never lost sight of the fact that all of this talk about my bravery was hollow and mistaken. I had no such courage and certainly did not in any way intend or even wish to partake in the terrifying fighting. It is perhaps true that most of us, myself included, had been "hardened" by years of witnessing and living with violence – the Intifada, after all, had been raging for almost three years by then – but I was as terrified as everyone, perhaps even more so. Alas, I was unable to articulate to anyone why it was that I stood still, because I did not even know. So I played along with their narrative and assured them that from that day on, I would focus only on my studies and nothing else.

I don't know if I'm better placed today to answer the question of why I stood still. The best I can do is to suggest that it was perhaps the mysteriousness of violence that captured me in its grip in that moment. And from that moment on, I have been trying to better understand that very mysteriousness, knowing full well that I'll never be able to capture violence as it is, in its full and fixed totality. This work is an extension of that eleven-year-old's encounter with violence. And I can say that, just like then, this work is not driven by courage, but rather by a fixated gaze at something terrifying – a thing that is beyond the ability of the gaze to capture.

The concern of this book is "political violence," but to define violence from the outset is an exercise in futility. The multifaceted use of this concept within the social sciences makes it virtually impossible to establish a definition that can hold its ground by the end of the inquiry. This is especially the case with the increasing necessity and tendency in academia to examine violence through an interdisciplinary mode of inquiry. Though there are attempts to delimit violence in fields such as the sociology of violence, (e.g., Collins, 2008; Walby, 2012) the anthropology of violence, (e.g., Krohn-Hansen, 1997; Schmidt & Schröder, 2001), security studies within international relations (e.g., Shapiro, 1997; Burke, 2007), or the philosophy of violence (e.g., Gallie, 1978; Bufacchi, 2007), to name some of the more prominent fields in the social sciences, the study of violence simply cannot be limited to one specialized and highly restricted field or even subfield of study (as all of the works just cited, with perhaps the exception of Bufacchi, themselves attest). This book is driven rather than discouraged by this futility. The evasiveness of a firm definition that would secure the concept of violence in one delimited space of analysis is not regarded as a failure or a shortcoming of academic study, but rather as constituting the very ground of theorizing violence. Yes, this ground will constantly shift and move, but that is precisely how an inquiry into violence ought to proceed. If there is one constant feature of violence, it is that violence is ever shifting and moving, and in order to understand this flux of violence, then the inquiry itself must accordingly shift and move.

In its fluctuation, the book develops a dialogical analytic for the study of violence that does not speak on/of/about violence, but rather "speaks with violence." By "speaking with violence," I do not suggest that the analyst ought to engage directly in violence, or to speak with blows instead of words. On the contrary, practising violence leads into a vortex where a critical gaze is impossible to reach. So by "speaking with violence," I am referring to a dialogical analytic that examines how violence is conceptualized and represented in academic discourses, and most crucially *follows violence as it escapes all of our understandings and significations of violence.* The dialogical analytic is therefore the name of an analytical movement that follows violence into the complex and hidden dimensions in and through which it eludes the collective comprehension and understanding of all who attempt to make sense of violence. Attention to the elusiveness of violence opens up a rich landscape of analysis whereby social scientists can examine the often-overlooked mimetic and transformative dimensions of violent acts. Within the dialogical analytic, violence is not the end of a discussion on an otherwise political, social, economic, or cultural story; rather, violence attains an epistemological status. Violence, as it were, speaks.

At its core, the dialogical analytic is both driven by and an outcome of a hermeneutics of violence. By "hermeneutics," I refer to a critical interpretive approach that, generally speaking, concerns the examination of the social world in accordance with its uniqueness and unpredictability, following the ways in which phenomena appear to us (whether in texts, acts, events) in order to dialogically discover what is left unsaid in what is being said (Moules, McCaffrey, Field, & Laing, 2015, pp. 61–69). A hermeneutics of any given phenomenon strives to build a new understanding of a subject matter by (re)interpreting what is already revealed about that subject matter and placing the different pieces of the puzzle within a new order of interpretation and understanding (i.e., within a hermeneutic circle). This new order will not be an absolute or fixed totality but rather a sort of loose assemblage of meanings that then invites a new set of (re)interpretations and so on (Moules et al., 2015, pp. 44, 117–135). Philosophically speaking, then, hermeneutics tends to move away from a priori concepts and analytical frameworks that claim to have access to knowledge that is superior to other forms of knowledge that make up, and inhabit, the social world (Gadamer, 2004 [1960]). *A Hermeneutics of Violence* strives to (re)interpret the already existing and vast set of meanings that have been assembled in texts on the subject matter of violence.

Of course, including all of this knowledge in one book, or giving equal interpretive attention to each text, is an impossible task. Specifically, then, I am interested in largely theoretical academic texts dealing with the subject. In the task of (re)interpretation, I am not searching for some hidden meaning of violence *behind* those texts. As Rabinow and Sullivan put it in their take on the interpretive turn in the social sciences:

> What we want to understand is not something behind the cultural object, the text, but rather something in front of it.... To understand a text is to follow its movements from sense to reference, *from what it says to what it talks about*. To understand an author better than he could understand

himself is to display the power of disclosure implied in his discourse *beyond the limited horizon of his own existential situation*. (1987, pp. 13–14; emphases added)

Similarly, though more strongly, Charles Taylor formulates the interpretive approach as such: "Our aim is to replace this confused, incomplete, partly erroneous self-interpretation by a correct one" (1985, p. 26). I do not quite follow this strong formulation, particularly in Taylor's claim that a "correct" – in the sense of "superior" (Rabinow & Sullivan, 1987, p. 8) – interpretation can replace what is erroneous, but I do agree with Taylor that a more complete interpretation is possible and worthy of our efforts. Hence my aim is to encompass various strands of theoretical interpretations of violence (what they say) into a new (more complete) theoretical framework that, without losing sight of their differences, connects these varied insights in a chase after the elusive thing called violence (what they talk about).

There are two reasons for focusing primarily on theoretical texts. The first concerns the need to (re)interpret theories of violence within a new order, or within a new hermeneutic circle. Theories of violence are numerous today, but conversations among and between these theories have been limited, especially across disciplines, which has resulted in unproductive repetition (e.g., discipline- or field-specific theorizations of "structural" or "objective" violence vs. "agentic" or "subjective" violence) and the formation of seemingly irreconcilable theoretical positions (e.g., a "realist" state-centred conception of violence vs. an everyday approach to the study of violence). *A Hermeneutics of Violence* seeks to remedy these problems by placing in dialogue various theories of violence from the disciplines of anthropology, sociology, international relations, and philosophy. This allows for a clearer view of the points that are repeated across these disciplines (which I sometimes trace in the endnotes only), but most crucially, it allows for a formation of an interpretation of violence that ties together the seemingly irreconcilable elements of our existing knowledge of this thing we call violence. I want to make clear that *A Hermeneutics of Violence* is not concerned with flattening differences and creating seamless totalities, but rather with (re)interpreting some of the *seemingly* irreconcilable elements, to show how such elements can indeed reconcile while remaining distinct, in order to highlight what are *actually* irreconcilable elements in our understanding of violence, which largely centre around the question of violence's knowability. The new (re)interpretation of violence advanced in this book is a four-dimensional view of violence that ties together what are usually viewed as irreconcilable theoretical positions, which I take up in each of the four dimensions. Far from irreconcilable, these positions, when placed within a four-dimensional outlook, open up new avenues for the study of particular cases of violence.

This brings up the second reason for focusing on theoretical texts as opposed to specific case studies. Even though I examine academic representations of the Palestinian–Israeli struggle in the last chapter, that examination will be primarily undertaken so as to further elucidate the theoretical arguments of the book. Having said that, this entire project indeed arises out of my study of the case of the Palestinian–Israeli struggle (Ayyash, 2010a). It was through my interpretive analysis of texts in that struggle that I first made the case for the operation of a dynamic called "violent dialogue" – the question-answer exchange between protagonists in and through violent acts. While that study made apparent what was unsaid (violent dialogue) in what was being said (texts that proclaimed violence), I was not able to further develop the theoretical implications of this dynamic while being ensconced in the particularities of the case. Too many questions were left unanswered, and some of the features of violence – for example, the formation of postures of incommensurability – were left underdeveloped or undeveloped. It became clear to me that there had to be a theoretical elaboration of the dynamic of violent dialogue that would properly place it among the other dynamics and features of violence, and that this would be possible only through an engagement with theoretical texts that have gained penetrating insights into the subject matter of violence. Thus, the impetus behind this theoretical project is indeed the perplexing and of course tragic and devastating case of the Israeli–Palestinian struggle, which is also why I come back to it in the last chapter of the book. It is my hope that this theoretical exegesis into violence will lead to a better understanding of violence in that case and others like it. The predominance of the Palestinian–Israeli case in my thinking also means that the book is primarily speaking to questions and concerns associated with the modern nation state and the settler-colonial context (i.e., the violent sorting of peoples and lands within bounded socio-politico-juridical entities). Much of the following analysis will thus deal with twentieth-century debates and theorizations of politics, society, the state, and violence that have emerged across co-constitutive colonizing and colonized spaces,[1] particularly in Europe and the Middle East. However, my hope is that the four-dimensional conception advanced in this book can help pave the way for a fresh approach to dealing with the problem of violence in a broader set of contexts, but such an examination remains beyond the limits of this study.

In addition to hermeneutics, the book's analysis is influenced by post-structuralism. While I think that hermeneutics is best suited for chasing the elusive thing we call violence – that is, while hermeneutics in its very philosophical structure operates upon the principle of understanding further what we cannot fully understand – there is also a weakness with the hermeneutic approach that should be noted here – namely, that hermeneutics tends to lose sight of the power dynamics and the political dimensions of the social world (Kögler, 1999 [1992]). The school tends to (re)interpret the social world without paying enough attention to the power dynamics that are operative within the social institutions and social relations that are being studied and analysed. This is where I think post-structuralism can be helpful, and this in fact is the main reason why readers will detect a post-structural influence in the (re)interpretation that is operative in this book. The school of post-structuralism, particularly the work of Jacques Derrida, highlights that language is more than just a transmitter of meaning (Derrida, 1973 [1967], 1988 [1972]). The kind of language that we use in describing something does not simply convey the thing as it is; rather, the language that we use will constitute that which is being studied in particular ways and produce specific effects on the very thing we are supposedly simply trying to understand. I develop these Derridean points later in the book since they directly apply to the structure of the dialogical analytic and of four-dimensional violence, but suffice it to say for now that post-structuralism brings to our awareness not only the fact that language is powerful and that it has important and significant effects, but also the idea that language is not neutral (i.e., that language is always political) and that the meanings that are circulated within our language cannot be fixed and controlled by our various attempts to do so. Both hermeneutics and post-structuralism encourage us to examine the ways in which academic knowledge does not simply (re)interpret the social world from a neutral perspective that is supposedly outside of this world; but unlike hermeneutics, post-structuralism also asserts, along with postcolonialism (e.g., Said, 2003 [1979]) and feminism (e.g., Smith, 1990), that academic knowledge in many ways *produces the very social world that it is studying*. This brings to the forefront of the book's analysis the moral, ethical, and political dimensions of social analysis, as well as, in a Foucauldian vein (Foucault, 1980), the power dynamics that are operative in the production of knowledge and the kinds of power that the production of knowledge makes possible and/or constitutes. This will be especially crucial to this project since its engagement with theoretical texts does not mean that it does not speak to the "real" world or to specific cases and events. The theories I am dealing with all resonate with different versions of political and social discourses surrounding the subject matter of violence – in fact, they do more than resonate in many cases, as they indeed shape how violence is understood or mystified, legitimized or delegitimized, justified or opposed, performed or resisted, supported or confronted, and everything in-between.

Throughout this project, I have done my best to combine these lessons and insights that these schools of thought offer. Following Hans Herbert Kögler's (1999 [1992]) fusion of Foucauldian insights into Gadamerian philosophical hermeneutics, I understand the dialogical character of interpretation, or a "critical hermeneutics," to encompass both an interpretive chase after the "truth" of the subject matter – the concealment and un-concealment of the subject matter and not the uncovering of a totalized fixed "truth" – as well as a critical attention to the operation of power dynamics, mechanisms, systems, and relations in discursive formations, without reducing one to the other (Kögler, 1999 [1992], pp. 1–7, 167). In a critical dialogue, the interpreter is constantly making explicit their own preunderstandings, which are the conditions of our understanding that we cannot do without and include life history/experience, the symbolic order through which we understand the world, and social power practices that limit how/what we can understand. Through a reciprocal dialogue that also makes explicit the preunderstandings of the social agents in question, we find the critical hermeneutic effort to produce new and critical concepts that can move beyond the previously implicit structures of our collective preunderstandings, creating new horizons of interpretation in the process, which can then be further dialogically interrogated and so on (Kögler, 1999, pp. 83–85, 91–93, 98–107, 171–172, 212–213). Hence, there is no endpoint or a final resting place where we reach the full "truth" of a subject matter. This is why the book is titled "*A* Hermeneutics of Violence" and not "*The* Hermeneutics of Violence." I do not claim that this book's critical hermeneutic effort provides or produces the final word on the (re)interpretation of violence but rather that it offers one possible direction that, even though I assert is useful for the study of violence and offers a more complete interpretation of violence, does not on that account close off other possible directions of (re)interpretation, and that indeed, as will become obvious later in the book, invites such acts of further (re)interpretation in its four-dimensional outlook.

In practical terms, then, whether I am dealing with one specific text from an author's oeuvre without paying much attention to that author's other writings (as I do in chapter 1, for example), or whether I am deeply engaging with a number of texts from the same author as well as other texts that this author builds their work upon (as I do in chapter 2, for example), I have striven, sometimes explicitly and sometimes implicitly, to (a) understand the knowledge that social actors create and produce about the subject matter of violence from their own point of view (and needless to say, I consider scholars as social actors) and (b) (re)interpret this knowledge in a manner that is attentive to the ways in which this knowledge constitutes its object of study as "violence," limiting in the process what can and cannot be said about it. Both of these guidelines move hand in hand throughout the analysis, creating a dialogical movement that asks certain questions of the works analysed in such a way as to not dismiss them, but to open up an interpretive space through and into which the analysis can move. In this analytical movement, *A Hermeneutics of Violence* both develops and employs a dialogical analytic in its reading of theoretical texts on violence. The dialogical analytic therefore can apply to specific case studies in the same way that it is employed in this book (I will come back to this in chapter 5 and the conclusion), but to be clear, it is primarily employed in this book to develop a theoretical framework for understanding violence.

In its employment, the dialogical analytic reveals a four-dimensional view of violence that illuminates the complex operation of violence in society. I prefer using "dimensions of violence" as opposed to, for example, "types of violence" or "kinds of violence" because I want to underscore that the different viewpoints into violence analysed in this book do not constitute different species of violence that reside or even operate at different vertical levels or separate horizontal plains; rather, they constitute different dimensions of the same phenomenon (this four-dimensional viewpoint into the phenomenon of violence is similar *only* in the sense of the simultaneous operation of different dimensions to the way science understands the four dimensions of space-time). Instead of positing different kinds of violence that do not necessarily speak to one another, the dimensions are interlinked and intertwined in a manner wherein they simultaneously enable and unsettle each other. I develop these ideas in chapter 4 through Derrida's work, but suffice it to say for now that four-dimensional violence does not constitute or refer to four levels of ascending abstraction, descending concreteness, or disparate (sub)species. The four dimensions will be presented in a gradual way for the sake of clarity. But in specific violent events and contexts, the four dimensions are intractably interlinked and operate simultaneously.

Conventional scholarly conceptualizations of violence predominantly operate on one-dimensional and sometimes two-dimensional views of violence. In challenging this restricted and narrow view, the book instead moves through four dimensions of violence. This movement is cumulative in the sense that each new dimension incorporates the previous dimension(s) within its analytical viewpoint and better illuminates violence. Broadly speaking, the one-dimensional view posits violence as an instrument of politics; the two-dimensional view incorporates the first and adds that violence produces complex effects long after its instrumental purposes have passed; the three-dimensional view incorporates the first two and adds that violent dialogue transforms the protagonists themselves in ways they could not foresee; the four-dimensional view of violence incorporates all of the previous dimensions and adds an explanation for the elusiveness of violence and the perpetual propagation of violence.

The arrangement of the book follows the structure of the argument and is divided into four chapters, each dedicated to one of the four dimensions. In addition, there is a fifth chapter in which I undertake a dialogical analysis of academic representations of the Israeli–Palestinian struggle to further elucidate the book's theoretical arguments. The analysis of the first two dimensions tackles academic conceptualizations of violence primarily in sociology, anthropology, and international relations. The third and fourth dimensions are derived largely from philosophical conceptualizations of violence. Once reached, the four-dimensional view of violence invites a new conversation on the problem of violence and shows that the difficulties that societies face in moving beyond violence – difficult as most commentators already believe them to be – are even more enormous than is conventionally believed or thought. An overview of the four dimensions will begin to show why the perpetual propagation of violence is such a difficult process to understand and to counter.

The first dimension of violence, explored in chapter 1, is found in the prevalent mode of explicating violent conflicts, which posits violence as fundamentally *instrumental* in nature. There is certainly some analytical validity to this approach, but it limits the conception of violence to a one-dimensional view that does not, and indeed cannot, take into account the flux of violence. Instrumental conceptualizations posit violence as that which does not need to be directly explained, and in effect, make violence inexplicable outside of a means-ends framework. Instead of delimiting violence, I argue for a "freeing" of the concept of violence, *not* in the sense of discussing the gruesome details of violence or in the sense of glorifying violence, but in the analytical sense of following the flux that is inherent to violence. The analysis shows how attempts to capture violence within fixed boundaries fail to subordinate the flux of violence. To capture violence is to think of it as residing within a delimited and fixed space from which it operates but never leaves. To free the concept of violence is to think of violence in its continuous movement. The dialogical analytic directs the inquiry onto that flux of violence by charting the movement out of the instrumentalist perspective and toward the two-dimensional view of violence.

The movement beyond the first dimension of violence does not lead into nonsense or irrationality as the instrumental viewpoint warns. Instead, it opens up a wide landscape of analysis where the relationship between violence and language, the *linguistic* dimension of violence, takes centre stage. In chapter 2, I investigate how this two-dimensional view shows that events of violence cannot be readily captured and compartmentalized within fixed or clearly defined boundaries. Rather, these violent events descend into the everyday in complex ways, maintaining an ever-elusive, yet paramount role in people's everyday lives. With this two-dimensional view, it becomes clear that violence does not end with its officially announced "end" and that violence continues to produce effects in the formations of subjectivity for the victims and survivors of violence.

Although not framed within a dimensional outlook, Veena Das's (2007) work is exemplary of such two-dimensional analyses of violence. In examining how victims and survivors of violent events form their subjectivity by living with, against, and through violence, her work asserts that the seepage of instrumental violence is restricted to a descending movement into the everyday. Any notion of an ascending movement is seen as a journey into the pure madness of inexpressible violence. However, the flux of violence cannot be divided into a descending movement that ought to be examined and an ascending movement that allegedly leads into madness and thus resists examination. A focus on the victims and survivors of violence is crucial, but it is equally important to develop an analytic that can explore the violent acts of the perpetrators, as opposed to casting them as pure moments of madness.

Despite her many strengths, Das does not guide us into that difficult dimension of supposed madness, but a movement into this third *mimetic* dimension of violence is of the utmost importance for our understanding of violence, which is the focus of chapter three. Building on Gadamer's (2004) philosophical hermeneutics, the dialogical analytic allows the analyst to become a voice of a different order in the conversation over violence by exploring what is said "over and above" those who proclaim and employ violence. Following Gadamer, the dialogical analytic accounts for the inexpressibility of violence without positing violence as radically inexplicable. Language is seen here as both bridge and barrier, in the sense that the limits we experience in language are not the end of language, but are indeed an invitation for a (re)interpretation of the subject matter in question. And in following the subject matter of violence, the dialogical analytic reveals a dynamic of violent dialogue in the third dimension of violence.

Participants in violence can never know precisely what they speak when proclaiming and employing violence. They fail to comprehend their violence, and/or their representations of violence, because they fail to understand that their violent acts create a dynamic of violent dialogue. In protracted exchanges and practices of violence, the participants have closed the question-answer exchange on the subject matters over which they fight, and thus a dialogue seems to disappear between them. However, violent dialogue, which emerges out of the violent acts, substitutes for the disappearance of this verbal dialogue precisely at the point where the latter reaches its limit. Irrespective of their intentions, the participants are engaged in a question-answer exchange in the realm of violence whereby a violent dialogue overtakes them. In doing so, the participants and their closed positions are transformed in ways they could not foresee and are indeed unaware of.

In violent dialogue, there are born certain important transformations of the protagonists' worldviews that are then carried into and indeed come to constitute the very interaction and relationship between the protagonists. Drawing on the works of René Girard (1977 [1972], 1986 [1982]) and Michael Taussig (1987, 1993) (Girard's work largely acting as a counter-conceptual apparatus), I argue that these transformations are of a mimetic character, in the sense that the sides involved in violent interaction come to resemble each other in some fundamental ways through violence. They become "enemy-siblings." Violent dialogue shows that what marks the violent interaction between the protagonists is not the end of a dialogue between the participants signalling their irreconcilability and separation; rather, we can see a peculiar kind of communion forming between the protagonists around the subject matter of violence.

The three-dimensional view of violence makes evident that the inexpressibility of violence does not reach its limit with the violent act itself; rather, violence forges a space in which the interaction between the protagonists forms, continues, and transforms. Far from moving into nonsense because it is inexpressible, violence indeed plays its most influential, impactful, and significant role precisely at the moment when it eludes us the most, which is the moment of its enactment. I argue not only that violent acts are beyond the ability of any political force to fully control, but also that rather than having the desired effect of destroying or expelling the enemy, violent acts indeed create a violent communion with the enemy. The violent acts between protagonists are not a simple continuation of the political process by other means, but they rather constitute a violent dialogue. In violent dialogue, not only are violent acts meaningful (in the sense that they constitute and communicate meanings), but they also create a violent communion between the sides. This communion is marked by postures of incommensurability that continuously produce incommensurable positions across a spectrum of time and space. On the surface, incommensurable positions *seem* to suggest a lack of a common basis between protagonists, but the assertion in this book is that the sides involved in violence do indeed share deep fundamental agreements in their hidden violent communion. Incommensurable positions, therefore, do not properly or fully explain the emergence or appearance of violence; rather, we must examine the postures of incommensurability.

The character of these postures is difficult to directly detect, which means that they cannot belong to the observable mimetic third dimension. Consequently, a yet even more elusive dimension is operative: the fourth dimension of *transcendental* violence, where I locate violence the "thing itself," which essentially concerns the very *knowability and unknowability* of violence (from this point on, I will denote this combination as "(un)knowability"). Drawing primarily on the work of Derrida (1978 [1964], 1988 [1972], 1997a [1967], 2002 [1990]), the book demonstrates how an emphasis on the (un)knowability of violence can allow the analyst to explore the elusiveness and flux of violence without falling into a mythological view or conception of violence. Violence the "thing itself" does not refer to a mystical, otherworldly, absolute creature or force (God or otherwise) that rules human affairs from a distance through violent acts and events controlled by an invisible hand. Nor does violence the "thing itself" fall into the effect of such a claim, whereby violence becomes an all-encompassing subject (as distinct from a subject matter). Rather, violence the "thing itself" is what escapes the signification of those caught in the midst of violent conflicts, events, and acts, as well as the signification of those who attempt to (re) present violence. And it reveals a complex four-dimensional violence that is operative above, underneath, and through the human hands that enact violence.

While the book ends its theoretical exegesis with a discussion of this fourth dimension, violence the "thing itself" is the very force that pulls the analysis in this direction and that direction, guiding the dialogical analytic all along, without necessarily announcing itself. There will not be a substantive discussion of violence the "thing itself" as *it is*, or, in the sense of settling the questions that violence the "thing itself" raises, once and for all. Rather, violence the "thing itself" will, in a sense, say very little in concrete or fixed terms, not because what it offers is grandiose and too abstract for the concrete (as if the concrete was ever easy and simple to understand), but because it is meant to account for how that which escapes us is not to be described and judged by its abstractness or concreteness, but is to be understood in accordance with its evasiveness. This fourth dimension is thus not the final destination of a journey into violence, nor is it the beginning. There are no beginnings or ends. There is only a four-dimensional view of violence that explains the presence and role of violence in society without ever coming to a last or final word on the matter, since this fourth dimension necessarily means that an element of violence will always be beyond our reach.

The dialogical analytic makes visible what is rendered invisible by the one- and two-dimensional views of violence. The one-dimensional view of violence compartmentalizes the political process and defends it against any encroachment from violence – this view says that violence appears as an instrument when the political positions are incommensurable and the sides incapable of reaching agreement, and that violence disappears when this instrument achieves its goals and/or an agreement is reached. The two-dimensional view of violence challenges such a neat separation between violence and politics, but then compartmentalizes the everyday and defends it from the encroachment of the madness of inexpressible violent acts – this view says that if the analyst chases this inexpressibility, then only madness and non-knowledge await. The dialogical analytic, in reaching for the third and fourth dimensions, destabilizes both forms of compartmentalization and explores the dynamic of violent dialogue and the evasiveness of violence the "thing itself." It opens up an avenue for examining postures of incommensurability, by which I mean the very disposition from which words emanate, or the disposition that gives as much meaning to the word as the word itself.

In their use of violence, the participants are indeed forging shared postures. In violence, these postures are made, remade, and communicated, formative of a communion between the seemingly separate sides as enemy-siblings, inextricably combining enemy-siblings with a simple but yet not so simple dash. A dash that is more significant than the words that lie on either side of it. This is a communion that is not very visible, never stable, and always transforming, because one of its elements is violence the "thing itself," where the (un)knowability of violence is drawn upon in so many different ways to commence, continue, and maintain a violent dialogue.

In order to better delineate the analytical space that this book is try-ing to open up for future analysis, chapter 5 engages with two promi-nent academic representations of the Israeli–Palestinian struggle. Specifically, I engage with Edward Said's critical mode of representa-tion, along with Benny Morris's objectivist/instrumentalist mode of representation, of the 1948 war in Palestine/Israel. I chose these two authors for a number of reasons, which I outline later in the book, but primarily because their works make for a difficult analysis. It would be much easier to locate the four-dimensional operation of violence in texts that promote and/or participate in violence, but my hope is that if I can show how four-dimensional violence operates in complex writ-ings that attempt to counter violence by either following through with its instrumental logic (Morris) or by challenging violence through jus-tice (Said), the overall case I am making for four-dimensional violence will be more convincing. The analysis in the chapter shows the manner in which violence the "thing itself" escapes these two representations of violence, and I begin to outline how the dynamic of violent dialogue reveals a certain kind of communion between the sides (although not specifically between the two sets of texts), which is missed by both rep-resentations, albeit differently.

I conclude that to change the bonds of violence, no political process that simply proclaims to counter violence can succeed. But this is not the debilitating dead end that it may seem at first. It is in fact an invita-tion to commence a fluid journey into a fluid thing we call violence, and the dialogical analytic is the vehicle for this journey. My hope is that peace activists, policymakers, academics, intellectuals, and anyone who is concerned about the question of violence in society will find much value in taking this journey, and my greatest hope is that in a sus-tained and collective effort, we are able to gain a deeper understanding of violence, so as to better counter postures of incommensurability and violent communions.

A Note on Terminology

Throughout the book's analyses, particularly those that involve the works of Das, Girard, Taussig, and Derrida, I will use various terms and concepts, such as "originary violence," "absolute violence," "world-annihilating violence," "founding violence," "maintaining violence," "unbound violence," and so on. These terms are not ones that I wish to include in the proposed four-dimensional conception of violence. Rather, they are terms that are integral to the theories of the authors examined, and where these terms and concepts appear, it is only in an effort to remain as fair and true as I can be to the text being analysed. For example, it is not my intent in chapter 2 to discuss Das's notion of "world-annihilating violence" for the sake of developing that concept later in the book – rather, I discuss it in order to better illuminate and understand Das's theory of violence, which is a theory that I ultimately move beyond. Thus, I do not wish for a concept of "world-annihilating violence" to be seen as a foundational concept for my own argument. This same caveat can be applied to the rest of the authors listed above (with the exception of Derrida, whose concepts I will translate into terms that are more amenable to my work – I will discuss this point later in the book). Throughout the book, I have tried to be mindful of balancing the need to continuously (re)engage with the different concepts from different authors with the need to avoid a clouding of the general direction of the analysis with countless forays into the particularity of each concept. One of the ways in which I attempted this balance is to carry out such forays in the endnotes – thus, I do not view the endnotes as afterthoughts or as marginal ideas, but rather as supplemental substantive materials that are placed in the notes so as to reduce the density of the argument in the main text.

Despite the differences between the authors analysed, however, there are two important features of violence that seem, in a general sense, to recur within their works and as such constitute a similarity that allows for a meaningful conjoining/disjoining of their different ideas. The first, which has already been mentioned, is the constant movement or flux inherent to violence. More or less, this can be found in the above works, and I will attempt to develop an inquiry that is itself in constant movement so as to properly account for this feature of violence – I refer to this as "freeing" the concept of violence. The second feature is the idea that there are two kinds of violence: one that is unknowable (often associated with words such as "absolute," "unbound," "world-annihilating," etc.) and one that is knowable (often associated with words such as "ordinary," "legitimate," "maintaining," "calculable," etc.). This feature is manifested in particular ways in the works above. Part of what I will try to accomplish through the work of Derrida, particularly in chapter 4, is to dissolve this distinction, but without losing the elements of knowability and unknowability altogether. Thus, I present a concept of violence the "thing itself," which does not approach an unknowable violence that supposedly *is* and which supposedly *is* different from a knowable violence, but rather brings to the forefront of the analysis the question of the (un)knowability of violence.

On a final note, when I use "us" or "we" in the writing, it is not in the spirit that all must agree with me or that any reasonable or logical mind would follow this line of inquiry as it is presented – I am not making universal claims or appealing to universal reason. I think that using "us" and "we" in this non-universalist manner is a feature of any writing that follows a hermeneutic path, since as I understand them, hermeneutic paths of inquiry tend to imagine a reader who is genuinely interested in following the path of inquiry taken, not for the sake of agreeing wholly with the analytical movement advanced but simply for the sake of understanding the path taken. So, uses of "we" and "us" are done in the spirit of asking the reader to join me, in whatever way, on this road of exploration I am walking on.

1 Instrumental Violence: To Capture and Fix Violence

The war started up again, and with it the long siege that destroyed the camp and the cemetery and the memories of the massacre. As with all disasters, the only thing that can make one forget a massacre is an even bigger massacre, and we're a people whose fate is to be forgotten as a result of its accumulated calamities. Massacre erases massacre, and all that remains in the memory is the smell of blood.

–Elias Khoury, Gate of the Sun

The one-dimensional view of violence conceptualizes violence as fundamentally instrumental in nature and posits it as inexplicable beyond a strictly means-ends calculus. Within this instrumentalist perspective, violence appears explicable strictly as an instrument of politics and is consequently posited as inexplicable outside of its instrumental purpose, often as chaos, a black hole, and/or nonsense (Singer, 1990, pp. 150–153). There are two major shortcomings to this approach: (1) in explicating violent acts, events, and conflicts, the instrumentalist perspective must subordinate violence to something greater that explains it – most often politics (understood as the mechanisms and structures of governance) or some conception of the political (understood as the theoretical ground of what constitutes a political act/event) – thus directing the analytical gaze away from violence; (2) the subordination of violence as means to political ends is always necessarily, even if unintentionally, driven by an unstable and untenable analytical distinction between so-called productive and destructive violence.

Taken together, these shortcomings indicate that while there is certainly some analytical validity to the view of violence as an instrument of some sort or another, this view reveals only one dimension of violence. To turn this one-dimensional view into an all-encompassing framework that can supposedly explain all that can be analytically said on/of/about violence is to miss the three other crucial dimensions of violence. From Engels (2007 [1878]), Gramsci (1971 [1929–1935]), Schmitt (1996 [1932]), and Sorel (1999 [1908]) to Arendt (1969) and Fanon (2004 [1961]) (and the list can be greatly expanded), social and political theory has advanced and entrenched the instrumental view of violence as the most dominant and conventional mode of analysing violence. These classics have rendered violence a secondary concept that is reducible to greater concepts of power, politics, and so on (Walby, 2012, p. 104). Such a view maintains its presence today in predominant schools of thought in sociology and political science (e.g., political sociology, political realism, military and strategic studies, security studies). Only certain strands of those disciplines that take seriously the experiences of the margins (e.g., taking into account race, ethnicity, gender, postcolonial wars and conflicts – Walby, 2012, p. 96) have moved toward a two-dimensional view of violence, and some of these will be analysed in later chapters (though I will focus mostly on the discipline of anthropology in outlining the second dimension).

In this chapter, I outline the instrumentalist view of violence, its limits, and the analytical path that can move beyond instrumentalism. I first carry out a brief overview of a variety of "violence and politics" texts that tend to conceptualize violence in instrumentalist terms (section i), (b) explore the "violence and modernity" approach, which argues for a non-instrumentalist analytic to the study of violence but which, I argue, ultimately fails to address the difficulties associated with such a task (section ii), (c) make the case for analytically "freeing" the concept of violence (section iii), and (d) set the stage for a move beyond the instrumentalist perspective toward the second dimension of violence by highlighting the complex relationship between violence and death (section iv). In the first section, I am interested in works that subordinate violence as a means that serves a political end. I begin with texts by Hannah Arendt and Frantz Fanon in order to delineate how the subordination of violence as means to political ends revolves around an analytical distinction between productive and destructive violence. The argument then turns to feminist gender analyses of violence (Cynthia Cockburn), which help us posit the productive-destructive distinction as a matter of perspective and thus as easily reversible in any given context. I conclude the first section with the assertion that the productive-destructive distinction cannot act as an analytical basis for the study of violence.

The question of limiting violence within the analytic occupies the second section. I critically examine three theorists of violence and modernity, Hans Joas, Philip Lawrence, and Michel Wieviorka, who argue for a non-instrumentalist approach to the study of violence but ultimately, I claim, fail to adequately address some of the difficulties associated with non-instrumental analytics. This analysis brings to view the critical consequence of failing to analytically limit violence: that is, the danger in non-instrumental analytics of positing violence as a foundational concept that can explain all aspects of social relations and political formations. I conclude this section with the claim that perhaps "freeing" the concept of violence may indeed be the best way to limit it.

In the third section, I visit texts from Carl Schmitt and Antonio Gramsci in order to examine two prominent attempts to delimit violence within the scope of "realist" and "critical" conceptions of the political. I argue that their attempts to delimit violence within a specified analytical space fails, and I draw on some of the work carried out by Michel Foucault as well as Gilles Deleuze and Félix Guattari in order to underscore the element of flux in violence. Foucault brings into view the ever-continuous role of violence in maintaining relationships of power and domination as well as the role of violence in initiating struggles against such configurations. Foucault's work accounts for the effects of the flux of violence but does not quite explain the flux itself. In Deleuze and Guattari's notions of scattering and metamorphosis, we are able to think of violence in its continuous movement rather than as residing within a delimited and firm space from which it operates but never leaves. Focusing on this movement and taking seriously the implications of an emphasis on the flux, I follow violence into a place where it supposedly ends: death.

In the final section, I examine the seminal work of Elaine Scarry, which brings the injured/dead body to the forefront of our understanding of violence. For Scarry, the imperative task ahead for social scientists is to never lose sight of the injured/dead body and to avoid an academic representation that appropriates the injured/dead body in order to advance a set of ideologies and beliefs. Going a step further, I argue through Agamben's work on the Nazi camps, the witness, and the testimony that not only is the injured/dead body integral, but the inevitable production of death in violence always comes with an elusive element, with a voice of death. And these elusive voices of the dead, of the loss of life that takes place in multiple forms, ultimately can never be silenced. The dead body can itself open up a different kind of language, commence a different kind of dialogue, a question-answer exchange on the question of violence. This opens up an analytical path for exploring the question of violence and language and the limits of the latter in (re)presenting the former, which leads to a discussion of the important work of Das in the next chapter.

It should be noted that, more or less, the texts discussed in this chapter operate on a similar definition of violence: the physical use of force (the injuring and killing of the body) in war, colonial conquest, and riots or instances of civil disobedience and unrest. Having said that, my intention here is not to cluster all of these different works together as if they all easily fit into one category or operate on identical conceptions of violence, politics, the political, and so on; rather, my goal is to offer a hermeneutic of violence through a critical engagement with specific texts (as opposed to an emphasis on the authors of the texts) that exemplify different aspects of the instrumentalist conceptualization of violence *and the nature of my move beyond it*. The latter point is important – since many of the texts in this chapter aid in moving beyond the instrumentalist perspective (Joas, Wieviorka, Foucault, Deleuze and Guattari, Agamben, and others), I do not suggest that all of the texts in this chapter fall within the instrumentalist framework and the first dimension of violence. Some of the texts that allow for a movement beyond instrumentalism could arguably be placed within later chapters, as they can help illuminate the other dimensions of violence. Throughout the analysis, I will state where I think the limitations are for these texts in illuminating these other dimensions, but I will come back to some of the ideas found in these non-instrumentalist texts in later chapters as well.

As for the texts that exemplify the instrumentalist viewpoint, notably Fanon's and Arendt's texts, the following analysis does not claim that Fanon is in the same theoretical camp as Arendt, nor will I claim that the two authors conceive of violence in exactly the same manner, and finally I will not claim that they are instrumentalist thinkers per se. Instead, I am interested in drawing out of each of the two texts certain aspects of the instrumentalist viewpoint that can then draw attention to my reasons for moving away from such a viewpoint. Put differently, in no way do I consider the following analysis a complete treatment of these thinkers (whose thought is much larger and deeper than what this chapter can accommodate); however, the instrumentalist themes in their conceptualizations of violence force my analysis to engage only with these specific themes in the specific texts that are analysed as opposed to a detailed engagement with these thinkers' works – the latter being the kind of engagement that I reserve for thinkers who are more directly significant, both in the positive and the negative sense, for the development of my four-dimensional viewpoint (e.g., Das, Gadamer, Derrida, Girard).

I. Violence and Politics

Perhaps nowhere else is the one-dimensional view of violence better illuminated and the two aforementioned limits revealed (subordination of violence and the productive-destructive distinction) than in Hannah Arendt's *On Violence* and her critique of Frantz Fanon's *The Wretched of the Earth*.[1] Arendt dismisses Fanon's call to arms in the struggle for decolonization as an instance of a well-intentioned thinker who has succumbed to the lure of violence and mistaken violence for power. In *On Violence*, Arendt argues, "Power and violence are opposites; where the one rules absolutely, the other is absent. Violence appears where power is in jeopardy.... Violence can destroy power; it is utterly incapable of creating it" (1969, p. 56). That is, when power (defined as the "human ability not just to act but to act in concert"; Arendt, 1969, p. 44) cannot (for whatever reason) prevent the appearance of violence, we can expect only the emergence of more violence and not the reinstatement of an existing power or the emergence of a new power – in short, we cannot expect the emergence of the political in violence.[2] The main reason for this is that "violence is by nature instrumental; like all means, it always stands in need of guidance and justification through the end it pursues" (Arendt, 1969, p. 51). But Arendt maintains that violence is a peculiar instrument because it usually appears with power, even though the two are opposites (1969, p. 52). This link stems from violence's appearance as a form of action that can disrupt the movement of the status quo (Arendt, 1969, p. 30). However, since violence is primarily marked by its tools (i.e., its action is marked by human weapons and not by the act of group formation), it fails to disrupt the status quo in a positive or progressive manner – it inevitably leads to more destruction (Arendt, 1969, pp. 52–53). Violence, thus, is the most dangerous means because the strength it can procure at the barrel of the gun is easily mistaken for power.

For Arendt, violence can serve only short-term goals, for "violence does not promote causes, neither history nor revolution, neither progress nor reaction; but it can serve to dramatize grievances and bring them to public attention" (1969, p. 79). If violence is allowed to stretch its use in time, then this can lead only to more violence because violence defeats power when it induces the end of the political – that is, the end of our very ability to usher in the progressive and the new.[3]

Among other events of her time, the haunting spectres of Nazism in particular and totalitarian regimes in general are at the heart of Arendt's conceptualization of violence (Birmingham, 2011, pp. 12–14). Whether in her analysis of the Adolf Eichmann trial, where the banality of evil is exposed (Arendt, 2006 [1963]), or whether in her analysis of Nazi and Soviet totalitarian regimes, where the delusion of their power is highlighted (Arendt, 1973 [1951]), Arendt's conceptualization of violence continuously affirms the main point that violence is devoid of meaning – violence refers only to an evil that is in itself meaningless (Birmingham, 2011, pp. 21–22). For Arendt, violence cannot itself explain the political institutions and movements of human history; violence is a mere tool that is limited and restricted to small, specific, and in the long run negligible (albeit sometimes devastating, horrific, and painful) roles (Arendt, 1969, pp. 68–69). While Arendt's many insights regarding the Eichmann trial and the nature of totalitarian regimes are penetrating and remain relevant to our understanding of similar contemporary phenomena, I think a more fruitful line of inquiry is found by engaging with one of the targets of her critique: Fanon. And so I turn to his work next in order to highlight what I think Arendt misses in her analysis: namely, a deeper explanation of an analytic that attempts to give at least a certain kind of violence a more prominent role in the explanation and institution of political movements and formations. When this productive-destructive distinction is brought to light, it becomes clear that despite her attempts to distance her thought from the likes of Fanon (and Sorel for that matter), Arendt indeed operates on a similar distinction of violence and shares the same shortcomings that she assigns to Fanon.

In *The Wretched of the Earth*, Fanon situates the question of violence within the interplay between colonizer and colonized. The relationship between the two is born of violence and is maintained by it (Fanon, 2004 [1961], pp. 2–3). Violence and exploitation are the key features of this colonial system, and one cannot do away with these features unless one destroys the entire system. There is no room for reform in Fanon on this question: the colonial system can be removed only by outright destruction. The violence of decolonization will (a) destroy the colonial system and expel the colonizer as colonizer, which does not mean expelling individuals based on their race or nationality, (b) create a new social and political unity that is worthy of the precepts of freedom and liberty that decolonization evokes, and (c) restore the humanity of each colonized individual (Fanon, 2004, pp. 6–10). Succinctly put, the colonized must revert to violence, not to "bring a grievance to the public's attention," as Arendt would have it in her restricted and short-term sense, but to destroy the ruthless colonizer, revive the humanity of the colonized, and create a new decolonized world that respects and elevates all human beings.

Fanon is not urging on violence unreflectively. He is well aware of the difficulties and dangers that the use of violence produces. In his last three chapters, he confronts the reader with all of the difficulties faced by the colonized in their fight for freedom. These difficulties range from ones posed by the petty bourgeoisie of the colonized, to ones posed by the colonizer's immaculate success in a divide-and-rule strategy, to ones posed by overcoming the psychological effects of violence and war. His discussion on "spontaneous" and "guided" violence captures these complexities. Fanon first speaks of the spontaneous violence of the "rural masses [who] have never ceased to pose the problem of their liberation in terms of violence" (2004, p. 79). These are the groups that receive the worst colonialism has to offer, and they respond with all of their strength and without any overarching plan or leadership to fight the injustices and violence wrought upon them. They act simply because that is what their condition demands of them. But on their own, such forces cannot and should not last. They cannot last because the colonizer has recourse to many more resources and can easily outlast them (Fanon, 2004, pp. 86–87). They should not last because their violence is too easily embroiled in revenge and feelings of hatred, rather than focused on the more important and higher ideal of national liberation (Fanon, 2004, p. 89). Therefore, a leadership is necessary to guide the spontaneous violence of these groups (Fanon, 2004, p. 86).

Fanon hopes that such leadership and guidance can contain the destructive elements of violence once the objective of national liberation is achieved. He anticipates that because the fight will demand so much of the colonized in death and brutality, it will allow them to realize the complexity of the world (Fanon, 2004, pp. 92–96). To bring about this nuanced view is the task of the leadership, for if "pure, total brutality is not immediately contained it will, without fail, bring down the movement within a few weeks" (Fanon, 2004, p. 95). As soon as Fanon raises the spectre of pure brutality, however, he avoids the question of precisely how it can be contained, and he reverts back to his belief in the righteousness and necessity of the fight (2004, p. 96). And perhaps Fanon is correct in that the all-too-apparent destructive violence of the colonizer is so extreme that what counters it is necessarily good. Perhaps the colonized, in reaching for violence, can grab hold of only what may be called productive violence.[4]

But how are we to avoid pure brutality? How is limited brutality even capable of bringing about a realization of the "complexity of the world"? We do not know, and Fanon provides no guarantees or even an idea of how pure brutality can be dealt with or avoided. All we are left with is a distinction between pure and limited brutality presented within an either/or picture. Violence, in Fanon, is essentially an instrument for the revolutionary masses to use in order to first remove the colonial system and its violence and then replace this system with a new decolonized and democratic political system. In Fanon, if the productive violence of decolonization loses its distinction from the destructive violence of pure brutality during the course of decolonization, then the movement of the people will basically destroy itself. This distinction, then, lies at the basis of Fanon's instrumental view of violence. Violence, in Fanon, is explained by the larger political and colonial context in which it takes place, and this subordination of violence is made possible because of a delimitation of the concept of violence within neatly distinct categories of productive violence (that is explained by the colonial context and that explains the means of its overthrow in order to create a new decolonial world) and destructive violence (of pure brutality that only destroys).

But even if so-called productive violence succeeds in the overthrow of the colonial regime in an attempt to set the stage for the new decolonial world, such "success" does not necessarily signal the end of the violence and cannot guarantee the avoidance of destructive violence. This distinction does not explain how violence may seep into the decolonized political and social system and institutions after the overthrow of the colonial regime.[5] While Fanon is very familiar with this possibility (e.g., see Said's analysis of Fanon's sophisticated understanding of the pitfalls of nationalist consciousness in decolonial movements and the danger of, for example, Arab systems of oppression and violence replacing French colonial violence; Said, 1994, pp. 267–76), he upholds and keeps intact the productive-destructive distinction of violence at the basis of his analytic. It is not enough to simply acknowledge the possibility that violence may be productive in one sense and destructive in another sense; it is imperative, rather, that we develop an analytic of violence that is able to account for this possibility from the outset, as opposed to an analytic that uses a productive-destructive distinction in order to avoid having to explain and understand this very possibility.

Violence is productive and destructive on different levels. At best, productive and destructive guidelines are blurred in the context of violence. What is productive for one side engaged in war is destructive for another. In fact, there are varying levels within each of the sides involved. This is one of the crucial points that analyses of gender relations and violence, from various theoretical frameworks and using diverse methodologies, have made abundantly clear despite being de/undervalued in academic disciplines and fields such as international relations and security studies (Enloe, 2013; Enloe, 2014; Kurtz & Kurtz,

2015; Sharoni, Welland, Steiner, & Pedersen, 2016). An important figure in feminist gender analyses of war, peace, and violence, Cynthia Cockburn argues that gender relations, as relations of power, operate within a "continuum of violence" that perpetuates the power imbalance in gender relations (Cockburn, 2004, pp. 24–25). Cockburn asserts that the distinctions between pre-conflict, conflict, and post-conflict lose their sharpness when examined through a gendered lens. For example, when we take into account sexual violence, we observe that pre-conflict masculine militarization of society, sexualized torture in war, and post-war domestic violence are not separate incidents but rather indicators of a continuum of violence that cuts across the supposed distinction between war and peace (Cockburn, 2004, pp. 30, 43; Cockburn, 2012, pp. 253–254). The destructiveness of violence on women's bodies across this particular continuum is often ignored in nationalist rhetoric that claims productivity in war (i.e., victory) (Cockburn, 2004, p. 44). Furthermore, Nira Yuval-Davis argues that such overarching claims of victory often carry with them claims that perpetuate an imbalance in gender relations, such as "we fought this war to defend our women and children," "we freed women from the barbarian other," or "women did not fight with the men in the war and are therefore not equal contributors to the community" (Yuval-Davis, 2004). Such formulations ensure the perpetuation of paternalistic gender relations at best and outright (often extremely violent) exclusion of women from the public sphere at worst (Yuval-Davis, 2004, p. 189).

The continuum of violence that comes to the fore in gender analyses thus helps us think of the continuity of violence across (a) temporal periods (pre- and post-armed-conflict), (b) types or kinds of violence (domestic, military), (c) scale of force (fist, drone attack) and/or social unit (group, nation), and (d) the different spaces and sites in which it is enacted (body, family, battlefield, schoolyard, military training facility, economic institution, etc.) (Cockburn, 2012, pp. 255–256). Gender analyses blur the sharp/rigid distinctions between productive and destructive violence by illustrating that violence is deemed productive to the detriment of far too many involved on all sides of the conflict (Giles & Hyndman, 2004, p. 301; Scheper-Hughes & Bourgois, 2004; for a seminal intersectional analysis of class, gender, and race in the context of the military and militarization, see Lutz, 2001).[6] They also highlight that the officially announced "end" of armed conflict and war does not truly "end" with the signing of a peace agreement or treaty; rather, violence continues to operate along a continuum often at the expense of marginalized gendered bodies that are rendered invisible (I come back to this point in chapter 2 through Das's analysis of the figure of the abducted woman).

What the continuum of violence teaches is that the productive-destructive distinction cannot hold as a stable and tenable analytical basis for the study of violence. Rather, this distinction acts as a vehicle built for politics to escape its complex relationship with violence by conceptually and analytically subordinating violence to politics, by viewing violence as "by nature instrumental," to go back to Arendt's quote. Only when a kind of violence is viewed as potentially productive and counterposed to another violence that is certainly destructive can politics summon its name and ask the people to kill and die for a cause greater than they – for example, to kill and die for the promise of a true(r) democracy/freedom/liberty to come. Effective at mobilization as they may be (and I do not argue that they are not effective and/or even necessary in certain cases, such as the struggle against colonization), *analytically speaking*, such productive-destructive distinctions fail to convincingly posit politics as the master of violence, since these distinctions necessarily rest on a narrow definition of what is productive and destructive, failing to take into account the mutations of violence and politics, and hence the impossibility of neatly separating violence into, on the one hand, a productive instrument that may be summoned and controlled by politics and, on the other, a somehow avoidable destructive force that is outside of politics or the political.

Seen in this light, despite Arendt's efforts to distance herself from the likes of Fanon, her own attempt to limit violence is fraught with similar difficulties.[7] When she divides violence into that which can be used for short-term goals and that which can only destroy, Arendt is essentially using a productive-destructive distinction for the purpose of analytically limiting violence. But if the productive-destructive distinction is a mere matter of perspective and cannot act as a tenable analytical framework, then the attempt to limit violence in Arendt can be easily broken by considering, for instance, the effects of these so-called short-term goals on gendered subjects/subjectivities in the mutations of violence and politics. Put differently, the concept of violence cannot be restricted by an attempt to posit a certain kind of violence as productive, and as such controllable and confined within something called "short-term" goals, for at what point can we definitively say that the violent means have ended, or more difficult yet, how are we to ensure the restriction of violence to those short-term goals and the elimination of any spread of violence beyond them? Can there be such a calculable end when it comes to the so-called instrument that is violence?[8]

Critically as well, the one-dimensional view must always subordinate violence to greater concepts, often to conceptions of politics or the political. Even in the work of Cockburn, which does much to break the rigid boundaries often drawn around conventional understandings of instrumental violence, the concept of violence becomes subordinated to gender relations, or more properly the intersectionality of power. It is undeniable that all of these texts offer important theoretical insights into violence and analytically rich accounts of their various areas of study. However, they all (from Arendt to Cockburn) analytically subordinate violence and as such miss a four-dimensional view that is of the utmost importance in the study of violence: a view that will forever remain beyond examination should we follow an instrumental analytic that is based on a distinction between productive and destructive violence (Fanon, Arendt) and/or if we analytically subordinate violence (Cockburn – though Cockburn's work does reach a two-dimensional view of violence in that it follows the dispersal of violence beyond its officially announced "end").

At this point, two important questions arise: in countering the productive-destructive distinction and moving beyond the instrumentalist perspective, is there a danger of hypostatizing the concept of violence? In other words, when we remove the limits provided by the view of violence as an instrument of politics (even if they are shifting limits, they are limits nonetheless), would this lead to an analytic where the concept of violence can appear everywhere and come to form the foundation of our explanation for all human life? Second, if the answer is yes, then ought social scientists replace the instrumentalist framework with a non-instrumentalist framework that would yet subordinate violence – this time under a concept that is grander than politics or the political, a concept that has long been held as antithetical to violence – that is, the concept of modernity?

II. Violence and Modernity

Much of the scholarship on modernity and war/violence has held, since the classics, the assertion that modernity's advance would slowly lead to the disappearance of war and violence (Walby, 2012, pp. 97–101).[9] One of the most prominent and sophisticated examples of this idea is Norbert Elias's work on violence and the civilizing process (Elias, 1982, 2000 [1939]). The thrust of Elias's argument is that the modern nation state, in its monopoly over violence and the overall civilizing trend toward the constraint of interpersonal violent impulse/conduct, is *generally* (not absolutely, definitively, or mechanically) moving humanity toward the elimination of "barbarism" (Van Krieken, 1998, pp. 81–129). Siniša Malešević argues that while this view has been reinforced in recent influential publications, most notably Pinker (2011) (also see Elias's influence on Andrew Linklater's voluminous work in international relations; Mennell 2017), it suffers from a decontextualized understanding of violence (Malešević, 2013, p. 274). Malešević examines the relationship of modernity with violence across three levels of analysis (micro, mezzo, and macro) and argues that, when compared with the pre-modern world, the modern era is indeed more violent on the mezzo and macro levels and not much different on the micro level. The main reason for this increase in violence concerns the scale and form of dehumanization that takes place in and through modernity (Malešević, 2013, p. 285). With its constant emphasis on the universal autonomy and liberty of all individuals, modernity forces, in a sense, the modern state to dehumanize its political opponents so as to deny them universal equality and justify the use of violence against them. Following Zygmunt Bauman's (1989) important work on the Holocaust, Malešević argues that this sophisticated system of dehumanization is sometimes less visible and is marked by a "detached callousness" that leads to the rational organization of mass killings on a scale never before seen (Malešević, 2013, pp. 285–286).

This is a claim that is supported, among others, by Michael Mann's (2005) important work on the workings of murderous ethnic cleansing (MEC) in the modern era, where Mann asserts that MEC is very much a *modern* phenomenon – one that is not possible without the capacities of the modern state and the modern conceptions of nation, citizenship, and "we, the people." Certainly, Elias (and others who follow his line of argumentation) is not oblivious to such violences and to the relationship between civilization and barbarism (Van Krieken, 1998, p. 118). However, he insists that the general trend of modern civilization remains directed toward less violence, explaining occurrences such as the great violences of the German Nazi regime by focusing on context-specific social, economic, cultural, and political factors as opposed to a larger problem with modernity itself (Van Krieken, 1998, pp. 105–111). But in positing the civilizing process as the tamer of the human primal inclination toward violence, as the opposite of a premised ontological human tendency to use violence (a claim that is very much disputed in Collins, 2008), Elias's theory fails to adequately account for the proliferation of violence and warfare as a mode of social and political organization and as a mode of action in modernity (Malešević & Ryan, 2013).

Since at least the Frankfurt School, critical theory has chipped away at the notion that modernity and violence are opposites, that the advance of modernity necessarily leads to the disappearance or decrease of violence, and has brought to the forefront the destructiveness and self-destructive side of modernity: that is, the existence of a strong relationship between violence and modernity. In *War and Modernity*, Hans Joas (2003) deals with this relationship in a non-instrumental way that is quite fruitful. Joas asserts that social theorists cannot think of violence as a mere instrument of politics but, in overcoming this instrumentalist view, must resist the temptation to make violence the basis of our understanding of all social relations (2003, pp. 41–42). Joas draws attention to the varied experiences of violence, its unintended consequences, the unexplored avenues in which these experiences may travel, and the unlikely and out-of-sight origins of violence (2003, pp. 10, 193–196). Broadly speaking, the appearance of violence involves the processes through which an individual's identity is affected and shaped before, during, and after the event and/or act of violence.

In order to analytically limit the experience of violence once the instrumentalist perspective is removed, Joas opts to subordinate violence within the larger context of the advance of modernity. Joas sees modernity as consisting of fluid and multiple processes, institutions, and values (which revolve, in Europe, around the interplay between the Enlightenment and Romanticism). He maintains that while it is possible to speak of universal or common features of modernity across its diverse shapes and forms, it is misleading to speak about these universalities as firm or absolute foundations. So to counter classical modernization theories that posit modernity as *the* universal force in civilized and non-violent human history, Joas advances a notion of a "modernity of war" in order to illuminate a fundamental connection between modernity and violence (war, genocide, riots, etc.) (Joas, 2003, pp. 53–54). Here, violence is not seen as prehistoric to modernity, but as an important part of modernity's advance (Joas, 2003, pp. 43, 52). This shakes the belief that modernity can lead only to peaceful resolutions of conflicts, and it points to the contingent success of modernity in war. But if modernity owes some of its successes (e.g., the fall of Nazism) and failures (e.g., colonialism) (Joas, 2003, p. 41) to war, then the experience of violence can affect the larger context of modernity just as much as modernity can affect our understanding and view of war. So, how is violence subordinate to modernity?

The crux of the difficulty of Joas's argument lies in his attempt to develop a schema whereby one can observe "both the affinity and the *ultimate disjunction* between creativity and violence" (Joas, 2003, p. 42; emphasis added). Central to this attempt is the idea that if social theorists can separate the instances where violence creates modernity's positive or progressive goals and ideals from the instances where it takes on a life of its own and can only destroy, we can then analytically limit violence, thus producing enlightened directions for praxis (Joas, 2003, pp. 193–194). We are left with the task of drawing on modernity (e.g., methodologies for understanding human action) in order to realize its potential to limit the destructiveness of its own creativity – a destructiveness born of the very creativity that Joas is seeking to use so as to subordinate destructive violence.

But how can an attempt to understand violence through the tools of modernity aid in this task after Joas has shown that modernity is imbued with violence? What if the "autonomous process" of violence is perpetuating itself through an undivorceable affinity with creativity? What is the reasoning behind Joas's claim of an "ultimate disjunction"? Critically, if this attempt at limiting violence fails, then does not violence indeed come to form the basis of our understanding of all social relations? Joas does not present clear answers to these questions, as he is largely interested in launching a campaign against the classical modernization theory that attempts to subordinate violence to rational means-ends analysis.[10] Joas's own attempt of a subordination that revolves around openness to the varying experiences of violence and faithfulness to modernity, however, is unsatisfactorily presented through his claim of an "ultimate disjunction" between creativity and violence. And this raises the question: Would a shift toward a postmodern analytical approach better illuminate the connection between modernity and violence and alleviate the destructive power of that connection?

In *Modernity and War*, Philip Lawrence makes similar points to Joas regarding modernity's relationship with war and violence (Lawrence, 1997, p. 11). Lawrence highlights three bases for this relationship: (1) modernity as the "age of instrumental reason" (1997, p. 12), where a modern culture/society/mind seeks to control anything and everything on the basis of a supposedly universal progress,[11] (2) the disregard and utter contempt for an "other" that is supposedly outside of modernity's universal values (1997, pp. 30–31), and (3) the emergence of more deadly and massive wars through changes in the forms of state, economy, and society in modernity (1997, p. 20).

Lawrence asserts that so-called postmodern wars (e.g., the 1991 Gulf War) are not, as some would say, evidence of the unveiling of a postmodern era of warfare, but are rather very modern in their character (1997, p. 159). While there are differences between the so-called "old modern wars" and the "new postmodern wars," Lawrence asserts that the bases mentioned above are still in operation, with one important exception: the shift from trench warfare to air warfare (with its aesthetics of distance and "precise" calculation of "military targets")[12] changes the mode of excluding the other: "Thus we have slipped from a concrete form of exclusion, based on xenophobia and racism, to an abstract form based on distance and invisibility" (Lawrence, 1997, p. 177). For Lawrence, this makes the task to "recognize the 'other' as a partner in moral discourse" a difficult one to accomplish, but it remains the quintessential task in any effort to limit violence (1997, p. 184).

Lawrence argues that attempts to formulate postmodern analyses based on contingency and undecidability alone (in opposition to modern instrumental reason) cannot limit violence analytically or practically (1997, p. 5). These postmodern attempts are themselves connected to the strategies and worldviews of the "new wars," which approach the enemy with concepts such as uncertainty, undecidability, contingency, particularity, and the like (e.g., see the analysis of Weizman, 2006a, 2006b). So, Lawrence advocates an analytic that focuses on the way in which war (in its technological, organizational, and structural innovations) shapes and moulds society and culture around the distancing of an "evil other." But he, like Joas, still wants to engage in a project whereby these destructive reaches of violence are located, isolated, extracted, and removed. But what tools are we to use for this task, when all of our tools (whether modern or postmodern) are already imbued with violence? And more precisely, is it even possible to isolate "bad" violence to begin with, let alone remove it? How far does the reach of violence really go? Lawrence's approach essentially suffers from the very same shortcomings that Joas faces.

The problem of the productive-destructive distinction of violence re-emerges once again. Joas and Lawrence want to use a so-called productive violence (creative destructiveness) to stop a so-called destructive violence (autonomous process of violence). In addition, Joas's attempt makes clear an important element that is at stake, which is that when the all-or-nothing effort to subordinate violence to a greater context fails, violence moves to the basis of our understanding of all forms of social and political life. The solution to this problem cannot come by way of an all-or-nothing subordination, for whom or what can subordinate violence? Perhaps it is imperative to not fight violence, but to allow it to play its role freely. In its analytic "freedom," which accounts for the incessant movement of violence, the concept of violence may be limited, in the sense that violence would not become the concept that unifies all explanations of social and political life. From Joas, a line of inquiry can already be found to move into this direction. This line involves Joas's analytical emphasis on the movement of violence, on the manner in which violence moves between the different realms in which it is experienced. Violence is not only connected to the politics of the state, but violence appears in various and diverse forms within and through everyday social relations. It is imperative to follow this movement and chase violence, especially when it moves into its most elusive and mysterious forms.

Michel Wieviorka's (2009 [2005]) modern/postmodern sociological approach to the study of violence, in highlighting the elusive elements of violence, can help move forward this book's theorization of the movement or flux of violence. Wieviorka argues that social and political theory in contemporary modernity (or postmodernity) must approach violence in both its objectivity ("modern" analytical tools that establish its factuality in, for example, homicide rates) and subjectivity ("postmodern" analytical tools that explore how it is diversely experienced, represented, perceived) (2009, pp. 2, 72). The objective universality of violence (facts of violence in numbers of people killed or injured, in amounts of property or infrastructure destroyed, and so on) can be used to offset the dangers of a predominant subjective relativity (specific representations of violence from particular perspectives), and vice versa (Wieviorka, 2009, p. 74). In opening up the analytical tools available for the study of violence, Wieviorka releases violence from its constrained typologies prevalent in classical modes of analysing violence. Violence here is not restricted to its "instrumental" form (cold violence, a calculated means serving desired ends) or "expressive" form (hot violence, uncontrolled crude expressions of individual, cultural, or social meanings or states of mind) (Wieviorka, 2009, pp. 88–92). The definition of violence is turned loose, and in the process opens up an analytical avenue for a wide array of forms of violence.

Wieviorka's approach then moves beyond the limited boundaries of the state and examines the "globalization of violence" in its diverse forms (2009, p. 30). Most notably, he differentiates two forms of violence, "infra-political" and "metapolitical" violence. These two forms are further differentiated from "political violence," which was prevalent in the modern era of the state (Wieviorka, 2009, p. 34). Infra-political violence is "less political," even "pre-political," as it is more interested in keeping a distance from the state in order to engage, for example, in criminal activity and create economic gain for groups such as gangs (Wieviorka, 2009, pp. 34–36). Metapolitical violence moves beyond the instrumentality of violence, as "it rises above the political and becomes a vector for meanings that give it an intransigent and non-negotiable quality" (Wieviorka, 2009, p. 37). Metapolitical violence has no frontiers; the political process certainly cannot capture it, nor does this violence reside within the delimited boundaries of the state. It evokes a set of meanings that refuse the political process and claims a mantle above the political in order to maintain an absolute distance from it. In Wieviorka, then, the political is situated in the centre, and in our globalized world, much violence is moving away from that centre. Some violences move below it and are indicative of a violence that is purely utilitarian, while some violences move above the political and are indicative of absolute cultural or religious convictions that cannot be compromised in the political. To the latter, Wieviorka suggests the examples of political Islamist violence (2009, pp. 37–38).

Wieviorka argues that if scholars want to understand violence as a central issue of social life, then they must "recognize that its most mysterious and elusive aspects are the most decisive" in enabling such an understanding (2009, p. 95). Scholars must turn to the most extreme, least comprehensible, forms of violence, beyond instrumental and expressive forms, in order to grasp the essential features of violence itself (Wieviorka, 2009, p. 96). While pointing in the right direction beyond instrumentalism and beyond secondary explanations of violence as expressions of psychological, cultural, or identitarian contexts, Wieviorka wants to name this unnameable violence: he gives it a specific form, a metapolitical form, and he then points to an exemplary manifestation of that form and names it political Islamist violence. But can violence's elusive elements appear in a specific form? Can the elusiveness of violence be approached as an apparent form that can be specifically named? And why is political Islamist violence exemplary of this metapolitical form? Is the violence of political Islamists any more incomprehensible than the violence of the American government's drones?[13] And conversely, is not the violence of political Islamists as calculated to achieve political ends as is the violence of the drones? There are many works across different disciplines that speak to the political calculations of "terrorist" violence by political Islamists (e.g., Euben, 2002; Pape, 2003; Baudrillard, 2003; Devji, 2005; Bloom, 2005). Hence, are they both not simultaneously comprehensible (in their calculations) and incomprehensible (the unspeakable violence that they unleash)? Reducing the problem of violence's mysterious and elusive aspects into a specific form already evades the radical challenge of elusive violence, the flux of violence.

Despite his efforts to combine the best of both worlds, or to let the concrete case under study determine the appropriate analytical tools for its study, Wieviorka ultimately reverts to modernity's obsession in making fixed and knowable every thing it encounters. It is precisely this limit of modern analytical thinking that must be transgressed in the study of violence. The language of modernity cannot capture violence as a fixed object whose essence can be captured once and for all. At the same time, the language of postmodernity cannot refuse the necessity of stretching language into violence and speaking with it. Simply accepting the elusive character of violence is not enough, I agree with Wieviorka, as it can reduce the problem to a matter of perspective and diminish our capacity to judge the validities of competing perspectives, which can have dangerous consequences on our ability to deal with violence. This does not contradict my earlier claim that the productive-destructive distinction of violence is a mere matter of perspective. My point then was that sound evidence exists within the theoretical perspective of gender power relations to put into question the neat productive-destructive distinction underlying some analytics of violence. The point here concerns the muddying of our very conception of violence that can take place in postmodern efforts to evade the task of directly gazing at violence. On this point, I am in agreement with Wieviorka.

The point of difference, however, between the dialogical approach and Wieviorka's approach is situated on the question of how to approach the elusiveness of violence. This is best seen around the issue of violence's relationship to "discussion," or as I prefer, the question of dialogue. For Wieviorka, "violence closes down discussions rather than opening them up. It makes debates and exchanges ... difficult and encourages ruptures or even pure power relations" (2009, p. 10). Here is neatly separated the political process of discussion and dialogue from the violent process/acts/events that presumably shut down the latter. In this assertion is found the conventional understanding that violence separates participants as it closes the dialogical exchange between them. Instead, the dialogical analytic follows the ways in which violent processes/acts/events commence a question-answer exchange between the participants in and through violence.

In the dialogical analytic, violence is followed into the hidden and elusive ways in which it opens up a different kind of dialogue, a violent dialogue that communicates deep meanings across the various participants involved and affected, creating not separation, but a violent communion in the process. This does not refer only to states at war with one another but rather, following Wieviorka, all strata of the social sphere. To understand this process, the concept of violence must thus be "freed" from analytical subordination, the flux of violence must be followed, and when it is, in contrast to Wieviorka, we must remain open to the radical unknowability of violence and avoid the temptation to give a name to what is nameless, a form to what is formless. The latter point will be made clear in the discussion on the fourth dimension of violence, but for now, a better articulation of what I mean by "freeing" the concept of violence is needed. This requires a closer look at the movement of violence, the flux of violence, which is often de-emphasized or simply remains hidden in analytical attempts to delimit violence within either realist or revolutionary conceptions of the political.

III. "Freeing" the Concept of Violence

To better understand the flux of violence, the first subsection examines how the analytical delimitation of violence occurs in Carl Schmitt (where violence is restricted within a "realist" conception of the political) and Antonio Gramsci (where violence is restricted within a "revolutionary" conception of the political). I chose these two thinkers because their theoretical positions have shaped intellectual trajectories that are very influential in scholarly understandings of violence and politics today (realists in the case of Schmitt; critical theorists in the case of Gramsci). My goal here is not to undertake an exhaustive study of these trajectories; rather, I have the much more modest aim of making manifest my critique of two opposing theoretical efforts at delimiting violence. For this task, it suffices to follow Richard Bernstein's critical reading of Schmitt and the "realist" trajectory of his thought, as well as Étienne Balibar's daring critical trajectory from Gramsci's work where he attempts to circumvent the problem of the spread of revolutionary violence beyond the revolutionary act/event through a conceptual mechanism he calls "risk." In addition, I briefly engage with Michael Hardt and Antonio Negri's theory of the multitude and states of war, as it forms a sort of bridge across the two thinkers and makes clear the nature of the difficulties associated with the efforts to delimit violence. Instead of delimiting efforts, the second subsection follows Foucault's work on the schemata for the analysis of power and Deleuze and Guattari's concepts of metamorphoses and scattering in delineating the flux of violence.

A. Delimiting Violence

Carl Schmitt's delimitation of violence within a "realist" conception of the political has been, directly and indirectly, influential on a number of schools of thought, the most prominent of which is the "realist" school of international relations, which tends to favour an allegedly sober and realistic assessment of humanity's propensity toward violence and hatred as opposed to the so-called "idealist" approaches that are often associated with liberalism. As Richard Bernstein puts it,

Schmitt's "trenchant analysis of liberalism has been taken to be one of the most penetrating and devastating critiques of contemporary liberalism" (2013, p. 13), and the perception that Schmitt's theory offers a "realistic" theoretical grounding of politics against rationalist/deliberative/liberal models helps explain his seductive attractiveness to scholars from the right and the left (2013, pp. 2–3, 14–15). Without delving into Schmitt's oeuvre, we can observe his delimitation of violence within the scope of the political in *The Concept of the Political*, where Schmitt asserts that the "logic of the political" entails the most fundamental antithesis in any form of human association: the friend/enemy antithesis (1996 [1932], p. 26).[14] This political enemy need not represent a repulsive other, just as long as it represents "existentially something different and alien, so that in the extreme case conflicts with him are possible" (Schmitt, 1996, p. 27). Thus the "real possibility of physical killing" must be present in order to establish the distinction of friend/enemy (Schmitt, 1996, p. 33) – though this possibility does not have to necessarily be realized for the distinction to serve its function.

The possibility of violence is thus the fundamental ground of our political existence (Schmitt, 1996, p. 38). At the very moment that a group attempts to alter its relation with the other, it must activate its ability to potentially exercise physical violence against its clearly demarcated enemy (Schmitt, 1996, p. 51).[15] The existing relations can really be worthy of mention (i.e., become historical) only when they are embedded in a continuous and ever-present possibility of violence, specifically war.[16] Otherwise, we are left with the myth of an apolitical world (Schmitt, 1996, p. 53). In short, social entities and groupings (Schmitt's understanding of the political is not limited to the state; Bernstein, 2013, pp. 17, 186) are empty without the (collective public, not individualistic private)[17] friend/enemy distinction and its actual and potential violence – the mere possibility of which feeds life into social entities and gives them their shape, form, and indeed, their very vibrancy.

For Schmitt, the decision over the friend/enemy distinction is solely in the hands of a sovereign power (1996, p. 44). It is the decision over the friend/enemy distinction that constitutes the sovereign power as sovereign. Thus, in Schmitt violence is delimited within the space of the sovereign. In its potential and actual form, violence lies in the hands of a sovereign power that directs it against a clearly demarcated enemy and alongside the interests of a clearly demarcated friend. It is useful here to follow Bernstein's reading of Schmitt's *Theory of the Partisan* and how Bernstein outlines Schmitt's typology of the three types of enemy and their corresponding type of enmity – a typology that moves in a chronological order for Schmitt. First is the "conventional" enemy of post-Westphalia Europe, where states pitted combatants against combatants in clearly demarcated battlefields within demarcated periods of wars between enemies who were neither treated as criminals nor demonized. The object of these wars was not to annihilate the enemy but to defeat the enemy, thus giving rise to a "humanized war" (Bernstein, 2013, pp. 36–37). Second is the "real" enemy, exemplified in Prussian and Spanish resistance to the French invasion in the early parts of the nineteenth century, where all of the rules and delimitations of battle are eradicated, and instead we find a fight to the death that does not respect, for example, the juridical distinctions between war and peace. This kind of partisan enmity makes of anything a weapon, of any member of the enemy a target, and of any space a battlefield (Bernstein, 2013, pp. 37–38). Third is the "absolute enemy," where, unlike with the partisan who is rooted in a specific territory and fights a specific invading enemy, the enemy is "not a specific enemy, but a universal enemy who becomes demonized" (Bernstein, 2013, p. 39). Exemplified in Lenin's revolutionary war, this type of enmity is without any limitations and posits the enemy as that which must be completely annihilated.

Schmitt laments these transformations of the friend/enemy distinctions, and Bernstein skillfully draws out Schmitt's lamentations in order to "bring into the open the normative-moral perspective that orients his analysis" (Bernstein, 2013, p. 40). Schmitt's moral allegiance to the "conventional type" is clearly what drives his earlier theorization of the enemy/friend distinction. His moral convictions explain his emphasis on an encounter between respected and equal enemies, and why he placed this dynamic at the core of his understanding of the political. Conventional enmity ensures the establishment of clear boundaries between groups or collectivities as well as boundaries between the manner in which they potentially/actually fight (Bernstein, 2013, p. 43). Bernstein's interpretive trope convincingly shows that Schmitt's typology is not merely descriptive but is indeed expressive of a normative-moral judgment (Bernstein, 2013, p. 44). In properly situating the problem of enmity within the sphere of normative-moral judgments, Bernstein is able to show the mistaken assumption of "realists" that scholarly analysis can be solely descriptive and realistic while dismissing normative-moral judgments in the process (also see a similar critique of "power-political realism" in Joas, 2003, p. 34) – even in Schmitt, this sort of scornful dismissal fails. But Bernstein's critique of Schmitt also, and more important for my purposes, allows him to clearly ask the important question of how we can think about the problem of limiting enmity, especially since he agrees with Schmitt's judgment that the post–World War II world very much features absolute enmity – where we are threatened with an unlimited and unrestricted form of violence and warfare that could annihilate all social and political orders (Bernstein, 2013, pp. 44–45). I follow and agree with Bernstein on the orientation of his question regarding the problem of limitation, and I also agree with Bernstein that Schmitt's theory and typology does not provide fruitful ways or avenues to address this problem (Bernstein, 2013, pp. 160–161; also see Mouffe's critique of Schmitt's inability to properly account for pluralism within the political; 2005, pp. 53–57). In support of Bernstein's thesis, it is useful to recall here Hardt and Negri's understanding of the nature of war in the transition from modern to postmodern sovereignty since their work also reveals a transformation that is similar to Schmitt's outline of the transformation from conventional enmity to absolute enmity – with an important difference from Bernstein in that Hardt and Negri connect more systematically and directly enmity with states of war (albeit ultimately in a problematic way that effaces actual warfare and violence).

Briefly, in *Multitude* Hardt and Negri assert that a new state of war operates in and shapes the contemporary global world: a new form of sovereignty, which no longer has the ability to distinguish between war and peace, characterizes this state of war. Whereas in modern sovereignty war was seen as a *"limited state of exception"* (Hardt & Negri, 2004, p. 6; original emphasis) that would be fought only between sovereign states, in postmodern sovereignty a state of exception becomes permanent, thus creating and continuously maintaining a global state of war (Hardt & Negri, 2004, p. 8).[18] This, for example, is most obviously seen in the "war on terror," which, theoretically speaking, has no end since it is waged against "indefinite, immaterial enemies" (Hardt & Negri, 2004, p. 14). This new state of war breaks the barrier and/or distinction between inter-state and intra-state conflict, affecting all social relations and politics within states in the process (Hardt & Negri, 2004, p. 12). As such, the new state of war cannot be definitively won, or it has to be won everyday and is thus forever continuous (Hardt & Negri, 2004, pp. 14, 19). This means that a state of war is then elevated to an ontological status whereby "war has passed from the final element of the sequences of power … to the first and primary element, the foundation of politics itself" (Hardt & Negri, 2004, p. 21). As a foundation, violence and war then form predominant understandings of politics, shaping social structures.

Like Bernstein, Hardt and Negri emphasize the immense dangers of our time as located in the potential/actual unleashing of an uninhibited type of enmity and violence. Bernstein looks to a vibrant political public debate and sphere (in the Arendtian sense of politics) to counter uninhibited violence and limit its spread (2013, pp. 179–184); similarly, Hardt and Negri look to the multitude as an answer to this problem. Both highlight a revolutionary project that would centre rational/normative political debate in an effort to quell the advance and spread of violence. I do not necessarily disagree with this solution as a practical matter, but what I want to insist on is to tackle this problem by focusing on violence itself, not enmity per se (the full consequences of this shift will become clearer in chapters three and four, where our gaze turns to enemy-siblings and not enemies), which reveals that the problem of revolutionary change concerns not just the violence (structural, symbolic, and physical) that prevents the change from taking place but also the violence that enables the change.[19] The difficult connection between violence and revolutionary change can be illuminated in Hardt and Negri's solution to the problem of uninhibited state violence – that is, to the problem of the state of exception.

Hardt and Negri state that out of war, a true democratic society may emerge (2004, pp. xiv, xviii). But in order to make such an argument, Hardt and Negri have to first do away with actual war and violence. They decide that for democracy to have a chance, they must repeat Hobbes's masterful manoeuvre; except this time, the order of the manoeuvre is reversed: "Whereas Hobbes moved from the nascent social class [bourgeoisie] to the new form of sovereignty … we work from the new form of sovereignty to the new global class" (Hardt & Negri, 2004, p. xvii). In order to accomplish this, all of the different types of wars and violence (intra/inter-state) have to first be placed under the rubric of a *"general global state of war"* (Hardt & Negri, 2004, p. 5; original emphasis). This permanent state of war is of course antithetical to the democratic ethos, since it necessarily posits a permanent state of exception. By definition, a constant state of exception means state exemption from the democratic process. This suspension of democracy is what concerns Hardt and Negri, and they strive to find a source/power/force of resistance in the global state of war that would rescue democracy from the state of exception and bring forth a new democratic order of the multitude. This is the crux of the manoeuvre they undertake. They are no longer interested in explicating the different frames of reference and contexts of all the different types of wars and violence; only one contextualization for them matters: "it is superimposed over all others: violence that preserves the contemporary hierarchy of global order and violence that threatens that order" (Hardt & Negri, 2004, p. 32). Only when all wars and forms of violence look the same under the rubric of a global state of war can Hardt and Negri then draw a fault line between the carriers of a democracy to come and those who suppress that effort. Democracy, in Hardt and Negri, could rise and flourish because it would have nothing to do with the means and manner of its rise – and this claim is made possible because the democratic outcome is first posited outside of the peculiarity and particularity of its context and placed in an abstract global state of war, the emergence of which it had nothing to do with.

But can such absolute dissociation between the initial violent processes of democratic institution and the democratic outcome ever hold? For Hardt and Negri, such dissociation is manifested in a productive-destructive distinction of violence (carriers of democracy vs. preservers of current global hierarchy), which in my view is a distinction that can be easily unravelled by the possibility that so-called productive and destructive violences are not two distinct species of violence but can be, and are indeed, closely interconnected, where the terms "productive" and "destructive" are indeed transferable to any given violence depending on whose perspective is involved; the problems of the productive-destructive distinction arise once more in this case.

But another point begins to emerge here: while a focus on warfare and violence between and within state and non-state entities tends to direct our analytical and moral gaze toward the "othering" of the "other," toward the demonization of the enemy and the drive to annihilate the enemy in an uninhibited use of violence (similar to the previous discussion of the "new wars" in Lawrence; also see Burke, 2007), the problem of uninhibited violence itself needs to be directly highlighted. Once again, it is important not to lose sight of violence by following the question of enmity per se. The problem of a violence that knows no bounds, a violence that spreads uncontrollably in the social/political spheres, is not restricted to the violence that maintains the status quo or upholds existing relations of domination wherein marginalized groups or "rogue" states tend to be singled out, demonized, or dehumanized in order to maintain the exploitative systems of the status quo; this problem also can appear in revolutionary violence. I think it is fruitful to bring in Gramsci at this stage in order to better understand how violence is delimited within theoretical models of revolutionary change where the question of violence's spread becomes especially acute.

Much of Gramsci's work revolves around two positions: the dominant social group and their hegemony over the subaltern, dominated ones. There are two conditions that the dominant group must meet: (1) it has to be able to forcefully dominate its antagonists, and (2) it must exercise moral and intellectual leadership (Gramsci, 1971 [1929–1935], p. 57). Indeed, it is in the second condition that one finds the birth of a hegemonic power, which knows how to make/spread its claims intellectually before it presses them forcefully (Gramsci, 1971, p. 59). Violence is thus a servant to the aspirations and goals of the social group that uses it.[20] This can be illustrated through Gramsci's three levels/moments of revolutionary change. First, we have the organic social relations (Gramsci, 1971, p. 176). These relations of "social forces" are indeed a "refractory reality" – no one can object to the truth of their characteristics (e.g., they may involve relations of production) (1971, pp. 180–181). From these, certain relations of "political forces" can emerge, wherein each group may develop a certain degree of organization and an awareness of their antagonistic condition (Gramsci, 1971, p. 181). Finally, we move into the relations of "military forces," where the position of each group can be decisively determined through the use of force (Gramsci, 1971, p. 183). Organic social relations basically form the basis of the coming moment of violence. Violence is the means through which the organic social group can realize itself and its potential.

There are two main interrelated forms of political struggle in Gramsci: a "war of position" and a "war of manoeuvre." Gramsci seems to alternate between different definitions of these two forms. Despite this, I think it is fair to say (with a fair deal of abstraction) that the connection Gramsci was working with involves the possibility of an "abruption" (one that is unexpected by the hegemonic power and unannounced by the subaltern; i.e., born through a war of position whereby the subaltern group places itself in valuable positions that are favourable for its coming victory; Gramsci, 1971 [1929–1935], p. 239), which shakes society's stability and brings forth a war of manoeuvre (a "frontal attack" directly targeting the defences of the enemy; 1971, p. 235) that then revolutionizes the social, economic, and political landscape.[21] I say a fair deal of abstraction because the two types do not unfold in a linear fashion as may be suggested above, but tend to vacillate depending on the circumstances.

Ultimately, "one cannot choose the form of war one wants," and this is why the different forms of war are looked at by Gramsci as so many options the organic social group can utilize to realize itself (Gramsci, 1971, p. 234). Violence gains its significance (analytical and practical) when it serves the organic social group by overturning hegemonic social relations. Doubtless there are the problems of subordinating violence as a means toward a socio-political end in Gramsci, but since I have already indicated the weaknesses and shortcomings of this kind of subordination, I would like to focus on a different question that is illuminated in Gramsci (and which can also be seen in Hardt and Negri and in Fanon): What about the violence that will likely maintain a presence in the new social, economic, and political relations follow-ing the revolution?[22] Can we simply delimit violence within a specified space of actual political struggle, which attempts to settle the antag-onism of refractory social relations once and for all? What about the potential of violence that seems to inhabit the to-be-overturned hege-monic relations, which appear in a state of apathy prior to the actualiza-tion of violence in the revolutionary moment?[23]

Following the trajectory of critical theory from Gramsci's work (among other Marxist theorists), Étienne Balibar attempts to answer these questions by posing them as the risks we must make, as the risks that accompany any political decision we make toward emancipation (Balibar, 2015, pp. ix–xv). Revolutionary change can be guided by what Balibar calls "antiviolence," which should form the foundation of a new and (re)activated political sphere (Balibar, 2015, p. viii). In coun-tering "extreme" violence,[24] civility as an expression of "antiviolence" can be distinguished from the notion of "counterviolence" (violence to overthrow violence) and the abstraction from violence we call "non-violence" (Balibar, 2015, pp. 22–23). Balibar emphasizes the "anti" as a way to declare a displacement (or even rejection) of violence from within politics at the same time that we remain alert to the possibil-ity that revolutionary politics and emancipatory projects can produce their own forms of barbarity and cruelty (Balibar, 2015, p. 24). This risk is inherent to this kind of politics that Balibar calls "antiviolence" (2015, pp. 16–17), but he insists on separating violence from politics in advancing this concept, and more so, on separating violence from within politics, always already subordinating violence under a concept of revolutionary politics. Indeed, without this kind of subordinate and distinct separation, his entire notion of civility would crumble. While I find myself in agreement, again from a practical standpoint, with much of the strategies of civility that Balibar outlines (2015, pp. 93–126), this kind of separation, analytically speaking, is ultimately untenable. The reason for this untenability is rather simple: fully aware of the inability of politics to subordinate and delimit violence, Balibar introduces "risk" to account for the dangers of the possibility that violence will spread and also to act as a conceptual mechanism to delimit violence. While I have focused on the failure of politics or the political to subordinate violence, my claim is that ultimately, there is no concept that can sub-ordinate violence, not even modernity. The same applies to the concept of risk – in Balibar, risk is meant to signify the *dangers* of the movement of violence, but risk itself cannot account for that very movement. The language of risk works to placate our fear of the dangers of violence's spread, but it does not account for the movement itself.

Whether viewed through the prism of the friend/enemy decision (Schmitt) and its accompanying "realist" school of thought or through the prism of revolutionary change (Gramsci) and its accompanying "critical" school of thought, the problem of violence cannot be delimited and the solution cannot come by way of introducing a more explicit or vibrant moral-normative dimension (Bernstein), by way of a sharp distinction between the multitude and the global elites (Hardt and Negri), or by way of opening up politics to the risks of the political (Balibar). We can begin to tackle the problem of violence only when we directly face its inherently paradoxical relation with the political. A paradoxical relation that is revealed in the movement of violence across social and political spheres; a movement that is too complex for any delimitation of violence (whether actual or potential) to work. While Balibar draws in his book on Foucault and Deleuze and Guattari to accentuate the problems of our contemporary politics around the identification and disidentification of the "self," I think those thinkers can also be drawn upon to illuminate the flux of violence.

B. The Flux of Violence

Foucault's discussion on the two schemata for the analysis of power – "war-repression" and "contract-oppression" – is the starting point here. It is important to first note that when Foucault discusses the discourses that fall within either of the two schemata, he is doing so to outline their genealogy in relation to one another, and the transformations that each set of discourses has undertaken throughout the last few centuries. Thus the war-repression schema can be derived, for example, from the discourse of "political historicism" that was marginalized by the dominant philosophico-juridical discourse of Thomas Hobbes (Foucault, 2003, pp. 87–111). Foucault puts back into play that which is marginalized in dominant discourse for the sake of disrupting our understanding of the contract-oppression schema, which for him has shaped much of modern understandings of power.[25] Thus when Foucault praises and advances the role of the marginalized discourse of war-repression, he is not necessarily endorsing or advancing every aspect of it, but rather using this discourse as a way of reaching a new or different understanding of power, which may or may not eventually do away with the concept or the word "repression" (Foucault, 2003, p. 40).

The following analysis is not concerned with the question of genealogy, or with the specific discourses that are analysed in Foucault. It is not even my intention to discuss Foucault's conception of power, although some discussion of it will be necessary shortly. My goal, rather, is to present a general outline of the two schemata and the form of their interconnectedness in order to think a different way of understanding the paradoxical relationship between violence and politics. The best way to accomplish this is to primarily focus the discussion on a few lectures in which the example of Hobbes and the discourse of "political historicism" take centre stage.

I begin with the war-repression schema. Foucault defines repression as "the effect and the continuation of a relationship of domination ... the implementation, within a pseudopeace that is being undermined by a continuous war, of a perpetual relationship of force" (2003, p. 17). In this schema, war acts as a "principle of intelligibility" rather than a "disruptive principle" in our understanding of power, law, history, and the state (Foucault, 2003, p. 163). The most important feature of this schema is that it focuses on the opposition between "struggle and submission," whereby relations of domination are fought over in the battlefields of history and continue to be fought over in the ensuing political/civil/juridical/racial orders.

The interplay of forces during battle arises out of already existing relations of domination and is meant to either reaffirm, invert, or establish new relations (Foucault, 2003, p. 160). This schema objects to the theory of sovereignty and argues that "law is not pacification, for beneath the law, war continues to rage in all the mechanisms of power.... War is the motor behind institutions and order" (Foucault, 2003, p. 50). Through its focus on "the contingency and injustice of battles," this schema aims to highlight the contingent element of power (Foucault, 2003, p. 72). For example, it brings forth the idea that the legitimacy of the rulers is born of their unjust victory on the battlefield. Simply put, war, and not some notion of "natural law," is seen in this schema as the basis upon which the very definition of the "principles of public right" comes to rest (Foucault, 2003, p. 124).

The second, dominant schema for the analysis of power is contract-oppression. This schema primarily rests on the theory of sovereignty. Its main concern is to analyse the abuses of power – the institutions and mechanisms whereby the state oversteps its limits and uses its power as an oppressive tool against its subjects (Foucault, 2003, p. 17). Rather than "struggle-submission," the opposition here is between "the legitimate and illegitimate" apparatuses, forms, and mechanisms of governance. In this case, oppression refers to the "transgression of the limit" by the sovereign, whereas contract is the "matrix of political power" whereby the sovereign gains its legitimacy through the wilful surrender of power by the individual (Foucault, 2003, p. 17).

As a result of its focus on the contract, this schema forms a fundamentally different view of war than the previous one. This is best seen in Foucault's discussion on Hobbes. In Hobbes, war is part of a larger and continuous "state of war," and it is this state of war that ought to be our main concern, not the real battles of history. This state of war is characterized by an "unending diplomacy between rivals who are naturally equal" (Foucault, 2003, p. 92) during peacetime as well as wartime, the result of which is an unending state of war where life is always threatened by death. The contract, or more precisely in Hobbes, the state acts as a shield against this permanent state of war, and this is accomplished through forms of sovereignty whose underlying mechanism is always characterized by the series of "will, fear, and sovereignty"[26] (Foucault, 2003, p. 96).

The creation of the state in Hobbes, therefore, is always legitimate since it is the opposite of war (whether real or not), or it is that which ends war (Foucault, 2003, p. 95). The programmatic is to then move forward, away from the sites of real battles, and realize the state's "just" form. In short, this schema is concerned with the capacities and potentialities of the state (Foucault, 2003, pp. 110–111, 222). It is concerned not with revolution and/or the reconstitution of the state, but rather with the ability of individuals to constitute a state (Foucault, 2003, pp. 223–224). War is no more than the battles that had finally led us to the universal and just totality of the state – and this state explains history, not war (Foucault, 2003, pp. 233–236).

What Hobbes was ultimately trying to eliminate from his discourse is thus, for Foucault, the "Conquest of England, that painful historical category, that difficult juridical category" (Foucault, 2003, p. 110). Specifically, Hobbes attempted to marginalize and eliminate the discourse of political historicism, which refused the language of sovereignty, emphasized that certain forms of sovereignty were based on relationships of domination born of real battles and wars, and called for a sort of eternal resistance that never stops challenging the outcome of such battles.

Beatrice Hanssen's (2000) *Critique of Violence* maintains that *Society Must Be Defended* highlights Foucault's attempt to challenge the boundaries that the contract-oppression schema erects between violence and power. She also argues that Foucault's "The Subject and Power" aims to address the dangers of completely blurring such boundaries and works to reconstitute distinct boundaries between power and violence but in a direction that would challenge the contract-oppression schema (Hanssen, 2000, pp. 38–40, 148–157). While my analysis shares many points of intersection with Hanssen's, I argue that the most important point that

Foucault's text makes visible is that while each schema aims to dissociate itself from the other strategically, they are connected in the sense that they are both concerned with the relations of domination and relations of power operating within political violence. What is crucial, then, is the idea that the relations of domination established through war do not simply terminate when the political project is initiated and underway (although that is precisely what the contract-oppression schema attempts to accomplish and what the war-repression schema aims to reawaken). Rather, these relations of domination will continue to shape and influence the political project – the forms it takes, its tensions, and the struggle over its future directions. Things would be relatively simple if this was the end of Foucault's argument, but the difference between power relations and relations of domination in Foucault complicates matters further. This difference is perhaps most clearly developed in "The Subject and Power" (Foucault, 1983). As opposed to Hanssen's emphasis on Foucault's reconstitution of boundaries and differentiation between violence and power, I argue that Foucault's work in this text indeed both differentiates and illuminates the connections between relations of power and relations of domination.

To understand power relations, Foucault revives suppressed struggles in order to study the techniques and technologies of modern political rationalities (Foucault, 1983, pp. 210–212), and he asks: By what means is power exercised? (Foucault, 1983, p. 217) This question leads Foucault to the insight that modern forms of power are not exercised in the sense of forcing individuals to act and behave in specific ways; rather, power acts upon actions (Foucault, 1983, p. 220). Contemporary struggles in Foucault are seen as forming not against "domination (ethnic, social, and religious)" or "exploitation which separate[s] individuals from what they produce" (although neither have disappeared), but primarily against "subjection," which "ties the individual to himself and submits him to others in this way" (1983, p. 212).

So the exercise of power in Foucault is not to be conflated with the use of violence or with the "obtaining of consent" (neither of which the exercise of power can do without); rather, the exercise of power "is a total structure of actions brought to bear upon possible actions" (Foucault, 1983, p. 220). Such a characterization of power leads Foucault to argue that the form or structure of power relations is that of government – acting upon actions must take place within the context of freedom, or subjection can work only on free subjects who may choose freely within a limited field of application (Foucault, 1983, p. 221). These limits, even though not overtly violent as in the spectacle of public torture and execution, for instance, are often hidden modern forms of violence that can indeed produce unprecedented scales of violence (Oksala, 2010, pp. 37–39).

Thus we have in Foucault an interplay between power and a freedom that refuses to submit to it. Absent this interplay, we would be faced with a master–slave relationship, which is not a relationship of power in Foucault, but rather "a physical relationship of constraint" (Foucault, 1983, p. 221).[27] Power and freedom are entangled to such an extent in the contemporary world that they form an "agonism": a permanent state of provocation between two forces that cannot engage in direct confrontation because such a confrontation would destroy or paralyze the two (Foucault, 1983, p. 222). This state of agonism between power and freedom is at the basis of power relations, and indeed modern social existence (Foucault, 1983, p. 224). Based on this understanding, we can analyse power relations in terms of the various strategies through which they operate.

Although Foucault distinguishes between three senses of "strategy" ("rationally functioning to arrive at an objective," "the way in which one seeks to have the advantage over others," and designating "the means destined to obtain victory") (1983, pp. 224–225), he also maintains that these three senses can "come together in situations of confrontation – war or games – where the objective is to act upon an adversary in such a manner as to render the struggle impossible for him" (1983, p. 225). These are situations of confrontation that aim to establish a solidified order by obtaining victory of one adversary over another. In these situations, relations of power are interlocked with relations of strategy, where the latter are implemented and advanced so as to gain the form and status of the former (relations of strategy becoming relations of power), and where the former, if it continues its line of development, can be turned into a winning strategy if and when it is faced with an adversary. Even if not interlocked, the constant interplay between the two relations can give rise to different sets of interpretations: "from inside the history of struggle or from the standpoint of the power relationships" (Foucault, 1983, p. 226). In other words, these interpretations can either overthrow relationships of power or they can aim to solidify them (this is not dissimilar from the strategic utilities that Foucault outlines for war-repression and contract-oppression, respectively).

Additionally, Foucault argues that when relations of strategy and power are interlocked, we cannot be talking about power relations since these must have an agonism between power and freedom that does not yield a victory for one or the other. Or, if power defeats all struggles against its forms and institutions – if the possibility of insubordination is eliminated – then we are faced with relations of domination, not relations of power (Foucault, 1983, p. 226). In short, when relations of power are apart from (yet connected to) relations of strategy, we have a set of complex systems of institutions, norms, mechanisms, and technologies of rule that operate on the agonism between power and freedom. When relations of power and strategy are interlocked, we have relations of domination wherein power has utterly defeated freedom and exhausted its possibilities – even if at least, and relatively speaking, momentarily.

I do not follow a reading of Foucault that emphasizes the claim that the modern world is marked by either relations of domination or relations of power (sovereign rule or biopolitics), or a reading that explores sovereign violence and biopolitical violence as two distinct species of violence that sometimes dangerously coincide (á la Oksala, 2010, pp. 41–43); instead, I highlight Foucault's line of thinking that focuses on the manner of the interconnection (not combination or mergence) between the two sets of relations (even as they remain distinct in some important ways), which can be better seen when we go back to the schemata for the analysis of power.

In each set of relations, the schema of war-repression strives to reawaken the battle: that is, reawaken the agonism in relations of domination; or reawaken our understanding of our restrictive freedom in relationships of power; the schema of contract-oppression aims to solidify the victory: that is, solidify the antagonistic system of physical constraint and prevent the agonism from re-emerging; or solidify the field of restriction on freedom so as to ensure the victory of certain configurations of power relationships. Put differently, we are left with four arrows operating within a complex field of interaction that is marked by a dual form: one form perpetuates itself by punishing (or threatening to punish) those who transgress the established relationships of power within a political and social formation (formation legitimizes force); the flipside keeps in view the violent founding moment of a political and social formation whereby "legitimacy" was up for grabs, which made it possible to challenge the legitimacy of the established formations because it was never absolute (formation legitimized on force).

Going back to Arendt and Fanon, they are correct in their insight into the paradoxical nature of the relationship between violence and politics: the aim/tendency of violence is to destroy politics, and the aim/ tendency of politics is to put an end to violence. But this does not mean that social scientists must consequently separate the two in the study of political violence. Foucault's work makes it possible to think of the interconnection of politics and violence in their paradoxical relationship. A given formation can establish itself as legitimate through violence (politics ending violence), but on that account opens up the possibility of its own violent annihilation since its continuing (oppressive state) violence serves as a reminder of its founding violence (violence ending politics). This is the crux of the paradoxical relationship between politics and violence. In its dual form, political violence maintains in our view the continued presence of the possibility to create and maintain relations of power *and* domination while simultaneously illustrating that these relations are not ever-lasting or absolute because their guardian – political violence – sits on a gateway that both protects these relations and can also lead to their executioner. Contra Arendt and Fanon, Foucault offers a kind of explanation that does not shy away from or attempt to circumvent the paradox of political violence, but is rather a kind of explanation that gives this paradox its due attention.

Violence, therefore, cannot be captured within conceptual frameworks such as Arendt's or Fanon's, wherein violence must be divided along a destructive-productive axis. The paradoxical relationship between violence and politics that is made visible in Foucault further illuminates the underlying reason why it is virtually impossible to neatly separate violence and politics in these seminal texts. If the relation between politics and violence is essentially paradoxical, then this does not mean that the two cannot and do not meet and conjoin. Indeed, non-violence or a violence that can be controlled is not easily imagined or practised – violence plays an important part in human society.

Even if we are against violence, perhaps *because* we are against violence, this part must be understood. The four arrows that Foucault provides us go some way in understanding this role. For instance, Arendt attempts to posit violence through an arrow that deprives violence of the ability to institute the political, yet she does this for the sake of a peculiar Arendtian agonism that, briefly, seeks to revive the human ability to constitute something new for the cause of human freedom. Her argument, however, cannot be thus neatly separated, as at least two arrows crisscross in this instance: when she downplays the role of violence, she solidifies the field of restriction on freedom by naturalizing certain political and social formations that were born of war (e.g., American democracy); and she simultaneously reawakens the agonism in relations of domination. The interaction between at least these two arrows can produce, for example, the wide range of reactions with/against Arendt, with some calling her conservative and some radical, and both being somewhat correct in their claims. This is what occurs in the paradoxical condition of political violence, and it constitutes the basic reason why it is best for scholarly analysis to pursue the study of political violence in its inherently paradoxical condition, as opposed to an attempt to theoretically circumvent it through a productive-destructive distinction.

Thus, to understand the role of violence in human society, we should not ask if politics is the continuation of violence by other means (á la war-repression) or if violence is the continuation of politics by other means (á la contract-oppression). I think that this question misguides our efforts since violence and politics are not two separate entities; rather, they form a continuum in which relations of domination and power are established, but also continuously resisted, modified, inverted, and negotiated. A debate centred on causality and precedence will inevitably subordinate politics to violence (which Joas warns against) or violence to politics or the political (Arendt, Fanon, Schmitt, Gramsci).

Foucault brings into view the ever-continuous role of violence in maintaining relationships of power and domination as well as the role of violence in initiating struggles against such configurations. The four arrows that his work makes visible operate in a field of interaction that can point them in many different directions at once. This, I argue, is where the idea of a flux that is inherent to political violence is found, yet it is not properly accounted for in Foucault. Foucault's work points out a state of flux in which we may understand violence, but does not quite home in on this flux. His work makes visible the effects of this flux, as he meticulously studies the diverse avenues, mechanisms, technologies, systems in which power operates, making his analyses and many of the subsequent Foucauldian schools' analyses all crucial to our understanding of (post)modern forms of power. Having said that, if we are to understand the movement of violence, then a strict focus on the paradox of political violence will, in a sense, hide as much as it would reveal. Such a focus on violence, where it is viewed only from the vantage point of politics or as always inherently connected to politics and the political, misses the complex and varied ways in which violence plays a role in human society. These complex ways can be brought into view more fully when the study of violence accords the flux inherent to violence its due analytical attention – an attention that can be most properly developed and advanced if the relationship between violence and language comes to the fore of our analysis. Consequently, I argue that it is only in this relationship between violence and language that an analysis *in accordance with the flux* can be advanced – this is the most fruitful way of "freeing" the concept of violence, which will help us understand the diverse impacts, significances, paths, roles of violence in society. This is the task of the dialogical analytic: to move in accordance with the flux of violence. I will draw on Derrida later in chapter 4 to expand on this latter statement, but at this stage this point can be illuminated by briefly examining a similar idea that is found in the work of Gilles Deleuze and Félix Guattari (1987), beginning with their notion of the war machine.

For Deleuze and Guattari, the war machine is not to be confused with war,[28] but is rather a force that overthrows, displaces, interrupts, and mutates the ordered arrangements of things found in the state (1987, p. 417). In this relation, the war machine "seems to be irreducible to the state apparatus, to be outside its sovereignty and prior to its laws: it comes from elsewhere" (Deleuze & Guattari, 1987, p. 352). Accordingly, Deleuze and Guattari differentiate between the military institutions of the state (which reflect the state's attempt to appropriate the war machine) and a war machine that is exterior to the state (1987, pp. 354–355). The war machine constantly evades the capturing efforts of the state and continuously threatens it with counter-attacks.

This takes place in two steps. First, at the moment that the state launches its attack, the war machine defends itself by scattering into "thinking, loving, dying, or creating machines that have at their disposal vital or revolutionary powers capable of challenging the conquering state" (Deleuze & Guattari, 1987, p. 356). In its scattering, the war machine is reconstituted "in sometimes quite unforeseen forms – in specific assemblages such as building bridges or cathedrals or rendering judgments or making music or instituting science, a technology" (Deleuze & Guattari, 1987, p. 366). This leads to the second step, where the war machine awaits its moment to rise once again in a new form that then launches a counter-attack at the state. In short, the relationship between the state and the war machine is marked by

> coexistence and competition *in a perpetual field of interaction,* [by which] we must conceive of exteriority and interiority, war machines of metamorphosis and State apparatuses of identity, bands, and kingdoms, megamachines and empires. The same field circumscribes its interiority in States, but describes its exteriority in what escapes States or stands against States. (Deleuze & Guattari, 1987, pp. 360–361; original emphasis)

Phrased differently, the war machine cannot be reined in by a state apparatus (a greater force that delimits) because it is built to break any attempt at its subordination by subordinating itself before its mortal enemy reaches it. But this self-subordination produces only an illusion of victory for the conqueror: it is indeed a defence mechanism whereby the war machine scatters itself everywhere, and then awaits its moment to rise again in metamorphosis.

In Deleuze and Guattari, violence is always moving, continuously taking on new forms (what Bernstein calls the "protean quality" of violence; 2013, p. 177); although violence itself develops into nothing – although it can never gain an absolute form or manifest itself as such – violence simultaneously plays a significant role in the production and development of systems of rule, social institutions, cultural practices, politics, thinking, loving, etcetera (Deleuze & Guattari, 1987, pp. 356–361). Their most important lesson is that the concept of violence resists all attempts at delimitation. Like the scattering of the war machine when confronted with the state apparatus, every locus into which social and political theorists centralize and restrict violence disappears into a host of directions the moment it is approached. The more social and political theorists attempt to fix and delimit violence (Schmitt and Gramsci), the more it disperses within the analytic, and in this dispersion, violence is largely missed and its effects and emergences are not accounted for.

On a few occasions in this chapter, I separated my theoretical critique from the practical solutions/applications of various thinkers (Fanon, Hardt and Negri, Balibar). I stated that theoretically, I found their positions untenable while at the same I did not necessarily disagree with their practical propositions. The reason for this ambivalent stance is that my critique does not dismiss the instrumentalist view of violence altogether, but rather treats it as a valid perspective that speaks to one dimension of violence. Since it is valid, it of course necessarily produces valid directions for praxis, and hence why I do not disagree with some of the practical solutions. But although it is a valid perspective, it is an incomplete view of violence – the instrumentalist view constitutes but one dimension of violence, and it fails in its attempts to control violence as an instrument of some sort or another and hence does not, cannot, account for the dispersion of violence. For example, since violence cannot ever be captured and held, delimited and contained within the hands of any kind of leadership, then Fanon's hope in the guidance of a strong leadership is misplaced. The task of controlling violence is precisely what national liberation leaderships seek to accomplish, and at which they often fail (as was the case in Algeria). Just as violence emerges from a host of directions, it disperses into a host of directions, most of which are left unseen, unheard, and never captured within the discourse of national liberation (regardless of whether that discourse is genuine or corrupt, honest or delusional, etc.). This movement can travel to an individual's broken heart at having lost a loved one in violence, to a refugee camp and spaces of exile in faraway places, to the building of a shrine, to art, culture, thinking, belonging, loving and dying, to rituals and cultural practices, books, poems, talking, new friendships and severed friendships, and the list is indeed too large to enumerate. This is the second dimension of violence. This is precisely what a one-dimensional view hides and masks from view, and indeed can never grasp, and at the gates of which one-dimensional political projects often falter.

Regardless of their intentions, theoretical attempts to delimit violence in an effort to end "destructive" violence in the employment of "productive" violence fail to control and fix violence. And this theoretical failure is often found in all sorts of specific political projects throughout history.[29] There can be varied reasons for this, each set of reasons belonging to the specificity of each context. But ultimately, the main reason is the one-dimensional view of violence, which, in its inability to properly account for the flux of violence, cannot move into the complexity of the relationship between violence and language, cannot speak to the voices of the dead.

IV. Violence and Death

We have on this earth what makes life worth living: April's hesitation, the aroma of bread at dawn, a woman's point of view about men, the works of Aeschylus, the beginning of love, grass on a stone, mothers living on a flute's sigh and the invaders' fear of memories.

–Mahmoud Darwish, *Unfortunately, It Was Paradise*

How can we think of the relationship between violence and language when the very structure of that relationship consists primarily of the inexpressibility of the former in/through/by the latter? In other words, since violence is intimately connected with death and injury, with the dead and injured, then we must pose the question of its relationship with language as consisting of an inexpressible material, perhaps even an immaterial material – i.e., when death/injury is material (when we come face to face with the dead/injured body), then language is immaterial (we are often at a loss for words), and when language is material (where words attempt to capture death/injury), then death/injury is immaterial (it becomes hidden by our words). While there may never be a satisfactory posing of this problematic, let alone an answer to it, the political and ethical consequences are paramount and unavoidable. A reading of Scarry with Agamben can elaborate the problematic we are dealing with.

In her seminal *The Body in Pain*, Scarry (1985) argues that the uniqueness of expressing physical pain lies in the dynamic of it being at once that which cannot be denied (by the person in pain) and that which cannot be confirmed (by the person hearing about another's pain) (1985, p. 4). Physical pain is inexpressible because it is ultimately unshareable – it constitutes an inner state/consciousness that is unshareable because pain not only resists language but also actively destroys it (Scarry, 1985, p. 172). As an interior state, pain is like no other state because it has no object that is external to it that can make it shareable (Scarry, 1985, p. 5). And yet individuals, social institutions, and states continuously attempt to externalize and objectify pain, which can have two sets of political consequences (Scarry, 1985, pp. 11–19). First, when groups such as Amnesty International attempt to objectify the pain of the tortured and abused so as to terminate torture/abuse, or when medical institutions attempt to measure pain so as to alleviate a patient's pain, the political consequences tend to at least move in the right direction in that there is an effort to eliminate the pain of the sufferer (other examples can be found in the criminal justice system and art). I will examine such a direction toward healing through Das in the next chapter, but of the greatest prevalence for Scarry, and for my purposes at this stage, is the second set of consequences, where the externalization of pain occurs in a way that hides the existence of pain, which allows for the continued use of violence against the person in pain, exemplified in the torture chamber and in war. The key feature of both arenas is the disembodiment of pain, often through a material object (a telephone used in torture, a bullet used in battle, and so on), onto an immaterial imaginary (an ideology, a nationalist idea, a value system), thus concealing the pain of the sufferer (Scarry, 1985, pp. 161–180). More precisely, the act of injuring in war – of opening the body, of presenting the hurt and dead body – serves to (a) determine which set of beliefs and ideas wins and which loses, and to (b) substantiate, or provide a referential stability to these unanchored beliefs and ideas (Scarry, 1985, p. 120). Furthermore, Scarry argues that the act of injuring can have this reality-conferring function because of (a) the experience of injuring and of the injured body is the site of reality par excellence, or compels us toward the ultimate reality of the human condition, and (b) this reality readily provides its stamp of reality on any given set of beliefs and ideas because of the inherent *"referential instability* of the hurt body" (1985, p. 121; original emphasis).

Taken together, this means that the act of injuring is "able to open up a source of reality that can give the [unanchored] issue force and holding power" (Scarry, 1985, p. 124) precisely because the act of injuring is inexpressible at the same time that it releases the full force of reality itself – convincing us that reality is real. In the act of injuring, this sense of the reality of the real is transferred and bestowed onto unanchored beliefs and ideas, compelling the *"incontestable reality of the physical body to now become an attribute of an issue that at that moment has no independent reality of its own"* (Scarry, 1985, pp. 124–125; original emphasis). The experience of the act of injuring, of being injured, and of observing the act of injuring is perceived as the reality – as the materialization and embodiment – of the disembodied immaterial idea (e.g., "nationalism" or "freedom") that is being fought out, precisely because this experience is itself inexpressible and cannot be substantiated in its reality as injured/injuring (Scarry, 1985, pp. 124–133).

I want to go a step further from Scarry's analysis and argue that the reality of violence is both knowable and unknowable – is both reality conferring and reality destructing: not in the Scarry sense of conferring the reality of the winner and destructing the reality of the loser, even if not absolutely and definitively (Scarry, 1985, p. 137), but in the sense that it is both conferring and destructing of all the sides involved, for winner and loser alike (albeit very differently) because it is ultimately transforming all sides involved. Thus I want to understand how this reality of violence, in its ever-elusive character, in its flux, indeed creates a communion between the ideas and beliefs of the sides. The injured/ dead body must indeed come to the fore of the analysis to counter the inscription of this body onto the disputed set of beliefs and ideas (à la Scarry), but I also think that such an inscription is always already challenged by the injured/injuring, dead/killing body – that the injured/ injuring, dead/killing body always already transforms the beliefs and ideas that it is injured/injuring, dying/killing for; and I argue that we need to explore this kind of transformation *without equating* the dead/ injured body with the injuring/killing body. The main reason why the dead/injured, killing/injuring body always already transforms the beliefs and ideas it is killing/dying for is that the inevitable production of death in violence always comes with an elusive element, which, as Giorgio Agamben shows in *Remnants of Auschwitz*, concerns testimonies of witnesses and survivors that operate somewhere between the claim to know everything about the violence and the claim that one cannot know or comprehend the violence at all (2005 [1999], p. 13).

Agamben approaches the question of violence's comprehensibility from a ground similar to Scarry – the violence in the Nazi concentration camps is experienced and remembered by the survivors as the truest reality one has ever experienced and witnessed (that which cannot be denied) at the same time that this reality is irreducible to the facts that constitute it (the reality that exceeds the facts is that which cannot be confirmed)[30] (Agamben, 2005, p. 12). Drawing mainly on Foucault's (1972 [1969]) *The Archaeology of Knowledge* and reorienting it, Agamben attempts to find a location between the two poles of verifying the violence through facts and the inability to comprehend the violence in its full truth, or the sayability and unsayability of violence (Agamben, 2005, pp. 12–14). Agamben argues that Foucault's archaeological method, in examining the taking place of enunciation as opposed to the text that is being enunciated, presents language as a certain being that exists in its taking place. It is the outside of language (its taking place in enunciation – i.e., as discourse) that becomes the object of study for Foucault and not the inside of language (meaning in the enunciation) (Agamben, 2005, pp. 138–140). The emphasis on this system of enunciation redirects the analytical gaze toward the set of rules that define the taking place of discourse as an event – in other words, the site for Foucault's archaeological method lies "between discourse and its taking place" (Agamben, 2005, pp. 143–144). Foucault asserts that a general system forming and transforming statements that he calls the archive constitutes a non-semantic (unsayable) dimension that accompanies any enunciated (sayable) discourse as a function of its enunciation. The archaeological dig takes place in the "system of relations between the unsaid and the said in every act of speech ... between the outside and the inside of language" (Agamben, 2005, p. 144). The effect of Foucault's position (which Foucault begins to reflect on in his later writings), Agamben argues, is the effacement of the subject, of the author of enunciation – since archaeology is preoccupied with a "metasemantics of knowledge" that elucidates the systematic enunciation of statements, the subject necessarily disperses in the saying of the text as opposed to being firmly placed as the enunciator of what is said in the text (2005, pp. 141–142).[31] This effacement becomes especially problematic when the subject of enunciation is attempting to enunciate the subject's desubjectification, as is the case with the survivors of Auschwitz.[32]

Agamben therefore wants to reorient Foucault's method toward the difference between language (which, as opposed to discourse, is the potentiality of speech, the sayable and unsayable of every language) and testimony (which, as opposed to the archive, is language's potentiality, its taking place) (2005, pp. 144–145). The reorientation reintroduces the subject in between the possibility and impossibility, the potentiality and impotentiality of language because the utterance itself is now diminished in favour of the potentiality and impotentiality of the utterance in language. What is said in language, what appears as speech is always accompanied by the potentiality of not being said, not in the sense that a subject may or may not utter a speech, but in the sense that the subject is

> the possibility that language … takes place only through its possibility of not being there … [that] subjectivity … in its very possibility of speech, bears witness to an impossibility of speech. This is why subjectivity appears as *witness*; this is why it can speak for those who cannot speak. Testimony is a potentiality that becomes actual through an impotentiality of speech; it is, moreover, an impossibility that gives itself existence through a possibility of speaking. (Agamben, 2005, p. 146; original emphasis)

In Primo Levi's paradoxical assertion that "the *Muselmann* is the complete witness" of Auschwitz, Agamben explores the said and the unsaid in testimony. The *Muselmann* is the true witness to the destruction of the human being, to de-subjectification, at the same time that the *Muselmann* cannot bear witness, cannot put into speech the de-subjectification. Therefore, the subject of testimony "is the subject who bears witness to de-subjectification" (Agamben, 2005, p. 151). The relation between the witness (human) and the *Muselmann* (non-human) can never be complete/harmonious or separated/disjunctured, the testimony always remaining in-between, always maintaining the possibility of the witness on the basis of the impossibility of the *Muselmann* and vice versa. For Agamben, the very destruction of the *Muselmann* as a non-human always already inscribes the witness's survival of the inhuman (2005, pp. 77, 81–82), not by claiming that the events of the camps were simply unspeakable, thus detaching language from reality and consequently blurring that reality, but by ensuring the accompaniment of unsayability to every sayable word about the camps (2005, pp. 151, 155–157). Testimony consists, in a sense, of terms that recount or make present a remnant, which can be spoken of only through a bearing witness of the subject's incapacity to speak (Agamben, 2005, pp. 133–135, 158–159). By "bringing to speech [the human witness] an impossibility of speech [the non-human *Muselmann*]," the testimony provides an absolute refutation of the denial of Auschwitz at its very foundations, since it brings to bear the fundamental objective or logic of the camps: the complete annihilation and destruction of the subject in both life and death, where the *Muselmann* is produced as the final step along the biopolitical continuum, a step that does not even allow the subject to die, as it eliminates the distinction between life and death before the final step of the gas chamber (Agamben, 2005, pp. 85–86, 164–165). When Agamben leaves the "last word" for the *Muselmann* in his book, this is done not only in reverence to the victims of the German genocide of European Jewry, but also because the testimony that functions on a paradoxical relation between the non-human and the human eliminates the notion of a complete/definable subject, an "I" who can speak as the subject of testimony, since such testimony takes place in a nonplace of which and in which there is no articulation, and in bearing witness to the inhuman, the human becomes eternally connected to, even defined as human in relation to, the inhuman (Agamben, 2005, pp. 102–104, 120–121, 129–130): in short, the voices of the dead, in taking place in testimony, *always get the last word*. Certainly the voices of the dead, which we cannot hear but can only bear witness to their impossibility, can be misheard or hidden from view (as the Nazis attempted to do and their apologists/followers continue to do), but ultimately, they cannot be silenced; something always remains in the destruction of the human (Agamben, 2005, p. 134), and when heard, when we bear witness to them, they can never be unheard.

In addition to the many historical/philosophical analyses of testimonies of trauma and memorialization of suffering (e.g., Edkins, 2003;[33] Jay, 2003, pp. 77–85; Alexander, 2012; Miller, 2014), I think that literature provides the most illuminating illustrations of the difficulty of unhearing the voices of the dead.[34] While the plethora of writings on the theme of "haunting" seems to be the appropriate illustration in this case, I think it can be more usefully seen through the connected theme of the "voices of the dead," which features in one of the short stories written by the Iraqi writer Hassan Blasim. In "An Army Newspaper" (dedicated to the dead of the Iran–Iraq War), Blasim (2009) writes a fictional story of a man who worked for an army newspaper during the war. The short story begins with a scene where the living dig out the man's body from the grave and demand to hear his story, which they are convinced will be an honest account of what had taken place since they believe that even the "bastards" among the dead are "honest." The dead man thanks them for the opportunity and begins to tell the story of how he once worked on the cultural page of the army newspaper. His ultimate dream was to move up the ranks and become minister of culture. Most of the stories and poems he received from front-line soldiers were rather dry and unimaginative, so his role was to make some minor modifications, not to censor the soldiers (since they already censored themselves) but to elevate and heroize their stories.

The turning point came when he received five exquisite stories from one soldier. Each story was written in a different exercise book (the kind used in primary schools) and bore a different name; each story was about the experiences of a different soldier, whose name was written on the cover of the book. The quality of these stories not only dwarfed that of all other submissions to the army newspaper; it dwarfed much of what passes as literature anywhere. Each story was more eloquent, creative, and extraordinary than the previous one. Instead of publishing these stories, the man saw an opportunity to advance his career – what if he convinced the soldier that these writings were subversive to the Ba'athist regime's authority, threatened him with the charge of treason, and then went on to publish the stories as his own? So he sent the soldier a threatening letter.

To his pleasant surprise, he received a letter from the soldier's army corps indicating that the soldier in question had recently been killed in combat. He was delighted that he could now freely publish the stories as his own without fear of being discovered. Upon the publication of the first story, he became internationally famous, such was the superb sophistication of the stories. He became the minister of culture, a world-renowned literary figure, and assured of the Nobel Prize in Literature upon publishing all five stories. But matters were disrupted when months later, he received twenty new stories, from the same soldier, written in the same exercise books, again with different names on the covers of each of the books. In his confusion and terror, he hid the new stories, hoping the problem would simply disappear on its own, but parcels atop parcels continued to flood his office in the ministry. Months passed, and every day the stories would arrive in greater numbers, all still in the same format of the exercise books and the different names, but all from the same soldier, delivered from different locations on the front line, all the stories still of marvellous quality. He received so many parcels that he was forced to buy a warehouse in which to store them. He searched everywhere for this soldier, and every search conclusively proved that this soldier died long ago. He even went as far as finding the soldier's grave and burning his dead corpse. But none of this halted the flood of parcels; the stories kept coming. Eventually, he began to go mad; he resigned from his position at the ministry, divorced his wife, and secluded himself on an isolated piece of agricultural land, where he built an incinerator. He burnt all the stories, but others followed him now to this new address, still arriving every day as the war raged on. He hoped and wished for the war to stop so that the stories would stop flooding in. Finally, the war stopped, but a new one began, and that's when he threw himself into the incinerator. At the end of recounting the story, the dead man says, presumably addressing God, "I know you are the Omnipotent, the Wise, the Omniscient and the Imperious, but did you also once work for an army newspaper? And why do you need an incinerator for your characters?" (Blasim, 2009, p. 20).

As with any work of literature of such depth, there are various avenues of interpretation that open up before the reader. But I think that one of the most important insights that Blasim elucidates in the story is the impossibility of speaking on behalf of the dead, and the impossibility of unhearing the dead once they are heard. Even if misheard, as was the case here where the stories were viewed purely for the purposes of personal gain, the stories cannot but follow us to the point where if we refuse to properly account for them, we are driven into self-destruction. In other words, the inevitable production of death in violence always comes with an elusive element, with a voice of death. And these elusive voices of the dead, of the loss of life that takes place in multiple forms, ultimately can never be silenced. Once heard, these voices of death and loss cannot be unheard even as they continue to be misheard. As Agamben claims, the dead body, when misheard, can itself open up a different kind of language that reaches for the unsaid of violence, ensuring the survival of remnants even in the face of genocidal destruction. Building further on this claim, and following Gadamer/Derrida in later chapters, I will argue that the unsayable of violence indeed commences a different kind of dialogue, a question-answer exchange on the subject matter of violence. The dead body allows in its death for a different kind of inscription to take hold of it. As Scarry points out, this inscription can be one of nationalism, democracy, or even freedom and liberty, which all hear the dead body only in accordance with specific projects of national self-determination, nation-building, liberation, and so on. But all of these attempts cannot move or proceed unscathed by violence. Indeed, violence shapes and moulds all such inscriptions into specific directions that demand the release of violence.

Going a step further from Scarry, then, I argue that one of the main reasons that the inscription moves in this direction is precisely because the killing body always leaves a message for the killed body (again, the two should not be equated). Among a myriad of messages, the enactment of violence always delivers a simple enough message – a message that is always received by the vanquished in violence, a message that is directly coming from the actions of the victor, a message that makes it impossible to silence the dead body: *violence works*. As the discussion on Foucault makes clear, violence can create, maintain, and/or reconfigure relations of domination.[35] This message travels through all the inscriptions that attempt to mishear the voices of the dead. This is why the propagation of violence is always already underway, almost guaranteed, in its enactment.

This simple enough message, however, is not so simple. It is by no means definitive, self-contained, and final. It is but the simplest message that hides a complex myriad of paths and roads through which violence may move. In this movement, violence travels far too fluidly for any political force to capture. Its movement into the second dimension reveals this impossibility. But that is not all. Violence also travels elsewhere, somewhere far more hidden, not directly visible because it is obscured by violence itself, in the enactment of violence itself: a space where the enemies become enemy-siblings. Before reaching these third and fourth dimensions, a closer examination of the second dimension is necessary.

Conclusion

The first dimension of violence posits violence as fundamentally instrumental in nature, exemplified in the works of Arendt and Fanon. While there is analytical validity to this perspective, it limits the conception of violence to a one-dimensional view that cannot take into account the flux of violence. Instrumental conceptualizations posit violence as that which does not need to be directly explained, and in effect, make violence inexplicable outside of a means-ends framework. In Arendt, violence can serve only short-term, limited goals, beyond which violence becomes purely destructive and indeed antithetical to the political as such. In Fanon, if violence does not serve the grand goal of national liberation, the (re)humanization of the colonized, and the creation of a new decolonial world, then violence will degenerate into pure brutality. But these attempts at limiting violence within a productive-destructive distinction cannot analytically hold. Violence as productive or destructive is part of what is to be analysed, and should not form the basis of our analysis of violence.

We should be aware, however, of the dangers associated with the advancement of a non-instrumentalist perspective. As Joas observes, removing the limits of instrumentalism means that violence can become hypostasized, forming the basic foundation upon which we come to understand all aspects of society, state, and politics. As a result, Joas attempts to limit violence through modernity and its analytical tools. This book's analysis of Joas, Lawrence, and Wieviorka shows that whether we use modern or postmodern analytical tools, or a combination thereof, we are unable to limit the concept of violence through a greater concept that subordinates it. This suggests that limiting violence through modernity is bound to fail, and the book suggests that instead of delimiting violence, we ought to "free" the concept.

In Schmitt and the realist school, as well as Gramsci and the critical school, we find prominent attempts to delimit violence. These attempts begin to reveal how these opposing schools of thought make manifest the powerful flow or flux of violence. Following this movement of violence, I argue through Foucault and Deleuze and Guattari for a "freeing" of the concept of violence in the analytical sense of following the flux that is inherent to violence. Foucault brings into view the ever-continuous role of violence in maintaining relationships of power and domination, as well as the role of violence in initiating struggles against such configurations. Foucault's work reveals much about the operation of power in contemporary society, but it yields to a conception of violence where violence is viewed only from the vantage point of politics and the political. The complex movement of violence can be brought into view more fully only when the dialogical analytic moves in accordance with the flux of violence.

While Deleuze and Guattari move us closer to a thinking in accordance with the flux, there is a danger in following their model in that their de-subjectification of violence makes it appear as if it is an omnipresent force that is just there, creating everything around us, while maintaining a certain kind of independent existence that is beyond us. Deleuze and Guattari are right in their claim that the one-dimensional view of violence, where violence is held by the state apparatus, is misplaced and untenable. But this should not be opposed with an absolutely free-flowing violence. Hence "freeing" the concept of violence is indeed (even if counter-intuitively) the surest method of limiting violence within the analytic, as it avoids the critical danger of positing violence as a foundational concept that can explain all aspects of social relations and political formations. The limiting elements are already there within violence, particularly in the fourth dimension, violence the "thing itself." Far from falling into irrationality or chaos, moving beyond the one-dimensional view instead begins to reveal other dimensions and their limiting elements.

This book takes seriously the one-dimensional view and treats it as a valid viewpoint, but only to a certain extent. The limits of this viewpoint must be outlined, and a movement beyond it must be advanced by investigating the relationship between violence and language, highlighting the linguistic dimension of violence. The initial contours of this second dimension can be seen when we examine the voices of the dead. Through Scarry, Agamben, and Blasim, I argue that the voices of the dead, once heard, cannot be unheard, even when we continuously attempt to hear them in instrumental ways. It is in these voices that the movement of violence continues to flow, despite all attempts at delimitation and instrumentalization. Precisely where this movement flows is the path followed next.

The dialogical analytic directs the inquiry onto the flux of violence by charting the movement out of the instrumentalist perspective and toward the two-dimensional view of violence. The analytic will indeed show that the space beyond instrumentalism is multidimensional, that it can and should be outlined, that analysts can and should follow its path, at the same time as showing that this "space" can never be arrived at, in the sense of settling in "it" and describing it as if it "is." Thus the dialogical analytic commences a journey into the other dimensions of violence, without ever leaving behind any one of the dimensions. And what is found in the second dimension is a complex relationship between violence and language, where violence moves into everyday life in a manner that is similar to what Deleuze and Guattari discuss as the war machine's scattering and metamorphosis, but which is better illuminated in the anthropology of Das.

2 Linguistic Violence: The Dispersal of Violence

I have not tamed violence by and into the representations of writing. Indeed one cannot. But neither can one overcome the will to try nor forget the fact of one's trials in so willing.

–E. Valentine Daniel, Charred Lullabies

In subordinating violence, the instrumentalist approach fails to deeply examine the complex relation between violence and language. Exemplary of this shortcoming is Charles Tilly's *The Politics of Collective Violence*, which makes of collective violence a form of "contentious politics" (Tilly, 2003, p. 26). Tilly sees violence as "a kind of conversation" that concerns the processes whereby different groups press claims on each other and where the objects of these claims are likely to raise violent responses (2003, pp. 6, 30). His analysis revolves around a transition from a non-violent civil debate to a violent one, wherein we remain under the heading of contentious politics throughout.

Found here is the conventional notion that the appearance of violence indicates a *transition* from the political process to violence (i.e., from the linguistic exchange of diplomacy, meetings, negotiations, demonstrations to the violent exchange of bombings, killings, displacement). The underlying claim is that when the political process fails to produce an outcome that the parties involved can agree to, then we are likely to witness a resort to violent acts that are meant to reach the political, economic, social, and/or cultural ends sought by the different sides. Tilly's model essentially operates on an instrumental view of violence, and in so doing, maintains the primacy of the political process in our understanding of any given violent conflict. But are violent acts a mere continuation of the political conversation by other means? Do "violent means" simply signal the cessation of a linguistic exchange, and conversely, does such dialogue signal the defeat of violence?

The idea that violence and language are opposites, or at the very least should be separated, is entrenched within the instrumentalist perspective. Such a tendency toward a neat separation between violence and language can be found in Max Weber's (1958a, 1958b) influential essays on the vocations of politics and science. For Weber, science and politics belong to different value spheres that can and should be separated. Politics is intimately connected with domination and both overt violence (e.g., police, military) as well as hidden/subtle violence (e.g., the violence and weaponization of words), whereas science speaks a language of rationality and reason (Weber, 1958a, pp. 78, 115–116, 121; Weber, 1958b, pp. 145–146). The latter's language does not transcend the world through universal reason, since the scientific vocation is a never-ending endeavour of accumulating and progressing specialized bodies of knowledge (Weber, 1958b, p. 138); it rather clarifies, through rational evidence-based analysis, the complexity and chaos of the world (Weber, 1958b, pp. 150–152). In his attempt to secure a language for the specialized expert who could speak about violence from a distance that is safe from the "diabolic" forces and effects of violence, Weber posited a neutral observer of violence who could explain it to the person of politics in rationalist and contextualized terms (Weber, 1958a, pp. 123–127). Underpinning this approach is the image of the academic consultant who provides the politician (or following Tilly, the social movement activist) with rational advice on the proper and improper usages of violence.

While it does have its political and ethical merits, the ethical limits of the Weberian approach have long been discussed, and are convincingly captured in the idea that the scientist, in claiming a distance from the ethics of political decision-making, ends up unwittingly contributing to the state machinery of violence, which is exemplified in the construction of the atomic bomb (Thorpe, 2004). In short, Weber's "ethos of soldierly discipline and value-neutrality facilitates the mobilization of science in the rationalized violence of the modern state" (Thorpe, 2004, p. 64). In addition to these ethical limits, the analytical limits of Weber's approach are best exemplified in the instrumentalist approach's failure to complicate and theorize the relationship between violence and language. Since violence is viewed as fundamentally irrational and in need of the rational language of the specialized expert who can guide policymakers on how to use the instrument of violence, the instrumentalist perspective fails to speak to the social scientist's ability to represent, in language, the movement of violence beyond the policy know-how of violence, following the dispersal of violence in the second dimension and the dialogic moment of violence in the third dimension.

Deleuze and Guattari's ideas point us in this direction, but perhaps a little too far in this direction in that everything becomes flux in their work. Analytically speaking, the work of Das comes closest to outlining the space beyond instrumentalism. Her work in particular, and the anthropological field of "violence and subjectivity" in general,[1] is very much concerned with theorizing violence in a manner that does not overlook the unpredictable flow of violence and its effects on subjectivity, at the same time that the analytic does not completely de-subjectify violence and excuse specific individuals for their violent acts by virtue of the floating character of violence. When discussing the agency-structure debate in the study of violence, Das and Arthur Kleinman pose this difficulty as such: "If we constrain agency in an explanatory framing so fully that no individual persons are to blame, then ethical responsibility cannot be assigned. Make everything agency, and local moral worlds lose the sense of powerful social constraints that organize collective experience" (Das & Kleinman, 2000, p. 17). Citing various studies on violence in the introduction to a collected edition of works, Das and Kleinman explain the fundamental feature of their approach in the following:

> Violence is seen in these ethnographies as having a temporal depth that influences the patterns of sociality.... Violence that is multiple and mundane may be all the more fundamental, because it is out of such hidden or secret violence that images of people are shaped and experiences of groups are coerced.... It is imperative to see how the violences which may have become buried in the routines of the everyday may acquire life – how unfinished social stories may be resumed at different times to animate feelings of hate and anger. (Das & Kleinman, 2000, p. 15)

In their emphasis on the intricate connections between violence and the formation of subjectivity, the various ethnographic studies of the "violence and subjectivity" school highlight the unpredictable and incessant movement of violence and show that there can be no definitive instrumental "end" when it comes to violent acts, events, and conflicts (Das, Kleinman, Ramphele, & Reynolds, 2000). This emphasis on the dispersal of violence through the prism of the limits of language is, in my view, the main contribution of this school and what makes this type of research constitutive of a second dimension of violence. We are not dealing here with the "violence of language" type of analysis, which, while important and insightful, often tends to subordinate violence to language and/or fixate on the instrumental uses of languages in inflicting violence and on using violent language as an instrument toward a political end; rather, in following the dispersal of violence *beyond* language, this school brings to the fore what I call a linguistic dimension of violence: a dimension where the complexity of the relationship between violence and language begins to take shape, revealing the wide range of effects, roles, manifestations, and metamorphoses of violence as it moves beyond the instrumental limits we impose on it – as violence moves beyond the "violent event." While it may not be so obvious at first sight, I think that Slavoj Žižek's (2008) arguments in *Violence* prove helpful in more precisely positioning the significance and uniqueness of Das's contribution, showcasing why I focus almost exclusively on her work as constituting a second dimension of violence, as opposed to the wider engagement with different authors found in chapter 1.

I. Navigating Violence in the Event and the Everyday

Implicitly following a long tradition in peace and conflict studies,[2] Žižek maintains that violence cannot be reduced to its most visible acts, such as school shootings, violent crimes, terrorist attacks, violent riots, and so on. He calls these acts, which are always carried out by an identifiable agent, a form of "subjective violence." The shock, horror, and terror of such acts force us to fixate on this form, whereby we come to understand violence only in and through the terms of subjective violence. But while they are the most visible acts of violence, most worrisome are forms of "objective violence," which are made up of both "symbolic" and "systemic" violences (Žižek, 2008, pp. 1–2, 9–10). Symbolic violence does not only concern discourse or language that incites violence, but primarily refers to the universe of meanings that serves to shape what we see and define as violent and as non-violent – when we describe an act as violent, we are always also normalizing various social, economic, and political structures as non-violent, which ensures the smooth functioning of those very structures: structures that are in fact extremely violent, as they constitute the systemic violences Žižek wants to emphasize (Žižek, 2008, pp. 58–73) (e.g., how universes of meaning in Western discourse hide from view the massive violences that colonial Belgium committed in the Congo, and how the violent conditions in the Congo and affluent conditions in Belgium today are very much shaped by these (post)colonial systems/processes; Žižek, 2008, pp. 2–3; for another example, see Žižek's critique of "liberal-communism"; 2008, pp. 24–27, 36–39).

The problem for Žižek is that objective and subjective violence cannot be observed from the same vantage point: subjective violence is experienced and observed as a disruption to the normalcy of social life, to the peaceful character of that normalcy; objective violence is the violence inherent to that normalcy, the violence of the background itself (Žižek, 2008, p. 2).[3] This leads him to conclude that scholars, activists, and critical intellectuals should not directly observe and examine subjective violence, since that gaze will always prevent us from observing objective violence. The horror of violent acts will always mystify violence, "and the empathy with the victims inexorably function[s] as a lure which prevents us from thinking" critically about violence, so he proposes instead a set of sideway glances at violence (Žižek, 2008, pp. 3–4).

Žižek's points are significant in their critique of instrumentalist conceptions of violence, which tend to ignore how violence, in its systemic and symbolic forms, cannot be observed when one is fixated on measuring the calculations, projects, and effects of identifiable agents who carry out violent acts, whether on an individual level (school shooter) or on a massive scale (military campaigns). The operation of the most extreme violent systems (capitalism, [neo]colonialism, patriarchy) almost always lacks this identifiable subject or agent, and with it the neat means-ends calculations that the instrumentalist perspective continuously strives to find. But Žižek's suggestion of sideway glances that turn away from the victim, not out of cruelty of course, but out of his desire to critically examine violence, is limited for one main reason: Das can speak to what Žižek would call objective violence by indeed better listening to the victim and following the victim. Her work achieves the critical distance that Žižek pursues, but in a more fruitful direction that can direct the analysis toward healing from the outset. In addition, I argue that looking directly at violence (as opposed to glancing sideways at it) is absolutely necessary for scholars to better understand the hidden dimensions of its operations.[4] Indeed, like Žižek, Das does not advocate for a direct gaze at violence, though for different reasons. To reach this discussion, I first examine Das's different approach toward the victims of violence.

There are a number of themes in Das's work on violence in *Life and Words*, two of which especially stand out. The first concerns violence and language, dealing with questions surrounding the (in)ability of language to express events of violence, both in the positive sense that language refuses to emanate from violence (the role of silence), and in the negative sense that language does not dare venture into the sphere of world-annihilating violence. The second theme concerns founding violence and maintaining violence, and the role of such distinct yet interconnected moments of violence in community and state formations.

I should note from the outset that while I share some of Das's ethical and theoretical stances as a scholar attempting to theorize and write violence, I do have some differences regarding the *direction* of the overall thesis of her work, which runs across the themes mentioned above. I am referring to her notion of a descent into the ordinary, into the everyday. So I organize my reading of her work around the two themes in order to highlight some of the important theoretical points (though not necessarily her concepts) that I will develop in chapters 3 and 4, but ultimately, this book differs from Das in that it refuses the choice between either descent or ascent.

In her book, Das advances an analytical framework that descends into the ordinary, into the everyday, in order to study violence. This approach derives from her refusal to subordinate the everyday to the event. Such a subordination, which underpins most conventional studies of violent conflict, she asserts, occurs when a given violent event is considered so powerful and unexpected, so horrific and incomprehensible, that it comes to occupy a special place in the analysis. This special place, because it is powerful, comes to mark the general outline of a given history, but because it is incomprehensible, it comes to also mark an anomaly in the unfolding of history. The anomaly is basically a moment when civilization is seen to have broken down and where human barbarity and savagery take over for, relatively speaking, a brief moment.[5] What underlies this conventional approach to the study of violent events is the notion that the human subject is left intact and almost unaffected by this anomaly, which is seen by the time of analysis and writing as having passed (Das, 2007, p. 79).[6] The ordinary, seen in such approaches as the simple unfolding of life in the everyday, is at best placed in the background, receiving minimal if any attention in the analytical process (Das, 2007, pp. 1–11).

Das's descent into the ordinary does not question the notion that something extraordinary does indeed occur when violent events, such as the 1984 riots in Delhi, take place, but she does question whether that is reason enough to downplay or subordinate the ordinary. For her, such subordination stems from the fact that "our theoretical impulse is often to think of agency in terms of escaping the ordinary rather than as a descent into it" (Das, 2007, pp. 6–7).[7] Not only does this theoretical impulse miss the extent to which a violent event makes and remakes the subject well after the event's occurrence, but it also misses how in such instances the subject makes and remakes subjectivity and the world. Thus both suffering and recovery, both destruction and (re)construction, are perhaps most poignantly seen in the everyday, and not necessarily in the violent event per se. The everyday here – rather than the event – is the "anchor" (Das, 2007, p. 7). This is not the same as saying that the everyday is the cause, and the event is the effect. The everyday is an anchor in the sense that it is the space where violent events and their effects are negotiated and understood, thus forming the soil out of which violent events may grow, as well as the soil out of which peace and reconciliation may flourish (Das, 2007, pp. 136, 149). In Das, subjects are formed through the complex interplay between the event and the everyday.

It is in this mediation that analysts can study violent events, which neither academic nor ordinary languages have grammar for. Das's assertion is that the moment of world-annihilating violence in the event is where language falters and fails. Language, for her, comes after this moment of world-annihilating violence, and often this language comes in the form of silence in the face of world-annihilating violence; but the sphere of world-annihilating violence cannot be said to be even silence. Thus Das emphasizes the (in)ability of language to express events of violence, both in the negative sense that language does not dare venture into the sphere of world-annihilating violence, and in the positive sense that language refuses to emanate from violence (the role of silence).

In Das, silence in the face of world-annihilating violence is to be viewed as both a tool for recovery (as subjects attempt to re-inhabit their world of devastation and loss) and as a tool to combat the excess of speech found in nationalist discourse (e.g., discourse that promulgates images of abducted Hindu women by lustful Muslim men for the sake of the state's strategic interests). In both cases, silence evades the abyss of world-annihilating violence, which does not reside in a transcendent world, but rather occupies a space within oneself and within everyday relationships. It is a space that contains poisonous knowledge, which must be contained within walls of silence (Das, 2007, p. 54).[8] Das warns anthropology against a transcendental view of the abyss, where anthropologists adopt the speaking genre of certain poets and novelists – those who push language where it does not dare venture, although like many before and many since them, they never allow the reader (or themselves?) to directly gaze at the violent event.[9] Das here follows the notion that "those who tried to name it [that which died with world-annihilating violence] … touched madness and died in fierce regret for the loss of the radical dream of transforming India" (2007, p. 58).

Looking at the abyss through a descent into the ordinary also has to be undertaken with extreme care. Madness is never far off, whether one approaches the abyss through an ascent to the transcendent or a descent into the ordinary. But in descent, the danger of opening up the abyss is also for Das the opportunity to let the other's pain mark the ethnographer. She relates to the pain of the other by underpinning the notion of language's refusal to emanate from violence for the sake of healing (i.e., the positive sense of the limits of language vis-à-vis violence). Put another way, the failure of language in this sphere of world-annihilating violence is not necessarily due to the weakness of language, but due to the danger lurking beyond the limits of language. Thus, the ascent to the transcendent, where only certain kinds of poets venture, moves into nowhere, or better yet, into pure madness (i.e., beyond the limits of language – a space marking the negative sense of the limits of language vis-à-vis violence); the descent into the ordinary, where only the sufferer can and must visit (and where ethnographers like Das may follow) but never enter (for entrance would be madness), moves into a space of loss and recovery, pain, and healing (Das, 2007, pp. 60–62, 74). More specifically, they can visit it by rewriting and reworking the violence that seeped into their everyday relations, but they can never move through the walls that surround world-annihilating violence (Das, 2007, p. 86). This is essentially the meaning of Das's observation of women inhabiting the world in a "gesture of mourning for it" (2007, p. 77).

In her discussion on the figure of the abducted woman during the 1947 partition of India, Das shows how state formation was founded on a story of abduction and recovery of women during the violence of the partition. She argues that a social contract, in which men formed the sphere of the political, had as its counterpart a sexual contract in which women were forced into the domestic sphere, where the "right" kind of men (i.e., protectors of women) would be produced for the political sphere (2007, pp. 19–22, 33). The figure of the abducted woman emerged in nationalist state discourse through a sexual contract that allowed the institution of a masculine social contract – both contracts were part of the state's inaugural moment (Das, 2007, p. 179). In this case, state discourse "recognized their [women's] suffering as relevant only for the inauguration of sovereignty" (Das, 2007, p. 37). For Das, "the 'foundational' event of inaugurating the nation then is itself anchored to the already circulating imaginary of abduction of women that signaled a state of disorder since it dismantled the orderly exchange of women" (2007, p. 21).[10] So here, the founding violence does not institute something from nowhere, but is "anchored to imageries that already haunt Hindu-Muslim relations" (Das, 2007, p. 22). Everything from the lustful Muslim, to the purity of the household and childbearing, to the innocent and passive Hindu woman, to the changing role of the Hindu man (e.g., loyalty toward kinship is replaced by a loyalty toward the state) – all of these and more both explain and are themselves explained by the violence of the partition (Das, 2007, pp. 34–36).

Here, Das avoids the determinism of the state-centric view by highlighting how women still manage to form their subjectivity despite the suffocating influence of state discourse at the same time that she does not downplay such influence (2007, p. 59). Das undertakes this manoeuvre by first describing the oscillation between what she calls the "rational-bureaucratic organization" of the state and the "magical" form of the state (2007, p. 162). By the rational mode, Das refers to "the structure of rules and regulations embodied in the law as well as in the institutions for its implementation" (2007, p. 162). By the magical mode, she refers to the local practices (such as petitions or inquiries into state practices through the law) through which "the state acquires a presence in the life of communities" (2007, p. 163). She uses the word "magical" to denote the uncertainty, vulnerability, and consequentiality involved for the local communities that undergo such practices, as well as the sort of other-worldly stature of law for them (i.e., law is viewed by local communities as a force that is up there, beyond us down here, not transparent, cannot be pointed at, etc.) (Das, 2007, p. 163).

The oscillation between these two modes is explained through Derrida's notion of signature. Das borrows from Derrida the "idea of writing as occurring in a context that is never fully saturated" (Das, 2007, p. 163).[11] According to Das, Derrida challenges the notion of intentionality in writing (i.e., the idea that whatever one intends in one's writing is all that piece of writing can be capable of accomplishing, to varying degrees, of course), and presents us with "the force of breaking that is inherent in the act of writing itself" (Das, 2007, p. 163). So when the state writes itself, as it were, through its rational mode, it opens itself up to a variety of local practices that can take this writing in unpredictable directions (unpredictable for the state and the local community alike) – in other words, it opens itself up to its magical mode, where the state can no longer control the manner in which its laws may function. The state, then, is present in the life of the community in the sense that its laws (rational mode) give the community its validity (e.g., it is a legally recognized part of the nation state) and in the sense that its laws can be used against it to stop the encroachment of the state upon the local community (e.g., using the law, often an extra-legal use of the law, to stop the demolition of houses within a given community) (Das, 2007, pp. 166–167).

This for Das explains why in scenes of violent riots, the crowds may chant in the name of the law. The lines between the founding and maintaining violence of the law are blurred because of state oscillation between a rational and a magical mode, not only during times of exception or crisis, but as an ongoing process in the everyday (Das, 2007, pp. 168, 177). Whether through rumour or official public inquiries into state practices, the lines between what is legal and illegal are always questioned in the everyday relationships of local communities. The process of legitimization that begins in the inaugural moment of the state (founding violence) does not cease there, but continues in the maintaining violence of the state, where it can be observed most poignantly in the life of the community. While such community practices and spaces are marginal to the state, Das claims that they are certainly not peripheral either to the community itself or analytically speaking. State discourse cannot simply manipulate or produce subjects in local communities, because the state signature on the law cannot lay full or complete claim on what is written in the law (Das, 2007, pp. 177–183).

Let us go back to the figure of the abducted woman, which at this point can make clear Das's superior ability to speak to what Žižek would call objective violence, not by avoiding the victim but rather by carefully following the victim. While the suffering of the abducted woman is essentially drowned out by the excess of speech found in state discourse, the walls of silence around world-annihilating violence within the subject ensure the development of a certain agency and allow these women to form their subjectivity in and through the relationships of the everyday: "The formation of the subject as a gendered subject is then molded through complex transactions between the violence as the originary moment and the violence as it seeps into the ongoing relationships and becomes a kind of atmosphere that cannot be expelled to an 'outside'" (Das, 2007, p. 62). Norm-setting legislation, as Das calls it, and transgression move hand in hand here. The subject transgresses the norms constituted by state discourse concerning the violent event by moving back toward the inexpressible abyss in a gesture of mourning. Not through words necessarily, but through the recovery of damaged relationships, for example.

The founding violence of the state, then, does not cease with its officially announced end (i.e., rioters have returned to their homes, order has been restored, killings, abductions, and destruction have ceased, etc.), but this is the moment when such violence is only beginning. Violence seeps into the ongoing everyday relationships, and it is in the unfolding of life in the everyday that this founding violence keeps moving (Das, 2007, pp. 108–109). In Das's account of "the temporal depth in which such originary moments of violence are lived through, everyday life reveals itself to be both a quest and an inquest" (2007, p. 78).

Das argues that the difference between these two moments of violence, what makes them distinct yet interconnected, has to do with the work, not representation, of time. Das asserts that the narration of founding violence has a "frozen slide quality" to it – it is basically a "non-narration" (2007, p. 87). The violence that seeps into the everyday, on the other hand, is constantly worked on – reworked and rewritten through cultural symbols and practices, for example. In this sense, time "is an agent that 'works' on relationships … as different social actors struggle to author stories in which collectivities are created and re-created" (Das, 2007, p. 87). This reworking moves close to the silence surrounding the partition, but maintains a healthy distance from it so that speech can go on in the everyday (as I said earlier, in this sense it visits but does not enter the abyss):

> I have tried to conceptualize the violence that occurs within the weave of life as lived in the kinship universe as having a sense of the past continuous, while the sudden and traumatic violence that was part of the Partition experience seems to have been frozen. Time cannot perform its work of writing, re-writing, or revising in the case of the second kind of violence. (Das, 2007, p. 88)

The founding violence shatters not only bodies but also the language of everyday life (of our cultural, social, and political universes) to such an extent that speech becomes impossible (Das, 2007, p. 89). Das suggests "that what becomes the non-narrative of this violence is what is unsayable within the forms of everyday life" (2007, p. 90). Furthermore, this founding violence questions the very notion of the human – could humans commit such extreme acts of violence, is a question that plunges everyone's humanity into doubt, perpetrator (are they an animal?) and victim (are they a thing?) alike. Because of this, such violence remains unspeakable and contained within walls of silence, the breach of which may very well signal the onslaught of this violence once again. Time cannot do work on what is frozen, on what cannot be touched, and on what if unleashed could turn time back on itself.[12] So the events of the partition are indeed of the past, but as Das observes, the partition "did not have a *feeling* of pastness about it" (2007, p. 97; original emphasis). The partition is there in the present, and there for the future, always in the everyday, but is itself frozen or absent. So how can we account for the continuation of something that is, for all intents and purposes, absent?

Das explores the question of absence, not from the view of one's inability to express what is inexpressible (a view that tends to highlight only the weakness of language or the weakness, if not lack, of agency), but from the view of absence as (a) blindness to part(s) of one's experiences (whether this blindness is wilful or not is insignificant because the work of time simply makes it blindness) and (b) a loose connection to floating words. Put differently, absence concerns the connection one forms to a past experience through a dissociation from some of the horrific details (blindness), and an association with floating words that are free of authorship (i.e., they lack a signature) and that, as such, can bring the dissociated part of the past to the present (Das, 2007, pp. 104–105). In short, she wants to understand how it is that the event remains present in its absence.

Two directions can be taken from this point. The first Das associates with Achille Mbembe's work, which Das admires but is hesitant to accept. According to Das, Mbembe traces the African failure at self-writing (i.e., the persistence in writing Africa primarily through tropes of war, devastation, famine, etc. – in other words, through the trope of victimhood and not subjecthood) to a series of denials that fail to directly face the horrors of Africa's past (Das, 2007, pp. 212–224). The problem for Mbembe then becomes concerned with how we, in the present, can recover and master the memory of the horrific past and resolve the unfinished story of the victims and survivors (Das, 2007, p. 219). In this way, it is hoped that nihilistic escape from the past can then turn into affirmative self-writing: victim can turn into agent.

The second direction is Das's own. Rather than view unclaimed experiences of the past (blindness) as "escape," Das introduces the possibility that subjectivity can be formed through a gesture of mourning that inhabits the world of devastation with the full understanding that parts of that world are lost forever and thus cannot be reclaimed or recovered (2007, pp. 214–215). So Das does not see the problem as one of "writing the self," which focuses only on what language can or cannot express and how, but rather focuses on the "contrast between saying and showing" in understanding how subjects are already affirmatively forming their subjectivity even when they are seemingly blind to their horrific past (2007, p. 216). This contrast is what allows Das to explore words and gestures that point us toward ongoing everyday practices of dealing with, and living in, what is inexpressible. Descent into the ordinary shows the complex ways in which subjectivity is (re)made by dealing with violence through everyday means.[13] These means, these forms of inhabiting the world in a gesture of mourning, are marked not by what are conventionally understood as extraordinary acts, but by their careful attendance to limits (whether the limits of official state discourse, or the walls of silence that cannot be breached), and the careful transgression of these very same limits (Das, 2007, pp. 217–218).

Time for Das can work only on what is accessible, which is not to say that the violence that seeps into the everyday is easy to deal with and readily open for the work of time, of rewriting and overwriting everyday relationships. Extreme care is needed (e.g., observing the interplay between word and gesture) to understand the full scope of what this difficult process entails in both its successes and failures (Das, 2007, pp. 91–92). For example, Das finds the work of time in the feeling of the aforementioned absence, which some women embodied by sitting in stillness, as if letting their unclaimed and unspoken experiences speak for themselves through gesture, building relationships with the dead by a gesture of mourning that understands that it takes a stone-like gesture to speak with what has been turned into stone (Das, 2007, p. 107).

Another example is the language of rumour, which has the ability to ignite acts of carnival-like violence (where crowds act in ways that they normally would not) because the words of rumour are free of authorship. These are words that can be repeated by anyone at any time to touch a past that is frozen but, because iterable in the manner of floating words, is a past that does not, as Das observes, have a "feeling of pastness about it." Words describing what *they* did, how *we* suffered, how we lost, how they were animals and we were things, how they defied the law and we must restore it – all of these words are floated through a crowd that can then distance itself from its violent actions as far as the words are distanced from the crowd: authorship disappears. Das sees the work of the everyday as countering this tendency, and the task of anthropologists is thus to observe the processes "through which victims and survivors affirm the possibility of life by removing it from the circulation of words gone wild – leading words home, so to speak" (2007, p. 221).

I am not certain that we have to choose between Das and Mbembe, since they both share some key elements that are not necessarily opposed. Namely, they share the critical idea that violence disperses into our very subjectivity, shaping and forming our world long after the violent event has gone into the realm of our "past" without truly ever becoming "the past." From this shared critical basis, Das does veer in a slightly different direction from Mbembe, but both directions can coexist in the same analysis, where we can examine the role of silence in dealing with the horrors of the past while at the same time reclaiming those violent experiences within varying forms of self-writing that do not rest on silence – all for the sake of healing and countering violence.

I think that Alexander Weheliye's (2014) work makes manifest part of what is at stake when we concede and relegate past horrors only or primarily to silence.

Briefly, Weheliye draws on Hortense Spillers's concept of the "hieroglyphics of the flesh," arguing that flesh – "the living, speaking, thinking, feeling, and imagining flesh" that slaves were reduced to through torture, injury, death – antecedes the construction of the body (qua legal personhood) within hierarchical racializing assemblages (Weheliye, 2014, pp. 39–40). The destruction of black bodies through the violence of slavery into flesh (broken limbs, scarred skin) creates racializing assemblages and is not simply an outcome of hierarchical distinctions or the breakdown of all distinction (Weheliye, 2014, p. 43) – that is, the violence "supplies the symbolic source material for racialization" (Weheliye, 2014, p. 28). The injured/dead flesh carries with it the marks of violence that institute and constitute the world inhabited by the body, both in the sense of how the flesh comes to mark the body as, for example, subhuman in the liberal state, and in the sense of how the pain and suffering of the flesh can conjure or imagine new forms of freedom and of what it means to be human (Weheliye, 2014, pp. 11–14, 44–45, 124). The flesh becomes the very material that can both create and destroy our world (or, to go back to Scarry's terms, make and unmake the world). Thus, Weheliye introduces an approach that accounts for (1) moments where the body remains situated within the ideas and beliefs that attempt to gain referential stability (to use Scarry's terms) through the dead/injured flesh (e.g., the black body as subhuman) and (2) moments when the flesh, *in carrying the marks of violence*, unsettles and transforms those very ideas and beliefs (e.g., engendering new forms of freedom).

The second moment can be achieved only when we directly gaze at, reflect on, and reclaim past horrific violences. My concern with having to choose between Das and Mbembe is that Das's direction can miss the potential of (re)writing the moment of violence to counter the hegemonic attempts that use the "symbolic source material" of violence for the purpose of (re)constituting systems and ideologies of racialization, domination, and colonization. Das and Weheliye both understand that dominant social and political forces make use of the symbolic source material of violence in order to saturate the vacuum created by silence with their self-interested talking points. In Das, however, the heavy emphasis on the victims' use of silence in countering hegemonic discourse can, I think, lead to an analytical de-emphasis on how such source material itself, when directly examined and rewritten, can challenge and transform the symbolic universe of those dominant forces. And more directly for my purposes, how an attempt to (re)write the violences can lead the analysis toward the two other dimensions of violence.

I want to stress that I am not opposed to a focus on the victims. I certainly agree with Das's focus on the victims and survivors of violent events and favour it against Žižek's approach, which directs us away from the victim. I simply want to stress that in addition, the analytic has to account for the inexpressible horrors of violence *and the possibility of (re)writing them*. This limitation of Das's analytic is best observed in how she addresses the perpetrators of violence. On the infrequent occasion that Das speaks of the perpetrators of world-annihilating violence, she assigns this figure a kind of false subjectivity. For example, when discussing the violence in the streets of Sultanpuri, Das asserts that three "registers of speech" marked the crowd's chants: the caste, the nation, and the global world. In all three registers, the crowd drew up images that were far removed from their real conditions (i.e., from the reality of their everyday relationships). Das concludes that this is a case of "a 'brokered' subjectivity in which the publics created in the streets of Sultanpuri somehow transcended the local for those few days that they completely ruled the streets" (2007, p. 160). When this "brokered" subjectivity, a subversion of subjectivity at bottom, cannot be moved forward in time, then the suggestion is that one's actions are undertaken without knowing what one is actually acting, as indeed Das herself states (2007, p. 161). For instance, someone committing violent acts against another is not ridding the world of an evil other and thus restoring the law; rather, that perpetrator is killing another human being, under an illusion of who they are, who the other is, and what their world constitutes. This constitutes a predominant view of the perpetrators' subjectivity. Even in typologies that expand the kinds of subjectivities engaged in violence, the underlying assumption holds.

Going back to Wieviorka's work, he offers a sociological typology of the kinds of subjectivities that correspond to five different logics of violence. He distinguishes between a "floating subject" who responds to the negation of their identity, values, culture, beliefs by resorting to violent action as a means of forcing their subjectivity onto the social/political landscape (e.g., the rioters' violent actions in response to the injustice of the Rodney King case); a "hyper-subject" who responds to the plethora of meanings, the excess of meanings, by expecting violence to create new social and political spaces in accordance with what they are convinced to be the real set of meanings that ought to govern the social and political landscape (e.g., the German-born Arab who violently attacks Germany on behalf of Middle Eastern states or peoples); a "non-subject" who simply follows orders or the law in their enactment of violence – the disappearance of subjectivity in these cases enables the callous implementation of violence (e.g., the German soldier following Nazi orders); an "anti-subject" who engages in violence for the sake of violence, whose violence reduces the victim to a thing or an animal that can be tortured or killed with impunity, and is carried out for the sake of pleasure (e.g., serial killers); and a "survivor-subject" who is similar to the anti-subject but whose violence is carried out to secure a primal desire to survive as a subject, regardless of whether or not their fear of non-survival is real or perceived (Wieviorka, 2009, pp. 150–157).

Wieviorka does not posit the five figures as absolute types, distinct and isolated from one another in events and acts of violence. All five may coexist (within a collective or an individual) in any one given act, event, or experience (Wieviorka, 2009, pp. 157–159). The task of the researcher is to search for the variations, transformations, and complex configurations of all five subjectivities. But for Wieviorka the overall trend of violence when it is enacted is to move subjects toward a distortion or perversion of meanings, intentions, values, identities, and so on – in short, the overall trend moves toward a distortion and perversion of subjectivity (2009, p. 163). He insists that the main problem of our world today is the prevalence of a floating and a hyper-subject, as these are the forms of subjectivity most likely to engage in large-scale collective violence. And since both rest on a radical separation from the social, from social relations, the political process, community values, and so on, both can be dealt with through education and community engagements that establish or re-establish a social bond (Wieviorka, 2009, pp. 165–170). Succinctly put, the perpetrators of violence, while varied in their reasons for using violence, are always driven by their acts of violence toward a perversion of their subjectivity, which can be dealt with only through a proper integration into acceptable political avenues of action. Their violence is an action that knows not what it is indeed doing, as it leads them farther away from real action that can move their subjectivity forward in time. Thus, even though more detailed, Wieviorka's typology takes us back to Das's claim of a brokered subjectivity.

The difference between the dialogical analytic and Das's analytic (as well as Wieviorka's typology) centres precisely on the following point, and no matter how uncomfortable, terrifying, and disquieting it is, this point is to be insisted upon: the enactment of violence does not necessarily tend toward a space of distortions, perversions, and/or absolute madness. Rather than posit a sphere of so-called world-annihilating violence as pure madness and thus pass this sphere over in silence, the dialogical analytic directly tackles the problem of so-called world-annihilating violence and examines the relationship between violence and language in the very sphere where such a relationship supposedly dissipates or never forms at all. The dialogical analytic insists on, to go back to the discussion on Weheliye, the possibility of (re)writing the inexpressible horrors of violence. While I agree with Das's positive sense regarding the inability of language to express violence (the role of silence), I take a different stand on her negative sense that language dissipates in a sphere of world-annihilating violence that cannot be known. This different stance essentially concerns a shift of emphasis from what is expressed, or is not expressed, to the realm of (un)knowability.[14] Thus, despite the many strengths of her approach, Das leaves unexamined the two other dimensions of violence.

Das claims (as does Wieviorka albeit more indirectly) that perpetrators of violence do not know what they are actually doing, and thus she does not explore what they know when they know and do not know while committing acts of a horrific carnival-like violence. The third dimension is in fact revealed when the violent actions of the perpetrators are seen as being undertaken *without knowing what one knows in knowing, (not)knowing.* This claim is crucial and can be properly understood only through a sustained engagement with Gadamer, Derrida, and their encounter. To reach this discussion of knowledge and so-called world-annihilating violence, I will first need to transition the analysis from Das to Gadamer/Derrida via Wittgenstein's view of language. In Wittgenstein's view of language can be found Das's philosophical reason for theorizing against any type of ascent or any kind of talk of transcendence. Das sees transcendental thinking as that which opposes her favoured approach of a descent into the ordinary. Thus, in Das, we find a binary opposition between the descent into the ordinary and an ascent to the transcendent, whereby the latter concerns a transcendental thinking that moves into nowhere – into pure madness. Moreover, this transcendental thinking is where she locates the negative sense of the limitations of language vis-à-vis violence.

Needless to say, this is not the only definition one may give to the word "transcendence." I would not assert that I put forth a more "accurate" or "truer" definition of transcendence, but my argument is that there is a different understanding of transcendence that is more fruitful to the study of violence: an understanding that neither treats any attempt at transcendental thinking as destined to madness or nothing, nor instead posits transcendence as a reference to some other-worldly superior force or value, but rather an understanding that is *open* to the transcendental element that is operative in the "conversation" over violence – an element that I indeed argue operates in Das's work despite her efforts to expel transcendence from her writing.

II. The Limits of Language

Someone who, dreaming, says "I am dreaming," even if he speaks audibly in doing so, is no more right than if he said in his dream "it is raining," while it was in fact raining. Even if his dream were actually connected with the noise of the rain.

–Ludwig Wittgenstein, On Certainty

Das follows Stanley Cavell and the later Wittgenstein in asserting that "the experience of being a subject is the experience of a limit" (2007, p. 4).[15] The subject here does not invent the world, but rather makes and remakes the world as the world simultaneously makes and remakes the subject.[16] The interplay between subject and world, which primarily takes place in language, is in other words never-ending and non-absolute. As Cavell puts it, Wittgenstein's "vision of language" places the subject already in the world at the very moment of language; or when the subject speaks, gestures, writes, it is not from a position outside the world describing it as a thing – as *it is* – but from a position already initiated into the world by virtue of the very ability to speak, gesture, write (Cavell, 1979, pp. 168–190). Language does not convey our inner experience or our thoughts – or, language does not convey our thoughts about things as things-in-themselves – rather, our limits in language are our limits in the world; they are indicative of our limits in the world, not of our thought. In his preface to *Tractatus Logico-Philosophicus*, Wittgenstein articulates this point as such:

> What can be said at all can be said clearly, and what we cannot talk about we must pass over in silence. Thus the aim of the book is to draw a limit to thought, or rather – not to thought, but to the expression of thoughts: for in order to be able to draw a limit to thought, we should have to find both sides of the limit thinkable (i.e. we should have to be able to think what cannot be thought). It will therefore only be in language that the limit can be drawn, and what lies on the other side of the limit will simply be nonsense. (Wittgenstein, 2005 [1921], pp. 3–4)[17]

The world does not make predetermined subjects, and the subject does not simply invent the world, because "the subject does not belong to the world: rather, it is a limit of the world" (Wittgenstein, 2005, p. 69). This is where Wittgenstein affirms a "truth" in solipsism and says that "the limits of my language mean the limits of my world" (2005, p. 68). The existence of the world can never be known, and as such "the world is independent of my will" (Wittgenstein, 2005, p. 85), but it is my world because it is shown in my language.

Thus my will can alter the limits of my world, but not the world as world (i.e., as a referent). So what we end up with is a continuous interplay between the world and subject whereby the limits of the subject's world are forever shifting and changing. Hence, a subject, already initiated into the world, puts together different fragments of experience, of the subject's world, and develops a totality that must have certain limits or boundaries because the experience of being a subject is not limitless; but this totality cannot be said or thought, and the boundaries are always already incomplete because "what expresses *itself* in language, *we* cannot express by means of language" (Wittgenstein, 2005, p. 31; original emphasis), which means that the limits and boundaries we draw (which must ground us because subjects cannot be limitless) are not grounded (because we are unable to express the boundary; all we can say is that we have a boundary, or show *how* a boundary limits us, but not *what* the boundary is), and can therefore be shifted, negotiated, their fragments reassembled, but with certain restrictions, and so on (for an illustration of this type of analysis, see Das, 2007, pp. 63–78).

To understand Wittgenstein's view of language, it is useful to examine his views on the question of pain. In Wittgenstein, there need not be (there cannot be, in any event) an appeal to the sort of evidence that says this is what "being in pain is" in order to communicate that one is in pain[18] – that is, pain consists of this and that criteria, and if you meet those, then you are in pain. Rather, "Wittgensteinian criteria," as Stanley Cavell calls them, are the shared conventions that we are initiated into through language, and as such they point us toward the intricate relations (both implicit and explicit) we have with one another[19] – these are conventions that make possible our communication, but do not assure us that something external like pain exists (and thus can be discovered, defined, once and for all, by the natural sciences, certainly not by philosophy) (Cavell, 1979, pp. 48, 72–73).[20] Put differently, even in our innermost uncertainty, even in our radical inability to know whether or not our feelings or states of being are or can be known by others[21] (radical because "we do not know with certainty of the existence of the external world (or of other minds)"; Cavell, 1979, p. 45), we can yet communicate with others such radical uncertainties like pain.[22]

Consequently, if one fails to understand or grasp a given object or a state of being, then it is not because one is missing this or that piece of information; rather, such failures point toward a lack of initiation of this person into the world, into the culture, into the society in which one lives or is attempting to understand (Cavell, 1979, p. 77).[23] Or, as Wittgenstein states, it is not a question of what someone "learns," but a question of what someone "observes" and is "instructed" that points us toward how it is that we share (and do not share) forms of life (Wittgenstein, 2006 [1969], p. 36e, s. 279). Now, this lack could be due to a person's age (a child is not initiated into language all at once) or due to a subject's position in the world (e.g., certain groups of people are forbidden from initiation based on their class, gender, race, etc.).[24] But this lack can also be seen in the kind of philosophy that places the thinker outside of the world so that the world can be studied as it is. It is precisely this type of disposition that produces the kinds of works that are blind to the already working dynamics of language: for instance, the social worker who mistakenly thinks that they already know what the suffering of the patient is before speaking to the patient.

One does not immediately judge "I am in pain" against absolute objective criteria; rather, one *responds* to the call of the other when the other says, "I am in pain." "I am in pain" is not the end of a mental process whereby I felt a sensation and then described it in language. Rather it is the commencement of a language-game in which "I am in pain" is only the beginning, where the verbal announcement is itself part of the sensations I am feeling. This does not deny the possibility that I am describing a sensation, but the particular use of "describing" here would be part of the conventions upon which the statement is made and may be understood, or not; but description of a mental state, in the sense of identifying an inner object, cannot make visible the ordinary use of "I am in pain" and can only lead us astray into a metaphysics of pain (Wittgenstein, 1973 [1953], p. 99e, s. 290, 187e–189e). The realm of the language-game is one in which intellectual engagements can produce works that challenge our conventions and change them only as they can be changed – together, the philosopher being one of the ordinary people and not intellectually above them, and in fact such a distinction supposedly disappears altogether here. Das picks this up and develops it in her work in a way neither Cavell nor Wittgenstein could have through their many hypothetical examples.

In her reading of Wittgenstein, Das understood as well as anyone the notion that it is ultimately our shared "forms of life" that are already in our language (or that we are initiated into when we learn language) that make our communication possible. These are not prearranged agreements that people systematically come to, and we can never know in advance the depth of our agreement or what we accept as mutual between us (Das, 1998, pp. 179–180; also Cavell, 1979, pp. 28, 32). Citing Cavell's work, Das puts it as follows: "this agreement is a much more complicated affair [than understandings of consensual agreement] in which there is an entanglement of rules, customs, habits, examples, and practices" (Das, 1998, p. 176). Indeed, Wittgenstein asserts that "language did not emerge from some kind of ratiocination" (Wittgenstein, 2006, pp. 62e, s. 475), and our shared conventions are not born of our agreement of opinion but of our shared forms of life; that is, "it is what human beings *say* that is true and false; and they agree in the *language* they use" (Wittgenstein, 1973, pp. 88e, s. 241; original emphases). And as Cavell puts it, what Wittgenstein consequently finds so astonishing is "that the extent of agreement is so intimate and pervasive; that we communicate in language as rapidly and completely as we do" (Cavell, 1979, p. 31).

In a critical passage, Das says that it is to her "wonder and terror … that it is from such fragile and intimate moments [in the everyday] that a shared language had to be built and with no assurance that there were secure conventions on which such a language, in fact, could be found" (Das, 2007, p. 8). I agree, but as far as I can gather, that is precisely Wittgenstein's view of language in general. Communication is possible because of our shared forms of life, but it takes place through a language that does not contain any assurances regarding the existence of such conventions as such or regarding the security of conventions per se. This is what Cavell says he finds so wondrous about Wittgenstein's view of language (Cavell, 1979, p. 36). A subject is fragile, yet capable of solidity. A subject is intimate, despite or because of the inability to know an inner state. A shared language is present, without us having to meet and agree on what it is. A language can ground subjects, and subjects must be grounded and limited, when a language cannot itself be grounded. So why does Das feel terror? Her wonder is understandable, as it is an integral part of her anthropology to find wondrous what others pass by and cast as insignificant; but why terror? Why in the face of the supposed madness of terror does she then descend into the ordinary? I am not saying that she is escaping madness here. She believes that when she descends, she will indeed gain greater insight than whatever the madness of terror had to offer. If one must insist that she escapes, she might say, fine, but out of prudence and for the sake of knowledge, not out of cowardice and for the sake of self-maintenance. I think she would be right in asserting this.

She is following Wittgenstein to the very last detail here, not in the sense of faithfully copying or imitating him but in the sense of pushing

Wittgenstein to the limits of his thought. And in so doing, she makes clear the scope and depth of the connection between the early and late Wittgenstein. Wittgenstein ends *Tractatus* with the following:

> My propositions serve as elucidations in the following way: anyone who understands me eventually recognizes them as nonsensical, when he has used them – as steps – to climb up beyond them. (He must, so to speak, throw away the ladder after he has climbed up it.) He must transcend these propositions, and then he will see the world aright. What we cannot speak about we must pass over in silence. (Wittgenstein, 2005 [1921], p. 89, ss. 6.54, 7)

How could Wittgenstein not repudiate this early work in his later works? He has instructed all of those who read *Tractatus* and understood it, and hence himself included when he reread it later (and he does talk about rereading *Tractatus* while writing his later works; Wittgenstein, 1973 [1953], p. vi), to abandon it (Gadamer, 1977a, p. 177). I do not subscribe to the conventional view that the ladder referred to is a mere tool that Wittgenstein used in *Tractatus* and that it is only this tool that he is throwing away. In my view, *Tractatus* itself is the ladder that he threw away when he wrote the rest of his work. *Tractatus* is where he met with nonsense; when he turned back from nonsense in his later works (which is the overwhelming theme of his later writings and what Das picks up on to descend into the ordinary – i.e., turning back by a gesture of waiting), he did so only after he had been to nonsense. Wittgenstein is saying: "You move beyond nonsense by going back to sense – outside sense there is nothing; pass it over in silence" – (this part Das works with); but there is an asterisk here, and in small print it says, "I know this because I've been to nonsense, even described it" (this part Das ignores). Wittgenstein may say, "But I did not know nonsense, I merely showed it." But how did Wittgenstein show it? With words, with arguments, with propositions as pretentious to scientific logic as philosophical propositions can be. In other words, with propositions that are almost impossible to disprove because they are so logically ordered. And then, are we supposed to forget this because Wittgenstein instructed as much? Why throw away the ladder? And most importantly, where does it fall? Where it falls is precisely the place where we can never reach again should we follow Wittgenstein. Why can he travel to nonsense and no one else? And if others travel there, might they find something other than nonsense?

Let us go back to the epigraph of this section. I read it as saying that a dreamer's claim of dreaming is no more right than the same person's claim in their dream that it is raining. In the first claim, the dreamer is making a claim to a listener, suggested by Wittgenstein's mention of the element of audibility. The listener cannot verify the claim by their senses, of course, since all they can sense is a person sleeping (and of course even that may be questionable, for it is possible to confuse sleep for meditative stillness or for eternal stillness). Nevertheless, this claim is first set up by Wittgenstein as the *apparently* more certain of the two claims, since it is *no more* right than the claim that the dreamer says to themselves in the dream that it is raining. The second claim is not made on a listener but in an inner dialogue, as it were, where the dreamer, as far as we can tell from Wittgenstein's example, is making known to themselves the fact of rain. The "no more right" suggests that Wittgenstein wants to unsettle a distinction between the two claims, and in fact make the distinction a non-distinction on the plane of certainty. The two claims, while different in shape and form, are indistinguishable when it comes to the question of certainty. And then he says, this is so "even if" the claim in the dream happens to correspond to the fact of rain outside of the person who is dreaming. This shifts what *appears* to be the more certain of the two claims, because our senses can more easily correspond the fact of rain to the claim that it is raining (never with absolute certainty, of course, since we may confuse rain for a drizzle or freezing rain or a fire hose gone astray). Regardless of which is the more apparent of the two claims, however, neither can be said to be distinguishable from the other on the plane of certainty.

This is where my uneasiness with Wittgenstein emerges. The claim that it is raining is an internal one in the sense that there is no listener outside of the person making the claim. So when he says that "I am dreaming" is no more right than "it is raining," my question is, to whom is it no more right? The dreamer awakes, sees and hears the rain, and says, "My claim about the rain was right," which will strike the listener as odd, who consequently may respond with something like, "Your claim about your dreaming was right," which would surprise the dreamer. Wittgenstein thus shifts the significance of these claims from the plane of certainty and onto the plane of communication. This is a significant shift that, I would agree alongside thinkers like Das and Cavell, is very much a welcomed intervention into analytic philosophy in particular and philosophy in general.

But Wittgenstein is able to accomplish such a shift in emphasis only because he can discern, from what he knows about the dream state and the waking state of the interlocutors, the complexity of the relationship between the two states. But to reach this conclusion, there must be an analyser of this language-game – one who knows what is unknown to each participant. Or, only when an analyser of this language-game knows what is unknown to each participant can an understanding of it, such as Wittgenstein's, emerge. Who is this analyser? They are certainly not participating in the language-game as it is being played out. To this question, Wittgenstein is silent, and he is so because of what he saw as his failure in *Tractatus*. But is there not another way of seeing the role of the analyser than as that of the superior logician? Can there not be an analyser who is just as ordinary as the ordinary conversation, yet at the same time of a *different order*?

Without putting this in explicit terms, I think that Gadamer makes a similar point. In his essay "The Phenomenological Movement," Gadamer (1977a [1963]) engages in a discussion on the difference between Edmund Husserl's transcendental phenomenology and the works of Martin Heidegger (especially the later ones) that challenged it. In that piece, Gadamer also uses the example of Wittgenstein to illustrate how something similar occurred to the world of analytic philosophy (1977a, pp. 173–177). More specifically, he shows how the break between the early and late Wittgenstein brought the question of language away from the problematic of a thing's immediacy and into a questioning of language itself, or into a philosophy where the question of language becomes central.[25]

Gadamer likens the early Wittgenstein to the Husserlian project, which he earlier described in the essay as concerned with securing a ground that is free of unjustified assumptions for a philosophy that can then match the "ideal of rigorous science" (1977a, p. 134). Wittgenstein discovered the futility of such a project in or after *Tractatus*, and then abandoned it in his later works. Gadamer sees little difference between the late Wittgenstein and the foundations upon which his own work is built – Gadamer's foundations being the interplay between the school of phenomenology and the work of Heidegger. However, there is an important difference between Wittgenstein and Gadamer, which can be discerned from the following conclusion Gadamer draws from this discussion: Wittgenstein's failure in his earlier work created his prejudiced position against transcendence, and instead of laying bare his prejudice and putting it into play, Wittgenstein ignores it and instructs all who follow him to abandon it (1977a, p. 177). As far as I can see it, the difference is that Gadamer is more willing to confront the transcendental element in his work, which Wittgenstein wants to ignore because he associates it only with his failure in *Tractatus*. My point of emphasis regarding Wittgenstein is that this transcendental element is there nonetheless, and simply repudiating it does not suffice.

In his introduction to *Philosophical Hermeneutics*, a collection of Gadamer's essays in which the above essay appears, David Linge provides a helpful framing of the matter when he argues that Wittgenstein's prejudiced position against the excesses of transcendental rules creates a false opposition where *"either* one must settle for a plurality of relative games, *or* one has a metalanguage that does violence to the empirical richness of usages and life forms" (Linge, 1977, p. xxxvi; original emphases). Both Wittgenstein and Gadamer emphasize concrete interpersonal communication (not some objective/scientific criteria that apply to all languages) as the locus of specifying the meaning of a word or a sentence. Wittgenstein, however, reduces philosophy to the task of clarifying language-games when these go wrong or astray. It is certainly possible to draw on the late Wittgenstein to advocate for a radical and transformative politics (in contrast to a rationalist approach that bases itself in a supposedly absolute objective reality), as Chantal Mouffe does in her work on radical democracy. But as Mouffe puts it, such a radical approach would not "extract a political theory from Wittgenstein" and would instead draw on his work to create "a new way of theorizing about the political" (2005, pp. 60–61). For me, this means that Wittgenstein's philosophy is not inherently open to a theorist like Mouffe, who wants to assert the role of the academic/intellectual in creating counter-hegemonic change. Wittgenstein's philosophy is not actively engaged in the political as it is understood by Mouffe, but is largely therapeutic, primarily I think because he does not properly account for the language of philosophy as another, yet peculiar, participant in language-games. The moment any such notion is brought up, he associates it with his efforts in *Tractatus*.

Gadamer, on the other hand, accounts for the role of the analyser of language-games as that of another participant who is fusing different horizons and creating something new, which then fuses with other different horizons, and so on. In short, Gadamer is better at illustrating the dialectical element of interpersonal communication than Wittgenstein is (Linge, 1977, pp. xxxvii–xl). And this is made possible because Gadamer does not throw out transcendence with one failed attempt at it, since transcendence, by definition, is the very mark of our shortcomings as finite beings. So my attention will now move toward an understanding of how this transcendental element relates to language not in a manner that treats transcendence as an ascending movement beyond the ordinary and toward nonsense or madness (this is the crux of what I am leaving behind from Das and Wittgenstein), but rather in a manner that focuses on how transcendence constitutes our shortcomings as finite beings whereby the "thing itself" will always evade interpretation – remains "over-there" in Gadamerian terms – at the same time that it plays a role in the fusion of horizons.

Conclusion

Beyond instrumentalism is not chaos and irrationality but rather the dispersal of violence. Das's anthropology convincingly traces the dispersal of violence beyond the "violent event," leading us toward a deeper understanding of how subjectivities come to be formed in and through violence. I termed this dispersal the linguistic dimension of violence to denote how such subjectivities are revealed through verbal and non-verbal modes of communication that broaden our understanding of how violence moves and metamorphoses in and through ordinary, everyday life. Such movement is found in the language we use and do not use, in the modes of interaction we build, in a community's disposition toward the state, in friendships, gender relations, poetry, love and hatred, and the list is indeed too large to enumerate, but it can be traced and represented in the analyst's language.

Following this descending movement of violence is thus crucial for scholarly understanding of violence, particularly how violence can be dealt with for the purposes of healing. But I argue that equally important is attention to the dispersal of violence into more difficult terrains – one that Das associates with an ascending movement into nonsense and madness. I argue that, disquieting as this idea might be, social scientists must follow the dispersal of violence in its most elusive and terrifying moments. We cannot be satisfied with the very old adage of positing the perpetrators of violence as simply not knowing what they are actually doing, since this adage simply passes over the "madness" of violence in silence. Instead, the dialogical analytic seeks to follow this transcendental evasiveness of violence and asks how the perpetrators of violence act *without knowing what one knows in knowing, (not)knowing*. The full meaning of this approach and the reasoning behind it will be developed through Gadamer, Derrida, and their encounter. Their works show how violence evades interpretation for both analyst and actor and how violence produces fused horizons joining participants in a communion born of dialogue. Ultimately, the point of following the dispersal of violence more fully, beyond the linguistic dimension while not ignoring it, is to understand the dialogical moment of violence and the transcendental character of violence. Both of these interrelated elements, communion in dialogue and interpretive evasiveness, are developed in the next two chapters.

3 Mimetic Violence: Violent Dialogue

Hence reaching an understanding on the subject matter of a conversation necessarily means that a common language must first be worked out in the conversation. This is not an external matter of simply adjusting our tools; nor is it even right to say that the partners adapt themselves to one another but, rather, *in a successful conversation they both come under the influence of the truth of the object and are thus bound to one another in a new community*. To reach an understanding in a dialogue is not merely a matter of putting oneself forward and successfully asserting one's own point of view, but being transformed into a communion in which *we do not remain what we were*.

–Hans-Georg Gadamer, Truth and Method (emphases added)

When the analyst becomes a voice of a different order in the conversation over violence, a door is opened for exploring what is said "over and above" those who proclaim and employ violence. The modus operandi of the dialogical analytic is to follow violence whereby a perpetrator of violence acts without knowing what one knows in knowing, (not)knowing. In following the subject matter of violence, the dialogical analytic reveals a dynamic of violent dialogue in the third dimension of violence.[1] The appearance of violent acts represents not the end of a dialogue between the participants, but rather the emergence of a specific form of dialogue under the subject matter of violence: a violent dialogue that creates a violent communion between the participants. This communion is marked by a complex interaction between mimesis and alterity (enemy-siblings) in violent acts and in representations of violence. Forged as enemy-siblings, the sides come to resemble each other in some fundamental ways even as they maintain certain stark differences on the surface.

In this three-dimensional view of violence, the inexpressibility of violence does not reach its limit with the violent act itself; rather, violence forges a space in which the interaction between the protagonists forms, continues, and transforms. Far from moving into nonsense because it is inexpressible, violence plays its most influential, impactful, and significant role precisely at the moment when it eludes us the most, which is the moment of its enactment. In this moment, the formation of enemy-siblings becomes prominent. We often assume that separation and distance mark the taking place of violence, but it is counterintuitively an *intimate type of relationship* that takes shape in the taking place of violence.

This puzzling dynamic will not sound surprising to scholars of "domestic violence," or more properly, varied forms of violence (psychological, emotional, economic, physical, sexual) between people who are known to each other. While this book does not deal with the topic of domestic violence,[2] it does heed Jeff Hearn's (2013) call for all fields of sociological study to take seriously important analytical insights that have been generated in that field. Most significantly, this book takes into account the insight that violence and intimacy, while they are seemingly contradictory terms, indeed form a paradoxical relation. It is not the case that closer, more intimate relationships lead to less violence, but rather that in and through violence, intimate relationships are not only formed, but also maintained. This paradox suggests that the default sociological (and I would argue also political) assumption that closer and more intimate interpersonal and social relationships can lead toward harmony and peaceful coexistence, and away from violence, is at best a shaky one (Hearn, 2013, pp. 155–157). In the widely present social phenomenon we call "domestic violence," we find that intimacy, closeness, and knowledge of one another's weaknesses, strengths, histories, tendencies, and desires can indeed lead to a virulent pattern of violent behaviour. It is a troubling insight, without doubt, but one that, contra the social and political axiomatic equation of social intimacy with peace and non-violence, must be taken seriously if we are to delve into the problem of violence and explore the third mimetic dimension – if we are to speak with violence.

This chapter unfolds in three main sections. First, I explain the dialogical analytic's imperative to speak with violence through Gadamer's philosophical hermeneutics and his understanding of how analysts can and should participate in the conversation over a given subject matter, (re)interpreting what eludes the participants in dialogue. Simultaneously, Gadamer's conception of dialogue, when examined next to

Derrida's conception of the sign, clarifies the dynamic of violent dialogue that is revealed when the analyst speaks with violence. I argue that the transformative element in dialogue can lead the analyst toward the manner in which participants in violent dialogue come to operate within a violent communion. This leads the analysis toward the question of mimesis, where I delve into the work of René Girard in the second section in order to highlight his understanding of the manner in which the mimetic function produces enemy-siblings in and through violence. Girard points us toward the formation of enemy-siblings, but his work does not properly account for the radical instability of the formation of enemy-siblings, as he highlights mimesis at the expense of alterity.

To account for what I posit as the possibility and impossibility of enemy-siblings, the chapter then examines in section three certain postcolonial approaches to the question of self-other, namely focusing on the works of Edward Said and Paul Gilroy in an effort to better articulate the way in which interdependence and interconnection occur across the self-other "divide" in and through violence. This brings together the mimetic question with the notion of alterity, which will lead the discussion to the work of Michael Taussig, who examines the mimetic function in its double-sidedness of sameness and alterity. Taussig provides useful analytical tools for understanding the kind of interaction that takes place in violent conflicts, particularly as it pertains to representations of violence and to our understanding of the notion of enemy-siblings.

I. Speaking with Violence

In his seminal *Truth and Method*, Gadamer explores "what happens to us over and above our wanting and doing" when we go about understanding things (2004 [1960], p. xxvi). Gadamer's project is launched from the Heideggerian notion that understanding is not simply one more aspect of a subject's set of behaviours or actions but "the mode of being of Dasein itself" (Gadamer, 2004, p. xxvii). He removes understanding from a subjectivist philosophy and instead advances a philosophical hermeneutics, where understanding is "never a subjective relation to a given 'object' but to the history of its effects; in other words, understanding belongs to the being of that which is understood" (Gadamer, 2004, p. xxviii).

For Gadamer, the "truth of the object" involves not its definitive or correct account, but rather the "being" of the subject matter in question (2004, pp. xxviii, 457). The assumption here is that we can never know precisely what we speak or write or paint when we go about understanding things. In any given act of interpretation, there is bound to be "something else" that evades us. The task of interpretation can thus never be completed. Ordinary and philosophical languages often overlook this puzzling feature of language, but this is precisely the space where scholarly analysis may be useful: that is, in interpreting further what has been rendered stagnant for whatever reason (historical, political, philological, etc.) (Gadamer, 2006 [1970], p. 26). This idea is best illuminated in Gadamer's discussion on the mode of being of the work of art, and more specifically his notion of "play."

Gadamer asserts that the player knows that play is only play and that it exists in a world of seriousness. The player thus loses themselves in play by this knowledge, which is necessary for the success of play. This suggests, however, that the relation to seriousness is as integral in making play as is the relation to playing. But this piece of knowledge is not "known" by the player, in that they cannot "intend this relation to seriousness" if they are to lose themselves in play. This then suggests that the player necessarily *does not know what exactly he 'knows' in knowing* that play is play as opposed to seriousness (Gadamer, 2004, p. 103; emphasis added). The mode of being of play is thus beyond the subjective consciousness of the player (Gadamer, 2004, pp. 103–105). The absorption of the player into the game leaves Gadamer with the following general characteristic of the nature of play: "all playing is a being-played.... The real subject of the game ... is not the player but instead the game itself. What holds the player in its spell, draws him into play, and keeps him there is the game itself" (2004, p. 106).

This is the case not only for the player, but for the audience as well. When play is turned into *a* play, the player not only loses themselves in play, but has to represent their role in play to the audience so that the audience (and not just the player) is absorbed into play. The main point is that artistic presentation exists as much for someone as it is of something (Gadamer, 2004, pp. 109–110). It is this "of something" that drives our experience of the play, but it is our engagement – the "for someone" – with this something that moves it in various unpredictable directions. Put differently, the artwork is the presentation of the truth of the thing being-played, and each part of this equation is important. It is the mode of being of the work of art that makes it possible for Gadamer to pinpoint the hermeneutic structure that guides understanding, which is the mediation between the truth of the thing presented in the artwork and our experience of it in the contemporariness of its being-played.

The key here is that Gadamer gives the analyst a role in this mediation that is both bound within play and beyond it. With his assertion that the player necessarily *"does not know what exactly he 'knows' in knowing"* that play is play as opposed to seriousness, Gadamer opens the door for an analysis that is part and parcel of what is being analysed, yet of a different order in that the analyst can and must account for the knowledge that is evasive. Thus, the analysis here would not be posited as either purely therapeutic (à la Wittgenstein) nor as a space from which superior or absolute philosophical knowledge can be produced. I have already discussed the therapeutic approach and stated why I wish to move away from it in the previous chapter (i.e., Das/Wittgenstein's idea of transcendence as nonsense), so it is important to now examine the movement toward absolute knowledge and indicate how Gadamer (and following him, the dialogical analytic) avoids it.

The emphasis on mediation is what ties Gadamer to Hegel's thought, but Gadamer is careful not to subscribe to any notion of absolute knowledge or attend to a project concerned with the manifestation of Spirit. This is accomplished through a long discussion on Hegel, Dilthey, Husserl, Yorck, and finally Heidegger (see part 2 of *Truth and Method*). I cannot delve into this discussion here, but suffice it to say, Gadamer does not believe that to counter Hegel's projection of thought toward absolute knowledge, one needs to return to a pre-given, fixed universality or essence (à la Husserl and Dilthey),[3] nor can we use as our ground Yorck's attempt to affirm Hegel's correlation between life and self-consciousness while avoiding Hegel's metaphysicizing of life (since Yorck's attempt was never completed). Rather, Gadamer wants to draw out the mediation found in Hegel, here translated into that between tradition (life) and interpreter (self-consciousness) (à la Yorck, in a sense completing Yorck's attempt), and he intends to avoid the metaphysicizing of tradition by making it continuously active, and actionable, and thus ever-changing.

Heidegger makes this manoeuvre possible. Gadamer argues that contra Husserl, Heidegger asserts that if we are to understand what is pre-given, then we cannot approach it as if the pre-given were fixed and timeless. That is, in Heidegger, phenomenology is not simply a matter of letting the thing show itself and then definitively reporting the self-shown thing as self-shown; but rather, phenomenology concerns a way of access to the Being of entities, which shows itself in a way that just as much conceals as reveals itself (Heidegger, 1962 [1927], p. 60). To understand Being, and more specifically in this discussion, to understand the pre-given, is "the mode of being of Dasein itself." For my purposes, it suffices to define Dasein as the entity whose mode of Being inquires about the meaning of Being (Heidegger, 1962, pp. 26–28). Dasein is there in the "clearing" or openness that reveals and conceals Being, a clearing that is itself no-thing, resistant to any description (see Heidegger, 1993 [1961]) (this "reveal and conceal" is the mark of truth in Heidegger and Gadamer) (Gadamer, 2004, p. 248). Understanding, for Heidegger, is not a mere matter for methodology to judge and determine, but rather "the *original form of the realization of Dasein*, which is being-in-the-world" (Gadamer, 2004, p. 250; original emphasis). As such, understanding is always engaged with what both precedes and as such projects it.

This leads Gadamer to suggest that in the case of interpreting a classical text, for instance, an interpreter can understand such a text only because the knower and the object that is (to be) known share the mode of being of historicity. The interpreter will inevitably project meaning into a text during the very act of reading it. These projections are the pre-given (our fore-conceptions) that we receive from tradition, and as such they contain the future possibilities of what is (to be) known in tradition, and is then pushed further, and so on. In this push, there can appear a new terrain, which is full of its own new possibilities and projections. The appearance of the latter, however, is not guaranteed, and that is why I bracket "to be." To unleash the flexibility of such future possibilities and open up the various directions they may take, Gadamer follows Heidegger in asserting that we must lay bare our fore-conceptions, in so far as this is possible, for we are limited in our own historicity (Gadamer, 2004, pp. 268–272). The task requires a hermeneutic effort that is forever continuous and never-ending, since different historicities will push different limits and produce different readings of the texts, and so on.[4]

This interpretive structure is a general one in Gadamer, and it revolves around Gadamer's notion of dialogue, which is the locus of interpretation and understanding. Furthermore, this structure applies just as much to dialogue between people – the experience of their interaction – as it does to dialogue between people and texts (Kögler, 1999, pp. 45–49). What is central is the move away from an emphasis on subjective acts, for this move renders the intentions of the participants secondary if not irrelevant. Only the commitment of the participants to openness in a question-answer exchange, or to "uninterrupted listening," is necessary for the subject matter to appear and for an engagement with its truth, which can never be Absolute, to take place – in short, for dialogue to take place (Gadamer, 2004, pp. 385–391, 461).[5] In other words, Gadamer is not interested in confining himself within what is known by the participants in a dialogue, nor is he interested in imposing some absolute knowledge from outside the dialogue upon the participants; rather, he wants to explore what evades the knowledge of the participants in dialogue. This is essentially what Gadamer means when he says he is interested in exploring what "happens to us over and above our wanting and doing," as I quoted him earlier,[6] and it is an integral part of what is meant in this book by "speaking with violence."

So in Gadamer, the being of the subject matter in question – the "thing itself" – transcends its creators (both the "original" ones and those who encounter it thereafter) and on that account can never be "correctly" understood (i.e., it is not an Absolute thing-in-itself) since it is ultimately up to these creators to (re)interpret it in accordance with their finitude (Kögler, 1999, pp. 66–67). Thus, dialogue involves the unfolding of a subject matter that makes certain demands of the participants in conversation, but can be activated (in diverse ways) only by the participants themselves (Gadamer, 2004, pp. 118–121, 248, 453–454). In this sense, the subject matter encompasses the participants within a dialogue that is never-ending since the subject matter will always evade us – or more precisely, an ever-continuous dialogue since a transcendental element of the subject matter will always be "over-there" joining us in communion in our chase after "it" (Gadamer, 2004, p. 371). When the analyst follows the transcendental element that evades the participants, it becomes possible to understand the communion that is born between them, without ever discovering, describing, and fixing this subject matter as *it is*.

For Gadamer, this, however, is not visible in every kind of dialogue – only in an "authentic" one (2004, p. 356).[7] The latter is a dialogue that moves beyond the temptation to win the dialogue and simply follows the subject matter as it unfolds before the interlocutors (Gadamer, 2004, pp. 277–278, 298, 460). More specifically, it is the type of question asked that determines for Gadamer the in/authenticity of dialogue. In inauthentic dialogue, the question is meant to prove the interlocutor right, whereas in authentic dialogue, the question is meant to break open the subject matter that is placed in-between the interlocutors (Gadamer, 2004, pp. 356–361). Inauthentic dialogue is concerned with only domination; authentic dialogue is concerned with a question-answer exchange whereby the interlocutors do not speak past or over each other but rather enter into a proper conversation by letting the subject matter lead the question-answer exchange (Gadamer, 2004, pp. 360–361).

Language, for Gadamer, is the medium through which this question-answer exchange takes place and common understanding over the subject matter is achieved. In his account of dialogue, "it is not that the understanding is subsequently put into words; rather, the way understanding occurs … is the coming-into-language of the thing itself" (2004, pp. 370–371). The language of the interlocutors is not in their possession or at their disposal, but is rather the "language in which something comes to speak" (Gadamer, 2004, p. 371). Language, therefore, is not a reflection/copy of the thing, nor is the thing an image or product of language; rather, "language has its true being only in dialogue, in *coming to an understanding*" (Gadamer, 2004, p. 443; original emphasis). And for Gadamer, this is the case even when we meet the limits of our language. While certain subject matters may be beyond expression in language, this does not mean that such subject matters are outside the realm of language (Gadamer, 2006, p. 14). Language is both bridge and barrier, in the sense that the limits we experience in language are not its end, but are indeed an invitation for a (re)interpretation of the subject matter in question (Gadamer, 2004, pp. 402–403).

Since in authentic dialogue the object is revealed before the participants, they do not have to first agree on this or that definition of the object; rather, they "are always already in agreement" (Gadamer, 2004, p. 444). This is where it is easy to see why Gadamer would think that he and Wittgenstein are close to each other's thought. But in Gadamer, this notion of "already in agreement" is more substantive, I believe, since Wittgenstein stops when the wonderment strikes him. Wittgenstein only speaks of pointing out and describing language-games; he does not discuss the fusion of horizons or explore how it is that language-games indicate that the interlocutors are "already in agreement." His notion of language-games makes the assertion of "already in agreement" without deeply exploring it. Gadamer also has that same sense of wonderment – although it is not as grippingly arrived at in Gadamer's writing as it is in Wittgenstein's – but he does not stop there and proceeds to explore this "already in agreement" in his discussion on the "fusion of horizons."

Gadamer argues that when the interpreter meets a tradition in a text, they foreground the horizon of the past from their own present horizon, not to prove either horizon as right nor to prove their radical otherness, but to simultaneously supersede both horizons and come to an understanding of the communion in which both horizons properly exist (2004, pp. 303–306).[8] This fusion should not be confused with subordination of either of the horizons to the other. Rather, it seeks just the opposite effect, which involves a diffusion of the tension between what may initially seem as two separately existing horizons (Gadamer, 1989a [1984], p. 41).

Authentic dialogue, then, reveals this communion by the fusion of horizons and the creation of a common language, while inauthentic dialogue hides the communion from view for the sake of domination. Inauthentic dialogue has the appearance of dialogue (i.e., verbal/written exchange between the interlocutors), but it does not achieve dialogue's authentic form, which is to reveal our communion. But while it does not reveal this communion, there is nothing in Gadamer's philosophy to suggest that a communion must not take place in cases of inauthentic dialogue. It is this unrevealed communion that I argue is operative in the mimetic dimension of violence, and it is formed through a peculiar kind of dialogue, a violent dialogue. This idea can be advanced through the encounter between Derrida and Gadamer.

Fred Dallmayr is helpful in setting the stage for our understanding of this encounter and the central question it poses: What is the transformative element in dialogue? Or, what is it in dialogue that makes it transform those caught in its spell? Is it dialogue itself? Is it the subject matter in question? Or is it an element of an entirely different order that is opened up by dialogue? It is the transformative element that allows for my claim that violence "speaks."

Dallmayr (who falls more so on the Gadamerian side of the encounter) argues in *Dialogue and Deconstruction* that the transformative element in Gadamer's work is crucial to understanding his account of dialogue. Drawing on Gadamer's aforementioned discussion on "play," Dallmayr emphasizes that the transformation Gadamer is thinking of here "does not mean an incremental, continuous development, but rather a complete reversal or rupture" (Dallmayr, 1989, p. 79). Thus, transformation can be seen to have two features: (1) the participants are wholly turned into something else by the subject matter, and (2) this something else is the "true" being of the subject matter. Dallmayr argues that despite Gadamer's espousal of rupture here, he consistently falls back on a notion of an "unfolding meaning or continuity of understanding" (1989, p. 81). Derrida, on the other hand, sees rupture not as a challenge that can be (re)assimilated into an unfolding meaning, but rather as a challenge that questions the very notions of unfolding and continuity (Dallmayr, 1989, p. 81). Derrida, like Gadamer, does not ground his understanding of events, occurrences, or actions in the intentions of what Derrida calls an "empirical subject" (Dallmayr, 1989, pp. 82–83; Derrida, 1988 [1972], p. 8); Derrida, however, is interested not in how we then (re)interpret meaning, but in the way rupture leaves "meaning" itself in a constantly ambiguous state – or, the way rupture moves "meaning" off the firm ground that is all too often and all too easily posited for it in philosophy (Derrida, 1988).

Dallmayr, however, criticizes Derrida for his rather effortless slippage into indifference, and the tendency of his philosophy to move away from a dialogue that searches for a common horizon or ground, which Dallmayr deems of the utmost necessity in today's "global city" (Dallmayr, 1989, pp. 88–90). This criticism feeds into Dallmayr's later work, where he more explicitly falls on Gadamer's side, primarily for the latter's more promising ethico-political position, which highlights "mutual exposure and risk-taking" of one's identity in dialogue (Dallmayr, 1989, p. 91). Nevertheless, Dallmayr does not abandon Derrida's intervention, and stresses the latter's important role in continuously challenging us to "recognize otherness or the alien in oneself (or one's own)," rather than simply attempting to appropriate alterity, which too heavy an emphasis on continuity may lead us to do (Dallmayr, 1989, p. 92).

In *Dialogue among Civilizations*, Dallmayr reformulates the matter somewhat by having already opened Gadamer to Derrida's thought in *Dialogue and Deconstruction*, and argues that Gadamer's emphasis on continuity does not necessarily efface rupture after all, but is rather seen in this work as a balancing force that is deployed in the face of what some (on the postmodern left) have come to call an "irremediable rupture" between different cultures (Dallmayr, 2002, p. 26). Dallmayr is not interested in joining the celebration of such a rupture, which he accuses some of Derrida's followers (but not Derrida himself) of doing, since for Dallmayr such a celebratory stance necessarily ends in the outright separation of human beings rather than allow us to find a common ground in today's "global city." In other words, Dallmayr comes to treat Gadamer's philosophical hermeneutics as a foundation that has been fixed and reinforced in certain select aspects by Derrida's intervention.[9] Thus, Dallmayr no longer says that Gadamer's espousal of rupture is lacking, since he is longer seen to want to do away with rupture and radical transformation (as evidenced in Gadamer's commitment toward a decentred view of the self) (Dallmayr, 2002, pp. 45–46); Gadamer simply wants to do away with a rupture that builds and maintains an abyss in the space of the "in-between."

The latter notion of rupture is where Derrida's work has led some of its followers, and for Dallmayr, Gadamer instead offers "dialogical understanding as the 'true locus of hermeneutics,'" which "always hovers in the 'in-between': between self and other ... presence and absence" (Dallmayr, 2002, p. 27). Having said that, and in tune with his earlier arguments, Dallmayr does indeed draw on Derrida when it comes to unsettling the Eurocentric worldview that governs much of Western discourse regarding the rest of the world (i.e., the West vs. the

Rest discourse). Here, Dallmayr does not so much separate Derrida and Gadamer as call upon Derrida's sharper eye for deconstruction in order to challenge Eurocentrism. In his joining of the two thinkers, Dallmayr sees a similar effort on the part of both thinkers to simultaneously reinvigorate "Europe" and question it, or to retrieve both its accomplishments and its shortcomings, or to put it yet another way, to bring to view the promise of "Europe" and its limitations, which only a conversation with the other of "Europe" can bring to light (2002, pp. 51–55, 61–65). Perhaps Gadamer's thought is better equipped to retrieve the promise, and Derrida's thought is better equipped to retrieve the limitations, but ultimately their ground is similar (a decentred self directed toward transformation), and hence their combination is the most fruitful in Dallmayr's view.

But is not Derrida's intervention more challenging than what Dallmayr lets on? I raise this question for the crucial reason that Derrida cannot be made to go along with an intellectual endeavour bent on locating, shaping, and articulating the space in-between self and other, presence and absence. Derrida questions the possibility of finding such a space since the binary between absence and presence is altogether broken in his work (Derrida, 1973, pp. 101–102). Or, the space in-between is precisely the force that sets in motion the work of deconstruction, which breaks apart the rigid binary altogether. To my knowledge, Derrida never directly deconstructed Gadamer's work, but I think that exploring this break of the presence-absence binary can be helpful in illuminating what separates the two thinkers.[10]

Derrida, like Gadamer, does not treat the interlocutors of a dialogue as subjects who are in complete control of their words or of the meanings that they are trying to convey to one another, and like Gadamer, Derrida highlights how words and meanings come to attain a life of their own, as it were, and transform the interlocutors in the process. Unlike Gadamer, however, Derrida is not interested in how we then (re)interpret meaning, but in the way "ruptures" in dialogue leave meaning itself in a constantly ambiguous state. While he never directly deconstructs Gadamer, Derrida's work generally challenges distinctions between authenticity and inauthenticity in communication and dialogue. In such distinctions, authenticity tends to mean the proper transmission of the real present thing or subject matter over which we communicate, and inauthenticity is then posited as a distortion of the authentic process of transmission. Instead, Derrida highlights the break in presence that takes place in the representation of presence. Representation or writing does not simply supplant presence, hence purely transmitting the meaning/idea/truth/picture of a thing in its absence, but is rather a break in presence that shapes, forms, effects the very meaning/idea/truth/picture of a thing (Derrida, 1988 [1972], pp. 5–6). This break in presence, this absence, produces the very condition of possibility of writing, since absence is at the core of the element of iterability (of writing what is readable, repeatable) that is so pivotal to the functioning of writing (Derrida, 1988, p. 7). In other words, absence comes to form the very condition of possibility of writing, and as such absence brings to light writing's impossibility.

Every sign can be cited, repeated, cut off from the context in which it "emerged," and then grafted onto differential chains distinct from those it may have been customarily inserted into. A context cannot saturate the possibilities of a given sign (i.e., the context is not the centre that explains/determines/limits the sign); the sign "can break with every given context, engendering an infinity of new contexts" (Derrida, 1988, p. 12). This is all possible because the "sign carries with it a force that breaks with its context, that is, with the collectivity of presences organizing the moment of its inscription" (Derrida, 1988, p. 9). This force is the "the force of rupture," which (a) is not exclusive to the written sign but to all signs and for Derrida to all experience as well, and (b) is the possibility of repeating what is absent in the absence of receiver and sender – that is, iteration (Derrida, 1988, p. 10). In Derrida, the transmission of the message takes on an importance never assigned to it when one focuses on the content of the message being sent, which is one of Gadamer's tendencies.

Derrida further explores the possibility-impossibility of writing through J.L. Austin's *How to Do Things with Words*, and this brings the analysis closer to the question of in/authenticity. While Austin's discussion on performative utterances goes a long way in challenging the notion that communication is strictly concerned with the transmission of the meanings of things (i.e., referents), Austin nevertheless remains within the framework of a philosophy of consciousness that reduces performative communication to the presence of interlocutors who are in control of their intended meanings, even if those meanings have no external referents (Derrida, 1988, pp. 13–14). In short, Austin does not allow any residue of meaning that would escape communication if communication is to be successful, at the same time that he suggests that should any such residue hinder the "correct" transmission of intended meanings, then communication fails (Derrida, 1988, p. 15).[11] So, in his deconstruction of Austin's opposition of success/failure in illocution/perlocution, Derrida asserts that what Austin dismisses as failure is not the binary opposition of success, but the very condition of possibility of what Austin posits as success (Derrida, 1988, pp. 16–17).

To counter Austin, Derrida does not posit absence as the central/dominant side of a binary opposition with presence: he rather shows how that which is excluded from these models is not the opposite of what is present; rather, what is excluded (absence) is the very condition of possibility of what is present in these models (Derrida [1973] deconstructs Husserl's phenomenology on similar grounds). And this brings to light the force of rupture, which is essentially the play between presence and absence – the signature whose condition of possibility (which is that it marks a "presentness" that produces various effects, as on a contract, for example) is simultaneously its condition of impossibility (which is that it produces effects that are "impure" and "fragmentary" because the signature is iterable, capable of repeating what is non-present) (Derrida, 1988, pp. 19–21).

The consequences of Derrida's intervention are decisive for reconceptualizing Gadamer's authentic-inauthentic distinction. For Derrida's intervention suggests that if inauthentic dialogue reaches its limit when the interlocutors are reduced to who can shout their position the loudest, and where the common horizon of meaning between them is thus not revealed, then one cannot view this as simply a negative occurrence (i.e., as *not* revealing our communion), but one must take into account that this, at bottom, is a play between presence and absence, or the occurrence of an absence, a rupture. As such, the rupture takes precedence over the question of authenticity – or, inauthentic dialogue is just as integral to the possibility of Gadamer's general account of dialogue as authentic dialogue is. If dialogue moves in various unpredictable and transformative directions, it is because of the rupture and not because a given dialogue is authentic or inauthentic. Derrida argues that absence is not to be taken as a modification in the continuum of presence; rather, absence produces effects as absence (1988, pp. 5–10). Put differently, the transformative element in dialogue occurs not only in the case of an authentic dialogue, as Gadamer claims, but in both authentic and inauthentic dialogue. As such, I argue that the authentic-inauthentic distinction is not very useful in understanding the transformative element in dialogue, and it is more fruitful to examine the play of presence ("is") and absence ("is-not"), which takes place in different manners across a number of varied kinds of dialogue, whether it involves a dialogue between a reader and a text, in the shouting match, or in the exchange of violent acts.

If we follow Gadamer in asserting that the participants reach the form of inauthentic dialogue when announcing their subject matters for the sake of domination, then we can say that this inauthentic dialogue reaches its limit when the interlocutors are reduced to who can shout their position the loudest. The common horizon of meaning between them, so important to Gadamer's concept of authentic dialogue, is thus not revealed here. But – and this is why Derrida is so important – this is not simply a negative occurrence (whereby communion is not revealed); rather, we are confronted with the occurrence of an absence, the force of a rupture, the play between what is and what is-not. This latter point leads to the following formulation of violent acts: as opposed to separating authentic and inauthentic dialogue and assigning each form of dialogue the label of non-violence (authentic) and violence (inauthentic), the dialogical analytic posits that in the context of the continuous exchange and employment of violence, the absence of written/verbal exchange, which we can see once the shouting match has reached its limit, paradoxically occurs in the form of an appearance, and this appearance involves violent acts – it signals the emergence of a violent dialogue.

We remain with this question, however: Why is this appearance of an absence "dialogue"? If the absence is "non-dialogue," then how can its appearance (violent acts) produce "violent dialogue"? Derrida's understanding of presence-absence suggests that violent acts can be said to form a violent dialogue because, in their meeting, they constitute what I take from Gadamer to be the defining feature of dialogue, which concerns the idea of a subject matter that is placed in-between the participants, forming their communion, although in the case of violent acts, this meeting takes place in a peculiar manner in that the communion remains concealed and unrevealed. I am not making the claim that violent dialogue is the return or emergence of authentic dialogue, but rather that it is the emergence of something similar to authentic dialogue's form, yet of a different and a peculiar order.

The reason it is peculiar, the reason their communion is unrevealed, is that the participants in violence can never know precisely what they speak when proclaiming and employing violence. They fail to comprehend their violence, and/or their representations of violence, because they fail to understand the "something else" created through violent acts. They fail to grasp that which escapes them in both the Gadamerian notion of "over-there," ever-beyond our reach yet constituting that which may reveal our communion with one another; and in the Derridean sense of "is-not," that which constitutes a transformative and generative force but which itself remains the realm of unknowability, simultaneously unsettling and making possible what we know of the violence. That is the reasoning behind my claim that violence "speaks": the subject matter that holds the participants together is not only the issue(s) over which they fight; the fight itself becomes their subject matter. In conflict, we often find that the participants have closed the question-answer exchange on the subject matters over which they fight (land, nationhood, resources, security, freedom, etc.), and thus an authentic dialogue cannot be said to appear here; rather, we have a so-called inauthentic dialogue. But I argue that violent dialogue, which emerges out of the violent acts, *substitutes* for what is often understood as "inauthentic dialogue" precisely at the point where the latter reaches its limit, which is the moment of the enactment of violence.

Irrespective of their intentions, the participants are engaged in a question-answer exchange in the realm of violence whereby a violent dialogue overtakes them. In doing so, the participants and their closed positions are transformed in ways they could not foresee, and are indeed unaware of. In violent dialogue, I argue, are born certain important transformations of the protagonists' positions on the subject matters over which they fight – transformations that are then carried into and indeed can come to constitute the very interaction and relationship between the protagonists. These transformations can be observed in the mimetic dimension of violent acts. It is precisely in this unrevealed communion that a complex relationship forms, and it is one that is marked by mimesis/alterity.

To explore mimesis/alterity, the next section begins with an extensive engagement with René Girard's theory on mimetic violence, which is important for two reasons: (1) Girard's work reveals significant insights into the mimetic dynamics of violence, namely the formation of enemy-siblings and the idea that there are two main mutually exclusive forms of representing violence, and (2) his work's theorization of the relationship between violence and transcendence acts as a useful counter-conceptual apparatus that will enable the dialogical analytic's approach toward the fourth dimension of transcendental violence. While I discuss some elements of the second point in this chapter, I will delve into it in greater detail in chapter 4; in this chapter, I focus on the first point in order to begin to delineate how mimesis unfolds in the third dimension of violence.

II. Mimesis

In *Violence and the Sacred*, Girard sets out to show how "sacrifice serves to protect the entire community from *its own* violence" (Girard, 1977 [1972], p. 8; original emphasis). He argues that the violence of sacrifice serves the function of protecting the community from "a violence that knows no bounds" (Girard, 1977, p. 25). Girard is theorizing on a different level than the works discussed in chapter 1 that search for a productive violence that would end destructive violence. He is attempting to explain the continuous interplay between productive and destructive violence, whereby violence propagates itself. Succinctly put, Girard attempts to explain the destructive-productive distinction rather than use it as his analytical basis. The central concern in Girard is to explain the function that certain productive or legitimate forms of violence, like sacrifice, serve, in order to understand the mechanism behind such distinctions between legitimate and destructive violence (Girard, 1977, p. 92). But he never states that legitimate forms of violence can indeed lead to a world of non-violence, nor does he claim that they are capable of controlling violence once and for all (Girard, 1977, p. 268). He is, to a certain degree, theorizing the manner in which violence propagates itself through both its restricted, ritualized presence (productive or legitimate violence) and its potentiality for a catastrophic, unbound explosion into human society (destructive or unbound violence) (Girard, 1977, p. 307). His argument is built on two interrelated core concepts: "mimetic desire" and the "scapegoat."

Girard does not invoke mimesis to call to mind a harmony born of sameness or similarity.[12] Rather, his notion of mimetic desire concerns the moment when two desires converge on one object and violently clash in their quest over it (Girard, 1977, p. 146). One person violently protects/encases the object of desire; the other strives to violently wrestle it from this firm grasp (Girard, 1977, p. 175). Girard examines mimetic desire and rivalry in modern literature in his first book, *Deceit, Desire and the Novel* (Girard, 1965 [1961]), and in other works he explains and bases mimetic desire in ethology, anthropology, and sociobiology, but I find this concept best illuminated through his extensive engagement with Freud in particular and psychoanalysis in general (see Girard, 1977, pp. 169–222; book 3 in Girard, 1987 [1978], pp. 285–431; for a succinct summary of mimetic desire, see Girard, 2007, pp. 56–57). I cannot delve into all of the details of this engagement, much less engage with the concept of "interdividual psychology" under which this engagement is more or less placed, but for my purposes, a general picture will suffice.

According to Girard, Freud went astray with his emphasis on the object of desire between disciple and model. Whereas Freudian analysis operates, in Girardian terminology, on a scheme of model-disciple-object (father-son-mother), where the object of desire serves as the basis of this scheme, Girard asserts that conflict or fierce opposition emerges not because the disciple and his model happen to desire the same object; the disciple rather desires an object precisely because the model desires it. Thus, Girard's scheme contains the same three elements, but they are phrased as identification-choice of object-rivalry. It is the figure of the rival that is dominant in Girard's scheme. The object of desire is desirable because the rival desires it. When this occurs (for whatever reasons, the most prominent of which is a scarcity of resources), then what may have first begun with a model who says to a disciple, "Imitate me," is suddenly turned into a rivalry to the death. The object drops from the view of those engaged in a fight over it because it is the identification between model and disciple (their mimesis, or, as Girard sometimes calls it, "acquisitive mimesis"; 1987, p. 18) in the form of rivalry that lies at the foundation of the conflict. Once the object drops from view, mimetic desire takes hold, and the thirst for overcoming the rival cannot be quenched, not even by the acquisition of the object, since the logic of mimetic desire is not the acquisition of objects but overcoming one's rival. There will always be another model to overcome (the ultimate model being the one that cannot be overcome and can thus be counted on to constitute a continuous and constant rival). When this mimetic desire spreads in a society, and for Girard mimetic desire is contagious (i.e., it affects the bystanders as well as the original participants), mimetic violence (or "conflictual mimesis"; Girard, 1987, p. 26) is unleashed, and this is precisely what the moment of unbound violence involves for Girard: this moment is one whereby violence itself becomes the instrument, object, and all-encompassing subject. And what halts this moment can be found in the religious universe of the sacrificial rites first, and the Gospels second (albeit primarily).

In his study of sacrifice in so-called "primitive society," Girard claims that sacrificial rites are indices to a real event of unbound violence that lead to what Girard calls a "sacrificial crisis," which is an inability to distinguish between good and evil violence.[13] When such a crisis overtakes a given society (for whatever reasons), all and any ability to make any distinction withers away. Once this occurs, mimetic violence spreads uncontrollably in the community (Girard, 1977, p. 47). With the proliferation of "enemy siblings," an outside observer can no longer differentiate between those engaged in the fight; internally, however, the ability to see differences not only remains but is also accentuated (Girard, 1977, pp. 158–159). This is crucial because it allows those engaged in the fight to avoid becoming completely devoured by unbound violence. That is, if they were able to signify the unanimity and reciprocity of their violence (i.e., their mimetic violence), if the sign did not separate itself from its referent by creating a distorted signification of the unbound violence, then in a *sacrificial society*, those involved would easily succumb to the lure of unbound violence and submit to a fate of complete annihilation. Fortunately for these societies, human language is largely incapable of signifying the sacrificial crisis.

The failure of the sign to signify unbound violence as unbound violence (as violent reciprocity, which at bottom is the destruction of all signification) is thus what saves the community from the lure of unbound violence and its logical conclusion of total destruction (Girard, 1977, p. 64). Simultaneously, the community is saved by the failure of the sign that is manifested in the form of the surrogate victim, which substitutes for unbound violence and promises an end to the outbreak of violence. In other words, the failure of the sign to represent unbound violence introduces instead the sacrificial substitution (or more precisely, the double substitution), which marks the braking mechanism that saves the community from unbound violence – a mechanism that never comes to view (indeed cannot come into view if it is to function properly) to those engaged in the fight but is visible only to those outside of it: the mechanism of the surrogate victim (Girard, 1977, p. 67).

The appearance of such a victim is made possible by the monstrous double, whereby all involved become interchangeable with one another (Girard, 1977, p. 161) and therefore readily substitutable (Girard, 1977, p. 79).[14] To stop the thirst for vengeance and bloodshed, a surrogate victim is identified, differentiated within the group (Girard, 1977, pp. 164–166),[15] and unanimously sacrificed by the collective (Girard, 1977, pp. 81–83).[16] The sacrifice ends the spread of unbound violence and sends it to a sort of captivity. Bloodshed is replaced by bloodletting. This maintains the presence of blood so as to allow the sacrificial rite to resemble the original violence, while simultaneously maintaining a distance from it so as not to reintroduce it (Girard, 1977, pp. 37, 99). Accordingly, the violence that puts an end to unbound violence is named and ritualized as legitimate violence. This distinction between good and evil violence constitutes a new religious universe that ends the sacrificial crisis, allows the participants to truly differentiate from one another, and erects a new cultural order that then regulates mimetic desire (Girard, 1977, p. 96). When this legitimate violence loses its ability to function properly for whatever reasons, a new sacrificial crisis begins to unfold, unbound violence spreads, only to be stopped by a new sacrifice, and so on. This is the nature of the cycle of violence according to Girard.

Girard is arguing that if sacrificial societies demystified the violent acts that they believed to be legitimate, if they stripped them naked (by calling the executioner of a sacrifice a murderer, for instance), then they would run the risk of releasing the real naked violence that such legitimate forms were indeed guarding them against (1977, p. 82). He argues that legitimate forms, while violent, are ultimately geared toward peace (Girard, 1977, pp. 136–137). What he learns then is that if you do away with transcendence (whether it comes in the form of God, an idea, or a system), then violence (even if propagated by this relationship between violence and transcendence) loses any and all checks on it (Girard, 1977, pp. 134–135).

Girard suggests that the Greek tragic poets (most notably Euripides) and some of the early Greek philosophers (most notably Heraclitus) were all too willing to shrink back when faced with the entrance to the abyss of unbound violence (Girard, 1977, pp. 135–136). For Girard, these ancient thinkers exemplify the fear humanity faces when confronted with this abyss, and more importantly, exemplify the manner in which mythologies and tragedies have been built on top of this very real moment of unbound violence for the sole purpose of hiding it from view. When confronted with such myths and tragedies, the point for us today is not simply to proclaim them as mystifications or mere fantasies, but to understand what the consequences of making such proclamations would have been for these thinkers and writers (Girard, 1977, p. 130). So to demystify the sacrificial rite in purely rationalist terms for the purpose of dismissing it is to miss the point that mythology arises out of real events of unbound violence (Girard, 1986 [1982], pp. 24–44), and as such, that creating and maintaining a distinction between "good" and "evil" violence, and in turn establishing distinction per se, is what is at stake, and not the justness of who/what is distinguished as good or evil: to demystify is to attempt to remove the misconception and misrecognition so necessary for the survival of human society, at least as we have known it thus far (Girard, 1977, pp. 132–136, 236–237).[17]

Now clearly, the modern world no longer has any use for the sacrificial rites and the mythologies of so-called primitive societies. We are afforded a luxury that the likes of Euripides and Heraclitus did not have: "to expose to the light of reason the role played by violence in human society" (Girard, 1977, p. 318). But Girard maintains that our modern world is still a sacrificial society.[18] How so? Girard argues that the modern legal system has successfully, for the time being and relatively speaking, kept the explosion of unbound violence at bay.[19] Law manages to control vengeance by acting as the absolute voice and actor on all matters that carry the risk of releasing violence (Girard, 1977, p. 15). Law is an effective mechanism to counter naked violence: it is the "most efficient of all curative procedures" (Girard, 1977, p. 21). It does not require a surrogate victim, a sacrificial rite, or religious mystification. Rather, "it conforms more strictly to the principle of vengeance….

[It] *rationalizes* revenge and succeeds in limiting and isolating its effects in accordance with social demands" (Girard, 1977, p. 22; original emphasis). Additionally, the transcendence of the law ensures that the punished are not likely to retaliate against a specific person to avenge the penalty and harm imposed upon them.

But this was the Girard of *Violence and the Sacred*. In *The Scapegoat* (1986) and *Things Hidden since the Foundation of the World* (1987), Girard asserts that the modern legal system is a sort of stopgap solution. Ultimately, it is scripture that we must turn to in order to (a) gain a better understanding of how it is that we are able to see the mechanism of the surrogate victim in this world in the first place and (b) gain a better comprehension of what a non-sacrificial world would entail. According to Girard, the only way out of the sacrificial cycle, where violence constantly and continuously propagates itself, is through a careful reading of the Gospels, which offer us a new world: one that finally brings the mechanism of the surrogate victim into full view. In this new world, mimetic desire is countered not by re-establishing firm definitions and boundaries between inside and outside, between self (community) and other (scapegoat), but rather through a radical rethinking of the self-other relationship.

This new world is grounded in two distinct types of text: texts of persecution and texts of the victim. The former represent the real act of collective murder in the form of a mythology that hides that act precisely because it is always written from the perspective of the persecutor: that is, the mythology shows the sacrificed as the origin of the eruption of unbound violence at the same time that the sacrifice itself marks the beginning of violence's end. The sacrificed is presented as really guilty of the crimes the community charges against it/he/she: that is, what we end up with in the persecutor's text is the "righteous victim" of mythology (Girard, 2007, p. 85). The texts of the victim, on the other hand, shatter the persecutor's perspective by telling the same story of the real act of collective murder, but from the victim's perspective: that is, the scapegoat is shown as a scapegoat. The person killed is no longer a guilty god of violence in these latter texts but is rather a victim. Not only exemplary but originary among these latter texts are the Gospels, which reveal the mechanism of the surrogate victim by shattering the illusions of the persecutor (Girard, 1986, p. 101).

Seen from the vantage of the victim, the act of collective murder is shown free of the mythological illusions that arise in the texts of persecutors: that is, free of the illusions that turn the scapegoat into a god of violence (or, the illusions that result in "the false transcendence of a victim") (Girard, 1986, p. 166). We can speak of such a thing as a scapegoat today only because for the first time, the Gospels revealed this "god of violence" as a scapegoat.[20] The texts of the victim are not only not texts of persecution; they are texts that reveal the truth of persecution and the mechanisms by which texts of persecution operate, and as such destroy them (Girard, 1986, pp. 117–119).

The essential issue that faces us today then concerns the choice between the Kingdom of Satan (the rites and cultural orders that are built on "the unanimous and spontaneous murder of a scapegoat"; Girard, 1986, p. 187) and the Kingdom of God (a world of love and forgiveness that is built on the revelation of a non-violent God, where there are no violent expulsions and sacrifices that maintain the credo underpinning all of Satan's kingdoms: the use of violence to stop violence; Girard, 1986, pp. 189–191). Jesus is essentially the "Paraclete" who speaks in place of every victim to discredit Satan. In his battle against Satan, Jesus is able to accomplish his victory through the crucifixion first and the Word second. In his crucifixion, Jesus dies for God's message of non-violence rather than use violence to stop violence. In this sense, the death of Jesus is not a sacrifice (and according to Girard there is nothing in the Gospels to suggest that it is; Girard, 1987, p. 180), but rather an act that illustrates and announces the defeat of Satan by showing that it is humans and not gods who killed Jesus. This act consequently shatters the mystification of cyclic mythological violence (i.e., it shatters the relationship between violence and the sacred that has shaped human history; Girard, 1987, pp. 231–235). Second, the Word that Jesus leaves behind reveals the nature of cyclic mythological violence for centuries to come. The Word does not cease in bringing the truth of Satan to light (Girard, 1986, p. 207).[21]

The choice between these two kingdoms is absolute: the two kingdoms "cannot communicate with one another, since they are separated by a real abyss" (Girard, 1987, p. 199). With guidance from the Kingdom of God, mankind can cross this abyss and leave behind the world of cyclic mythological violence. But this crossing does not come about smoothly or peacefully. Basically, each time the moment of unbound violence erupts, the old sacrificial ways of dealing with it become less and less effective because the Kingdom of Satan is shown for what it is – "violence reveals its own game in such a way that its workings are compromised at their very source; the more it tries to conceal its ridiculous secret from now on, by forcing itself into action, the more it will succeed in revealing itself" (Girard, 1987, p. 209).[22] When the point is reached that cyclic mythological violence can no longer function at all, humanity is then presented with an absolute choice: perish in the all-ending explosion of unbound violence (and this is what the apocalyptic elements of the Gospels are referring to), or at the very moment where the Kingdom of Satan was previously called upon to end unbound violence, instead call upon and follow the Kingdom of God, which in giving humanity the choice, puts violence back in the human hands that enact it and shows humanity how it, with its choices, brought about the explosion of unbound violence with human hands and can with human hands usher in the world of non-violence (Girard, 1987, pp. 196–215, 260–262). This new world "reconciles without excluding anyone and no longer has any dealings with violence" (Girard, 1987, p. 445).

The non-sacrificial world radically rethinks the self-other relationship in that it eradicates the logic of exclusion that forms the foundation of modern society. The "other" is no longer excluded and sacrificed for the sake of securing the "self," but rather the process of "othering" a scapegoat is itself put into question and eradicated. In Girard, enemy-siblings, the core feature of unbound violence, which ensures the halt and simultaneously the propagation of violence, would no longer feature in the non-sacrificial world of Christ. Putting aside a critique of Girard's absolutist position on the question of "what is" (Jesus) and "what is-not" (Satan) and his untenable and baseless grounding of his position in the Word of God (which I tackle in chapter 4), I want to first scrutinize further the question of enemy-siblings as a particular configuration of the self-other relation. The latter is of course a complex topic with a massive literature that cannot be covered in this book. I am interested specifically in how the self-other relation has been understood in the context of violence and in relation to violent confrontations, which I argue is most insightfully found in postcolonial approaches. In certain postcolonial theory is found an understanding of the self-other relation that illuminates the simultaneous possibility and impossibility of enemy-siblings.

III. The Possibility and Impossibility of Enemy-Siblings

Framing the topic within the context of violence, Richard Kearney (2002) summarizes four main approaches to the question of otherness in contemporary social theory: (1) deconstruction, exemplified in Derrida and Levinas, posits an absolute other as a way of countering the logocentrism of Western philosophy and emphasizes the need to open ourselves up to alterity (Kearney, 2002, pp. 8–13); (2) psychoanalysis, exemplified in Kristeva and Freud, posits the other as the repressed self that the self wishes to purge from itself (Kearney, 2002, pp. 14–19); (3) Girardian anthropology posits the other as the scapegoat and formulates the ultimate challenge for non-sacrificial society as having to open itself up to the radical other (understood as the Word of Christ) (Kearney, 2002, pp. 19–25); (4) critical hermeneutics, exemplified in Gadamer and Ricoeur, recognizes oneself as another and "construes otherness less in opposition to selfhood than as a partner engaged in the very constitution of its most intimate meaning" (Kearney, 2002, p. 28). Kearney finds elements of the first three approaches useful but argues that "deconstruction too rapidly subordinates same to other, [and] psychoanalysis too rapidly subordinates other to same" (Kearney, 2002, p. 19), while Girard's work too easily falls into dogmatism and loses a self-critical gesture by grounding itself in the Word of God. A critical hermeneutics, in its insistence on the interconnection of self and other (of oneself as another and of the other as another self), better captures, for Kearney, the critical ethical task of a constant engagement with the other that can "offer some tentative judgments about what kinds of others we have before us" (i.e., the kind of other that wants to be loved, the kind that wants to kill us, and so on) (Kearney, 2002, p. 29). To these four approaches, there should be added a fifth approach that I argue proves most useful: a postcolonial[23] approach that combines different elements from the four above approaches and places them within a framework of the possibility-impossibility of enemy-siblings. While this broad postcolonial approach can be found in a variety of forms within a plethora of works (e.g., Bhabha, 1994; Bhambra, 2007, 2014; Mamdani, 1996; Weheliye, 2014; Young, 1995), it is articulated best for the purposes of my analysis in the influential works of Edward Said (1994, 1995, 2001, 2002a, 2002b), Paul Gilroy (1993, 2000), and Michael Taussig (1987, 1993).

A. A Postcolonial Understanding of the Self-Other Relation

To begin with, Paul Ricoeur's (1994 [1990]) thesis in *Oneself as Another* is subtler than is suggested in Kearney. For Ricoeur, the interconnection between self-other is so great, one cannot be thought of without the other, which not only means that "oneself [is] similar to another" but also suggests an implication of "oneself inasmuch as being other" (Ricoeur, 1994, p. 3). This insight can also be seen in my earlier discussion of Dallmayr's hermeneutics, which is built through the Gadamer–Derrida encounter. I think this understanding of self-other is as well ever present in postcolonial theory, which, perhaps more so than the hermeneutics of Ricoeur, tends to eradicate altogether any notion of a "sovereign self" that then must learn how to ethically and justly approach the other, while also directly tying the understanding of self-other to the question of violence and violent interactions. This sort of connection is very well articulated in Said's (1994) "contrapuntal" framework of analysis.

In *Culture and Imperialism*, Said examines, from a cultural perspective and contrapuntally, the different experiences within colonized, formerly colonized, colonizer, and contemporary imperial societies.[24] As opposed to being fixed, sovereign, and autonomous, Said understands culture as being an interconnected set of "hybrid, mixed, impure" forms (1994, p. 14) that traverse across a wide array of identities (be they conceived as ethnic, racial, religious, national, and so on). The crux of his contrapuntal analysis is to view the above varied experiences "as making up a set of ... intertwined and overlapping histories," allowing him "to formulate an alternative both to a politics of blame and to the even more destructive politics of confrontation and hostility" (Said, 1994, p. 18). The contrapuntal method therefore juxtaposes different experiences with one another, opening up an analytical viewpoint into their complex connections while still being attuned to the differences and discrepancies between those experiences. Thus the contrapuntal method examines how colonial/imperial cultural forms are constructed with and through the cultural forms of the colonized (e.g., how the resistance of the colonized shapes discourses of liberty and freedom in the dominating imperial centres; Said, 1994, pp. 239–261; see also Gilroy, 1993 for this point), as well as how the dominating forms come to act against the dominated cultural forms, excluding and hiding them from view and also hiding from view the very connections between the forms (Said, 1994, pp. 51, 66–67).[25]

It is precisely in those discrepancies, which are revealed only when we juxtapose different experiences, that we can observe the workings of a destructive and violent colonial/imperial power, and it is precisely in the connections that we can find an alternative to that violence (Said, 1994, pp. 111–132).[26] By highlighting the immense depth of our interconnectedness across the, for the sake of brevity, colonizer-colonized divide, by examining how seemingly distant and "discrepant experiences" are indeed intimately connected while maintaining the stark difference of the experiences, Said hopes to counter the easy and violent thesis of a supposedly inherent or natural hostility between the West and the non-West (1994, pp. 19, 32–33, 38, 312).

Said's alternative model is best seen in his discussion of "resistance culture." Just as the culture of empire and imperialism spreads before the appearance of colonialism, Said maintains that a culture of resistance spreads before the appearance of decolonialism. Drawing on Basil Davidson's (1978) work on resistance in Africa, Said asserts that this takes place in three steps: (1) there is first a period of physical "primary resistance" against the immediate intrusion of a foreign power on a given territory, which is (2) followed by a period of "ideological resistance" that attempts to reconstitute and rebuild the destroyed and shattered community, until (3) we reach a third moment where resistance to colonialism and imperialism seeks to reconceive human history, liberation, and community (Said, 1994, pp. 209–210, 215–216).[27] Said does not pay much attention to the first step, as it, for him, simply involves the justified and understandable impulse to physically, and violently if need be, defend one's territory and community from the physical onslaught of a colonial power. The second step is also understandable for Said, since the colonized must battle against the colonial campaign to eradicate the community of the colonized – to eradicate their very sense of humanity and their cultural identities. To counter this campaign, we find the appearance of many cultural forms that attempt to "rediscover" and "reconstitute" a precolonial identity, the construction and affirmation of which are meant to shed servitude to the colonial power. This approach is significant in raising the community's consciousness of its own servitude and subjection to the colonial power and of its belonging to the anti-imperialist nationalist struggle against colonial and imperial domination; however, it suffers from a significant shortcoming in that it often falls back upon a colonial grammar and worldview (e.g., accepting the colonial territorial boundaries imposed on the community or accepting narratives of linear historical development) and ends up essentializing the identity of the colonized along racial and ethnic lines established by colonial grammar/institutions (e.g., accepting the different legal and institutional statuses of certain "ethnic" and "racial" identities) (Said, 1994, pp. 210–214; also see Mamdani, 2001 for how this process unfolded in the tragic case of the genocide in Rwanda).

This shortcoming is addressed in the third step of resistance culture, where the idea of resistance, "far from being merely a reaction to imperialism, is an alternative way of conceiving human history" (Said, 1994, p. 216). Most significant is how such cultural forms break down the barriers between cultures and traverse across not just "native" or colonized cultures but across European and colonizing cultures as well (Said cites Salman Rushdie's novel *Midnight's Children* as an example of this). Here is found a sort of playful exploration of the interconnectedness between these cultures in such a way that also highlights the features of domination, exploitation, and marginalization that mark the relationship between the imperial centres and the territories of the colonized. Another significant feature of the third step "is a noticeable pull away from separatist nationalism toward a more integrative view of human community and human liberation" (Said, 1994, p. 216). Walking a tightrope that neither dismisses nationalism and the need for national self-determination nor places the establishment of nationalism and a nation state as the pinnacle achievement of decolonial resistance, Said maintains that the greatest promise (and to a limited extent) achievement of this resistance is the realization that human liberty can be achieved only in concert with one another, across all of the divides that separate us, including colonized-colonizer, and for the sake of building a truly integrated community based on equality and justice and not the sort of violent integration that is introduced and maintained by imperialism and colonialism (Said, 1994, pp. 216–220, 258–259, 276–279). It is worth quoting Said at length here in order to make clear how he sees the connections between the violence of imperialism/colonialism and the search for a new understanding of the self-other relation:

> The major task, then, is to match the new economic and socio-political dislocations and configurations of our time with the startling realities of human interdependence on a world scale.... We need to go on and to situate these [learned national identities and histories] in a geography of other identities, peoples, cultures, and then to study how, despite their differences, they have always overlapped one another, through unhierarchical influence, crossing, incorporation, recollection, deliberate forgetfulness, and, of course, conflict.... It is no exaggeration to say that liberation as an intellectual mission, born in the resistance and opposition to the confinements and ravages of imperialism, has now shifted from the settled, established, and domesticated dynamics of culture to its unhoused, decentered, and exilic energies.... From this perspective ... one can see "the complete consort dancing together" contrapuntally. (Said, 1994, pp. 330–332)

The exilic energies or exilic viewpoint, for Said, enables a contrapuntal framework that situates the ravages of imperialism, in its ultimately uncountable violences (though we can and have calculated much about its violences – but going back to Agamben, we must co-think what we calculate with the incalculability of violence), as the foundation of human interconnectedness. But this interdependence is precisely what the ravages of imperialism seek to conceal because imperialism can continue to ravage only on the basis of a supposed abyss that separates the civilized from the uncivilized, the superior races from the inferior ones, and so on. Thus the contrapuntal framework opposes this kind of exclusivist enmity by showing how we are interconnected to such an extent that the ability to separate from one another is not even feasible.

Violence, in other words, fuses different cultures together at the same time that this fusion must remain hidden and concealed in order for violence to continue ravaging the supposedly radically different/separate "other."

Around the same time Said was finishing his book, Paul Gilroy had completed a similar argument in *The Black Atlantic* (1993). Gilroy argues that "racist, nationalist, or ethnically absolutist discourses" have, since at least the eighteenth century, hermetically sealed "ethnic" identities from one another and obscured the hybridity of cultures (1993, p. 1). Using "rhetorical strategies that can be named 'cultural insiderism,'" such absolutist discourses proclaim notions of "pure" races, "autonomous" nationalities, and "authentic" ethnic identities, consequently casting as impure, inauthentic, and degenerative all and any concepts of mixture, hybridity, and interconnectedness (Gilroy, 1993, pp. 2–5). These rhetorical strategies posit the nation state as belonging to, and/or as a manifestation of, an "original" and "homogenous" ethnic identity – hence the entrance of foreign elements is seen as impure and as a threat to the ethno-national state.

Against this absolutist discourse, which remains vibrant in political discourses of both the left and the right and most alarmingly for Gilroy has appeared in black political culture (1993, pp. 5, 7–9, 31–32),[28] Gilroy advances the concept of hybridity so as to emphasize (similar to contrapuntal analysis) the depth of human interconnectedness, interdependence, and cultural mixture. Drawing on the transatlantic slave trade and the experiences of slaves and ex-slaves, this conception is best exemplified for Gilroy in the image of the ship, which focuses our attention on the space in-between, on the "middle passage," on the circulation and movement of people, ideas, and acts, as well as the movement of key cultural and political artefacts such as books and songs (1993, pp. 12–17). It is interesting that in his reading of W.E.B. Du Bois's work, particularly *The Souls of Black Folk*, Gilroy establishes a triad similar to Said's three steps of resistance, where Gilroy asserts that in Du Bois's thinking,

> double consciousness emerges from the unhappy symbiosis between three modes of thinking, being, and seeing. The first is racially particularistic, the second nationalistic in that it derives from the nation state in which the ex-slaves but not-yet-citizens find themselves, rather than from their aspiration towards a nation state of their own. The third is diasporic or hemispheric, sometimes global and occasionally universalist. (Gilroy, 1993, p. 127)

The third mode is indeed most visible, for Gilroy, in Du Bois's novel *Dark Princess*, where we find a "valuable" notion of "hybridity and intermixture" that does not entertain the idea that something pure is "lost" or "corrupted" in hybridity, but rather celebrates and emphasizes "a meeting of two heterogeneous multiplicities that in yielding themselves up to each other create something durable" (Gilroy, 1993, p. 144).

The parallels to Said are apparent in the move from localized and bounded modes of identification to more diasporic (Gilroy) and exilic (Said) ones. While Said favoured the term "exile" over "diaspora" (Said, 2002b, pp. 441–442) and Gilroy favoured "diaspora" over "exile" (Gilroy, 2000, pp. 122, 124), substantively speaking, they agreed that this third mode exemplified a movement away from hermetically sealed identities, which centralize and essentialize the "self," and toward more complex, interconnected, and transnational modes of understanding identity as (a) an always hidden (or repressed) relation of self-other (á la psychoanalysis) that must be unconcealed (á la Girardian anthropology), (b) a yielding of the self to the other (á la hermeneutics), (c) the self as always already other to itself (á la deconstruction), and (d) a *yielding of the self to its own multiplicities* (the postcolonial contribution). Gilroy (2000) further develops this last idea in his book *Against Race*, where he argues the centrality of the concept of identity to theoretical traditions that are concerned with questions of belonging, ethnicity, and nationalism (2000, p. 98). In the book, Gilroy examines how the ultranationalist and (neo)fascist movements of the twentieth century (his insights are indeed most relevant for this second decade of the twenty-first century that has seen an explosion of ultranationalisms across the globe) manufactured an "ideal and unnatural human uniformity" in place of the "inevitable, untidy diversity" of social life (2000, p. 102). In these movements, "identity ceases to be an ongoing process of self-making and social interaction," instead becoming "a thing to be possessed and displayed" (Gilroy, 2000, p. 103). Most crucial here is these movements' absolute disdain and contempt for mixture and hybridity. Unlike some of the theories discussed in chapter 1 (e.g., Bernstein, Lawrence), the emphasis in Gilroy is not on the "other" who is different, but rather on "the half-different and the partially familiar" (Gilroy, 2000, p. 106). This is not to deny the hatred and violence that continue to be directed against the different or differentiated "other," but the point for Gilroy is that in contemporary society, such antipathies and hatreds toward the alter "other" do not reach the level of animosity that we find directed toward the "mixture," which is seen as a "great betrayal" to the "tidy, bleached-out zones of impossibly pure culture" (Gilroy, 2000, pp. 105–106). The outcome of such ultranationalist ideologies can be only "separation and slaughter" (Gilroy, 2000, p. 106).

Against this ultranationalist and (neo)fascist trend, underpinned as a collection of movements with an ideology of race – of a "raciology" that reaches far beyond the extremist political movements and operates in most political groups, parties, movements, fields (Gilroy, 2000, pp. 11–53, 57–58, 62) – Gilroy outlines and explores three interconnected problems that are encountered in scholarly and social/political uses of the concept of identity. Gilroy asserts that these are (1) "understanding identity as subjectivity," which concerns the shift from a belief in a grounded and bounded identity that operates in an ordered and bounded polity/society to the anxious and uncertain forms of identity that are prevalent in contemporary or postmodern society, where clear boundaries are at best blurred if not altogether eradicated (e.g., due to information technologies) (Gilroy, 2000, pp. 108–109); (2) "the problem of sameness understood here as intersubjectivity," which concerns the establishment and categorization of sameness and difference, where we find again a challenge to the "unitary" self by the "deliberations about how selves – and their identities – are formed through relationships of exteriority, conflict, and exclusion" (Gilroy, 2000, p. 109); and (3) the problem of "social solidarity" in an age where identity is challenged through the first two problems, wherein Gilroy is interested in asking how else we can forge social and political solidarities and collective forms of action in order to address social and political injustices (Gilroy, 2000, pp. 109–110). It is here that Gilroy moves away from the absolutist discourses of raciology and instead advocates an emphasis on the movement, hybridity, and mixture of identity – *the multiplicities of the self* – which, unlike superficial notions of mixture that are found in public political discourse (e.g., the "melting pot"), are always uneven and unequal and do not produce a seamless consistency (Gilroy, 2000, pp. 275–276).

I certainly agree with Gilroy's direction in the third step – when faced with a problem for which the outcome is "separation and slaughter," we should certainly be fighting to instead introduce the alternative route of "solidarity" and hybrid understanding of self-other mixtures. But I want to further probe and question the second problem that he outlines. This point indeed articulates the foundation operating underneath Said's continuous imploring of humanity to move away from the violences that have brought a myriad of diverse cultures together into an interconnected web and instead find a new direction of cross-cultural and inter-cultural fertilizations (similar to Gilroy's direction in the third problem that he outlines). Gilroy provides an added dimension to this foundation by asserting that the very argument for opening ourselves up to our interconnections indeed can contribute to a crisis of identity and potentially feed the fires of (neo)fascist and ultranationalist ideologies. The scholarly work that has done much to reveal our interconnectedness cannot thus divorce itself from the (neo)fascist and ultranationalist drive, delusional and baseless as these ideologies are, toward establishing starker boundaries between same and other, between inside and outside.

I think that in formulating the problematic in this manner, linking the impossibility of a unitary and sovereign self with the violences that seek to separate, an important line of questioning opens up, one that is starting to move away from Gilroy's own formulation of the matter: How is it that exclusion, conflict, hatred, and the violence of separation (whether through war or economic displacement or ethnic cleansing) indeed come to constitute an impossible unitary self? Furthermore (and this is moving beyond Gilroy), can the impossibility of "purity" be understood, not as a reaction to scholarly understanding of human interconnections, but as an outcome and consequence of violence and violent efforts at exclusion and separation? And if so, how does that process unfold? Is there something about violence that inevitably and inextricably forges sameness with alterity while simultaneously concealing this forging?

These questions are crucial to our understanding of the possibility-impossibility of enemy-siblings. The multiplicities of the self – the almost infinite co-constituents of the "self" that render the "self" a set of multiplicities – point us toward a dynamic process that I call violent dialogue, whereby the conflictual character of enemy-siblings is not simply an external confrontation that takes places across separate and separated selves, but also a confrontation that takes place within the self, wherein it becomes (a) *impossible* to constitute a self without the enemy in two connected senses: (1) because the other enemy wants to eradicate or degrade the self, it becomes impossible to assert a sovereign self (i.e., the self is under threat), and (2) since the first sense moves in both directions (for simplicity's sake, let's picture just two sides who want to eradicate one another), the enemies become entangled to such an extent that one cannot be thought of without the other (or, at the very least, they become selves that can assert themselves only against the threat of the other); which means that the confrontation makes it (b) *possible* to constitute a self precisely when the enemy is revealed as co-constituent of the self (i.e., when we confront the fact of our mixture and hybridity). This is basically how I understand the possibility and impossibility of enemy-siblings. A dash is forged in and through violence (e.g., Israel–Palestine) that makes the terms on either side of the dash both possible (as co-constituents) and impossible (as sovereign selves).

Now, this would be the understanding of the possibility-impossibility of enemy-siblings through Gilroy's hybridity viewpoint and Said's contrapuntal viewpoint. The absolutist discourse or the culture of empire would exhibit different understandings, but the important point here is that the framework of possibility-impossibility itself holds. So in that discourse, a dash is still formed (e.g., Israeli–Palestinian conflict), and it still makes the terms on either side of the dash both possible (as sovereign selves) and impossible (by being under existential threats). Regardless of the viewpoints, then, whose difference must be maintained – and we cannot lose sight of the fact that Gilroy's and Said's viewpoints are superior scientifically, ethically, and politically – the structure of possibility-impossibility of enemy-siblings remains intact and paramount to enhancing our understanding of the formation of enemy-siblings in violence. At this point, I think we must turn to Taussig's work, which theorizes the topic of sameness-alterity within the problematic of mimesis, violence, and representation. This will more firmly explain and support the idea of the possibility and impossibility of enemy-siblings.

B. Mimesis-Alterity

In *Mimesis and Alterity*, Taussig (1993) sets out to resuscitate the concept of mimesis from simplistic notions of mere representation, where mimesis is understood as a straightforward process of copying a thing, simply highlighting the constructed nature of things. Instead, Taussig delineates the complex interplay between mimesis and alterity. He understands mimetic behaviour as illuminative of an ongoing interaction between different cultures whereby definitions of self and other are constantly being shaped and negotiated. Succinctly put, Taussig argues that mimetic behaviour is just as much concerned with the difference that is posited in one's identity formation as it is with a sameness that may be simultaneously pursued – which very much falls within the scope of the postcolonial understanding of the self-other relation already outlined. But in addition, Taussig introduces a phenomenological dimension when he highlights the ways in which objects, "things," are part and parcel of the mimetic function.

Taussig argues that mimetic behaviour is tied not to a quest that seeks to simply copy a thing, but to a quest that may allow us to weld into the thing copied. Taussig illuminates the two-layered nature of the mimetic faculty: "copying" and a "palpable, sensuous, connection between the very body of the perceiver and the perceived" (1993, p. 21). If the real thing is beyond our grasp intellectually and physically (for example, "spirits" that are sought in certain healing rituals/practices), we nevertheless seek to find a way to conjoin our very selves, bodies, and intellects with the ever-elusive "real" thing.

The mimetic faculty takes us outside of ourselves when it creates this sensuous connection between the perceiver and the perceived. The very act of copying a thing (of becoming the same) highlights for Taussig the notion that we are in the process of becoming the same as something other (1993, pp. 40–41). We become other to ourselves by deeply, sensuously seeping into the thing that we want to know or feel or experience, or put differently, by imitating and contacting the other thing. Thus sameness and alterity are intractably bound together (Taussig, 1993, p. 129). There are three different configurations that this intractable relationship between mimesis and alterity may take: (1) in certain magical practices, the impossible happens and mimesis becomes alterity to create a certain kind of electricity or the magical effect of such practices (Taussig, 1993, pp. 191–192); (2) in the "organized control of mimesis," or the mimesis of mimesis, movements such as fascism rationalize the mimetic faculty in a way that makes it useful only for domination (Taussig, 1993, pp. 66–69); and (3) through the "mimetic excess" of a postcolonial world, where Taussig speaks of an excess that allows for the "reflexive awareness as to the mimetic faculty," we may "become any Other and engage the image with the reality thus imagized" (e.g., the taking on today, through information technology, of various identities simultaneously – the use of "avatars" being a prime example) (Taussig, 1993, pp. 254–255).[29]

These three forms of mimesis are distinct from the three forms of mimesis found in Girard. In Girard there is (1) the mimesis between those caught in the moment of unbound violence; (2) the limited violence of the sacrifice, which mimics the onset and the end of the unbound originary violence; and (3) the mimesis of the sacrifice in the persecutor's text. In Girard, mimesis is lodged in desire – it is mimetic desire that lies at the basis of all three forms, and this is most visible in the third form of mimesis (i.e., in representation). Put differently, only a proper treatment and reading of the third form of mimesis can reveal mimetic desire, and henceforth the mechanism of the surrogate victim; the scapegoat; God's love; etcetera.

In Taussig, on the other hand, mimesis in all its forms is always tied to the sensuous welding of the body into the thing copied, highlighting for Taussig the complex relationship between mimesis and alterity. This important difference offers a way out of Girard's absolutism in that it dislodges mimesis from desire. Consequently, this allows us to maintain some of Girard's discussion on mimetic violence[30] while discarding Girard's absolutism, which comes through the notion of mimetic desire. Taussig's argument points out, essentially, that the notion of enemy-siblings, which emerges from mimetic desire in Girard, already has embedded in it, in the very combination of these two words, the complex interplay between mimesis (sibling) and alterity (enemy). The difference between the two thinkers suggests that the brackets could easily be switched depending on the manner of representation involved, since the dislodging of mimesis from desire (which I must do if I am to move beyond the absolutism of Girard) brings to the forefront the problem of representation, not as a matter of two absolute and competing perspectives that are separated by an abyss, but as that which concerns the seepage of the thing copied into the representation itself; or, in Taussig, the representation that mimics a thing becomes part and parcel of the mimetic function itself since the kind of representation involved will produce specific and differing effects.

Thus Taussig's notion of mimesis/alterity, broadly speaking, opens the door for an analysis that examines the manner in which the "object of representation" seeps into the representation itself. We can observe the seepage of violence into representations of violence whereby, generally speaking, enemy(alterity)-siblings(mimesis) (in discourses of empire and absolutist discourses) or enemy(mimesis)-siblings(alterity) (in discourses such as Gilroy's and Said's) form and transform in the very representation of violence; or, put differently, where the representation itself becomes part and parcel of the mimetic function that forms in violent interactions. Because Taussig's insights on seepage suggest that it is possible to trace the operation of the "thing" in representations, a dialogical analysis can reveal through textual analysis, as I will try to show in chapter 5, a third dimension of violence wherein enemy-siblings are formed. In this third dimension can be found a dynamic process of violent dialogue that is ever-changing, the contours, generals, and particulars of which can never be pre-assumed. In following violence, the dialogical analytic seeks to understand this dynamic as it unfolds in its specificity. I maintain that there is a limit to what can be said about violent dialogue and the third dimension in this book, precisely because the book's project is primarily theoretical, and the problem that the book is attempting to articulate is not a problem that is to be resolved theoretically. Rather, it is a context-specific puzzle that can be approached only in the details of a given case study. While I have broached this type of analysis previously

(Ayyash, 2010a), I believe that a more nuanced and detailed analysis of it is a task for future projects.

Conclusion

When we follow the evasiveness of violence at the moment of its enactment, we do not find madness, as Das warns, but rather the formation of enemy-siblings. Instead of limiting the analysis to the linguistic dimension and positing the perpetrators of violence as "brokered subjectivities" who know not what they do, the dialogical analytic launches into the evasiveness of violence at its moment of enactment, where a third dimension appears. This mimetic dimension reveals that the most significant role that violence plays occurs precisely at the moment when violence seems incomprehensible and unknowable. Building on Gadamer, Derrida, and their encounter, the dialogical analytic seeks to follow the incomprehensibility of the subject matter through the violent dialogue that takes place between participants engaged in the exchange of violent acts. Violent dialogue is a dynamic that reveals the formation of a violent communion that remains hidden from the view of the participants, but whose effects can be traced in the formation of enemy-siblings. We can understand this formation through Girard, Said, Gilroy, and Taussig as constituting the possibility-impossibility of self-other. In short, this formation alludes to the fact that enemy-siblings are forged in a certain kind of communion where the "self" comes to make possible and impossible the "other." Instead of outright separation, violent dialogue ensures that the sides become irrevocably co-constitutive of one another. None of these processes can be fully or properly analysed if we remain limited to the one- or two-dimensional conception of violence.

When we explore what escapes the significations of violence and analyse the notion of enemy-siblings as it is formed and transformed in violence between participants who can no longer be viewed as irreconcilable because together, they constitute enemy-siblings in mimesis/alterity, a new light is shed on the kind of interaction that is taking place between the participants: a kind of communion is revealed.

This communion itself does not necessitate the use of violence, but being forged in the use of violence ties the sides with even deeper structures that lead them toward violence. I call these deep structures "postures," by which I mean the very disposition from which words emanate, or the disposition that gives as much meaning to the word as the word itself. This shows that it is not the incommensurability of the positions that matters most, but rather *the postures of incommensurability*.

The character of these postures is difficult to directly detect, which means that they cannot belong to the observable mimetic third dimension. Consequently, a yet even more elusive dimension is operative, one that enables and makes possible the mimetic dimension: the fourth dimension of violence, violence the "thing itself."

These last points make more explicit the shadow of mysticism that seems to hover over this book, perhaps ever since the first mention of an elusive "thing itself." I do not intend to enter this debate at its abstract point (i.e., mysticism per se), for it would take this project in an altogether different direction. But the question of mysticism cannot be ignored since it is tied to the important question of transcendence, which I have begun to raise and address in this chapter. And so I will directly address the question of transcendence and violence by going back to Girard in the first steps of chapter 4. An interlude will set the stage for my re-engagement with Girard, where I utilize some of Girard's concepts (mimetic desire, the monstrous double) to read Kafka's *The Metamorphosis*, but in a different direction from Girard's theory of sacrifice. Instead of utilizing these concepts to posit the victim's perspective as a transcendent voice that reveals and absolutely opposes the perspective of the persecutor, I highlight an element of *substitution* that is different from Girard's understanding of the sacrificial substitution, which then paves the way for an understanding of transcendental violence that is more fruitful than what Girard can offer.

Interlude

In The Metamorphosis *(2002 [1915]), Kafka's main character, Gregor, finds himself transformed into a beast, incapable of communicating to others but yet still in control of his comprehensive abilities. Gregor's relationship with his family in general, and with his sister, Grete, in particular, is at the centre of this peculiar problem. It is apparent that Gregor had always been a family and selfless man. He had dedicated his entire young life to moving his family out of a financial crisis and was astonishingly successful in this undertaking. It is also clear that he had loved his sister and, despite his parents, had seen great potential in her musical abilities. Before the metamorphosis, Gregor was even preparing to announce that he was sending Grete to a conservatoire where she could pursue her love for playing the violin. Following the dreadful metamorphosis, however, Gregor's family endures a great deal of financial and emotional suffering, with Grete carrying the heaviest burden. As time passes, Grete and the rest of the family grow weary of Gregor and they (Grete especially) begin to question whether Gregor is at all alive inside this beast.*

On his fateful night, Gregor is energized out of his slumber by the sound of his sister's violin. The music has reminded him of the human communication and relations that once filled his life with meaning. It is as if he is once more speaking with Grete. He is weak and faint at this point, as the burden of becoming a burden grew on him, but the memory of warmness and human connection fills him with the drive he needs to move out of his room and reach Grete. When he arrives in the living room, Gregor notices that the lodgers at his parents' house are disinterested and unappreciative of Grete's music. This spurs Gregor on even more, and he recounts to himself his once good intentions of sending Grete to the conservatoire. He thinks that even though he can no longer offer Grete this glorious gift, he can at least offer her an appreciative ear. He hopes that even in his hideous state, he will reconnect and re-communicate with Grete through the violin. But when the lodgers take sight of him, chaos ensues, and after they storm out of the house, the lodgers take with them an important source of income for the family. Grete then demands to her parents that they rid themselves of Gregor. This beast, she pleads, is no longer Gregor at any rate, for it cannot communicate with them. Crushed by this turn of events, Gregor, weaker and fainter than before, retreats back into his room and passively perishes.

I ask: Did Gregor deserve his fate? Can we blame Grete — a young and promising woman — for not wanting to dedicate her youth to caring for a beast that could not even communicate? She seems all the more blameless because she could not have known about Gregor's good intentions toward her. And was he so selfless? Was he so "good" because he felt that it was his duty to bestow the "good" upon his sister, even though this act was detrimental to Gregor himself (for he hated the man his work was making him)? Gregor created the conditions (his career, for instance) that made it possible for him to bestow the "good" upon his sister: his income meant that Grete could leave behind the established values of the family; she could break the boundaries set for her; she could create her life and create her music, with the two creations going hand in hand. But what, then, are we to make of the last turn of events? At the very moment that Gregor attempts to definitively realize or act out his good intentions toward his sister, she seemingly shows herself as his true nemesis and brings about his ultimate demise. At the same time, it is his most forceful attempt at enacting his good intentions that is indeed his last act. This prompts the questions: Who or what was his nemesis? His sister or his "good intentions"?

Communication is at the centre of Gregor and Grete's relationship. We are first told that Gregor is preparing to communicate the wonderful news to Grete. This is the stage where Gregor is experiencing hubris: he is differentiating himself from his parents by believing in Grete's talents, and enacting the impossible by not only taking care of his family's basic needs, but also securing for Grete the luxury and privilege of attending the conservatoire. Not only this, but he is also sacrificing his happiness in this undertaking. After the metamorphosis, Gregor is completely forbidden from only one of his formerly human abilities: communication. He can no longer bestow the "good" he had planned for Grete. To Grete, Gregor is incapable of communication as a beast, and she thus has no way of connecting with her brother. Still, she carries the heaviest burden in caring for Gregor, and this suggests her hope of communicating with Gregor one day still. This is all the more evident when much of her argument in favour of disposing of the beast revolves around its inability to communicate. We can say from this that Grete and Gregor desire one object: communication.

Grete can still speak in the story, but like Gregor, she also cannot communicate after the metamorphosis. Communication, as Gregor now understands, is predominantly concerned with human connections and relations and not with the mere functionality of words. In this sense, Grete can no longer communicate because Gregor was her only companion in communication. The violin is her most precious gift for communication, and no one cared for her music except for Gregor. Grete can no longer communicate through the violin: she is reduced to an unwanted and unappreciated musician to the lodgers, appeasing them so as to ensure that her parents could maintain that source of income. It is not a coincidence that everything comes to an end on this night. On hearing the sounds of Grete's violin, Gregor feels that he can resuscitate their communication once more. The violin will break the barrier between them, where he, even as a beast, can yet bestow the "good" upon Grete. Hubris has not left Gregor, but this time, his failure is fatal.

His first failure (the onset of the metamorphosis) set the stage for the mimetic desire over communication. His second failure came at a point where mimesis had already spread: Grete and Gregor were the same person at that point. Grete's want and willingness to dispose of Gregor is all but understandable at this moment: she was disposing of her monstrous double. Gregor's nemesis was never his sister; it was always his good intentions. His good intentions led him to affirm his difference in a manner that asserted his will and his will alone upon their plane of communication (i.e., I am sacrificing myself for your own good). In this act, Gregor becomes the crucified who cannot be communicated with: he has stepped into the abyss of sacrifice, where only few dare venture. Who dares to communicate – who can communicate – with the one who was so daring in self-sacrifice? Impossible! Gregor meta-morphed into a beast because that is only what his bestowing of good intentions could have made him: that which cannot communicate or be communicated with. The beast is the substitute of the crucified: the beast is the non-communication that substitutes for the incommunicable. *The bestowed, left speechless, uncomprehending such self-sacrifice, is made into the same creature, but worse: living, left behind, incapable of communicating with the one who bestowed the good. After the death of the beast, we are told that Grete is reborn, and she boasts a glow that her parents had indeed never seen in her before. But it seems to me that when Grete effectively killed Gregor, he was already dead, and so was she. Indeed, Grete was never really reborn. For it was only after the beast that substituted for self-sacrifice was eradicated that she was ever truly born.*

4 Transcendental Violence: Violence the "Thing Itself"

Thereafter he became ever thinner and paler – became the "ideal," became "pure spirit," became "the absolute," became "the thing-in-itself." ... *The collapse of a god*: he became a "thing-in-itself."

–Friedrich Nietzsche, *The Anti-Christ* (original emphasis)

Girard posits two distinct horizons of interpretation: the satanic persecutor and the Christ victim. Instead of separating the horizons with an abyss where the victim's text reveals the truth of the persecutor's text (pointing out its originary point of violence) and then defeats it once and for all (halting the continuation of violence), I think we must, following my reading of Kafka's story, pay attention to the element of substitution: not Girard's focus on the sacrificial substitutions but rather the ways in which a substitution for what cannot be said/represented/made present constitutes a fundamental relation across the different moments of violence; or, as I will come to understand this, the ways in which the (un)knowability of violence provides clues as to the propagation of violence.

In this chapter, I first examine Girard's understanding of the relationship between "what is" and "what is-not" in order to use his work as a counter-conceptualization that enables the dialogical analytic to establish its domain of analysis. I distance myself from (a) the intellectual tendency to align oneself with an absolute source of love (Christ/God in Girard's case) in the effort to counteract a transcendent violence (which signals an account of violence as a thing-in-itself that *is*), and (b) Girard's claim that "mimetic desire" lies at the foundation of *the* problem of violence in every human society. In making this critique, I draw on Hayden White and Derrida in challenging Girard's distinction between mythological texts and the Word of the Gospels, and Girard's positing of a satanic "what is-not" in his concept of transcendence. I use this analysis to begin formulating a different understanding of the relationship between violence and transcendence.

Instead of positing mimetic desire as the firm ground and foundation of violence, I argue that a mimetic dimension is possible because of the groundless ground of violence, or violence the "thing itself." To illustrate what I mean by the latter, I revisit the Gadamer–Derrida encounter, this time by relying on John Caputo's framing of the encounter within the distinction between a metaphysics of presence and the flux. While Caputo is helpful as a starting point, there are some differences between his approach toward the flux and the dialogical analytic's chase after violence the "thing itself," mainly because my approach relies on Gadamer more than does Caputo. In highlighting Gadamer's emphasis on the interplay between understanding and elusiveness, as well as Derrida's understanding of violence, the book formulates the groundless (Derrida) ground (Gadamer) of violence as constituting a fourth dimension of violence, and I explain why I associate this transcendental dimension with the name of violence the "thing itself."

In translating Derrida's terminology on violence, I also illustrate how Derrida's work allows the dialogical analytic to link the fourth dimension of violence back into the first without subordinating the dimensions to one another. While the fourth dimension cannot be directly observed, analysts can, I argue, observe its effects as it links up with the other dimensions of violence. In emphasizing the movement of violence in its four-dimensional operation, we come back to the last bastion for dividing/delimiting violence that the book has yet to deconstruct: the absolute distinction between founding and continuing violence, which brings us back to Taussig, Das, and Girard. I argue that while Das and Taussig present important distinctions between the forms in which the inexpressibility of violence may take shape (i.e., between founding violence and two distinct forms of continuing violence), opening them up to Girard (without following Girard's path) points toward a different formulation of the question of violence's (un)knowability. Instead of the founding-continuing distinction, the question of (un)knowability points toward the formation of postures that demand the release of violence in the fourth dimension of violence.

Through Bourdieu's theory on deep dispositions and the symbolic-brutal moments of violence, Benjamin's "Critique of Violence," and Derrida's "Force of Law" and "Différance," I outline how the operation of deep postures of incommensurability produce incommensurable positions across a spectrum of time and space. It is these postures that must be analysed and understood if we are to properly account for the propagation of violence. I conclude that this posing of the question of violence's (un)knowability (which is basically how I come to understand the relationship between violence and transcendence) opens up an analytical space where one seems improbable, thus allowing for the exploration of violence the "thing itself" and enabling a four-dimensional view of violence.

I. Violence and Transcendence

Deconstruction seems content with a pure mirroring of the sacred that amounts to nothing, at this stage, but a purely literary effect.... If there is really "something" to Derrida, it is because there is something beyond: precisely a deconstruction that reaches the mechanisms of the sacred and no longer hesitates to come to terms with the surrogate victim.

–René Girard, *Things Hidden since the Foundation of the World*

Picking up where Girard was left off, it is religion (the Judeo-Christian scriptures specifically) that for Girard begins the process of demystification that governs our world today (Girard, 1987, p. 138). As already mentioned, this transition is far from peaceful or smooth: it is on the contrary quite violent in the sense that while "our knowledge of the victimage mechanism ... represents considerable progress ... in intellectual and ethical respects," it will also "mean a terrible recrudescence of that same [mimetic] violence, often in odious and atrocious forms, since sacrificial mechanisms become progressively less efficient and less capable of renewal" (Girard, 1987, pp. 127–128). For Girard, the violent events of the twentieth century attest to this recrudescence. As such, it is not Girard's books that are leading the way to the revelation made in the Gospels: the revelation is already there and has already been shaping human history for some time (for instance, in the form of totalitarian movements that have reacted to the dissolution of sacrificial institutions through an attempt to rationalize the victimage mechanism). If it were not Girard, it would be someone else who has presented us with a "scientific" understanding of this unfolding history and of the mechanism that explains everything (Girard, 1987, pp. 134–135). And if he is able to do so, it is simply because in the Gospels, *everything is already revealed*" (Girard, 1987, p. 138; original emphasis).

When Girard talks about what has been hidden since the foundation of the world, he is only quoting the Word of Christ in Psalm 78, where Jesus promises to reveal just those things in Matthew 13:35

(Girard, 1987, p. 164). What has been missed throughout the years, which Girard finds astonishing, is the actual thing that Jesus meant to reveal: the mechanism of the surrogate victim. Anyone who reads Girard knows that he is not reserved in his universal claims. Girard is adamant about the simplicity of his hypothesis and his ability to demonstrate it in seemingly disparate texts, traditions, and mythologies in a kind of seamless totality.

And how can Girard not make such universal claims? He is explicating a truth that has allegedly been revealing itself for centuries: a truth that asserted itself as universal, all-encompassing, and absolute from the outset. Girard agrees that there is no stance that allows us to discover what may be called an absolute truth. However, he does maintain (contra deconstruction as he views the movement – a view that often teeters on the edge of a caricature of deconstruction) that there is a world outside of language, and he does hold on to the possibility of gaining knowledge of the world as such (Girard, 2007, p. 28). The guarantor of the reality of the world, for Girard, is God (i.e., a supreme transcendent being that assures us of something that is outside us) (2007, p. 147).[1] Ultimately for Girard, what makes the Word such an absolute truth is that it is, by definition, not human (or not solely human at the very least): "the Word that states itself to be absolutely true never speaks except from the position of a victim in the process of being expelled. There is no human explanation for his presence among us" (Girard, 1987, p. 435). If Girard stumbles upon this revelation as it happens to ripen in our time (and the fact that it took this long to reveal itself – that it was misinterpreted by countless readers, followers, worshippers, theologians, humanists, priests, scientists, etc. – is evidence of the extra-human dimension of the Word), then how can he not carry in his own explication the universal, all-encompassing, and absolute characteristics of this truth? The answer is that he must. Let us combine these characteristics into one word since Girard's work is, to put it mildly, suggestive of such a combination: transcendence.

Girard basically argues that in sacrificial societies the victim is the "transcendental signifier," upon which a given society's distinctions of before/after, inside/outside, and community/sacred are built (1987, p. 102). This does not mean that the victim is the "*true* transcendental signifier," but that the victim functions in a manner where "the signified constitutes all actual and potential meaning the community confers on to the victim and, through its intermediary, on to all things" (Girard, 1987, p. 103; original emphasis). In the revelations of the Gospels, the transcendental signified is shattered: there can no longer be any myth that will convince us of the persecutor's perspective. Thanks to the work of the Gospels, we in the modern world are capable of seeing the persecutor as a persecutor and the victim as a scapegoat.

But this does not mean that the Gospels do away with "divine transcendence" altogether; rather, "transcendent violence," and all that has been signified in it (the cultural orders of human history), is what is done away with, and instead humanity is presented with a "transcendent love" that was previously hidden from view by the cycles of "transcendent violence" (Girard, 1987, p. 217). The transcendent love is not sacrificial, and to attempt to purge the Gospels of their transcendent dimension would amount to a sacrificial practice itself; it is rather a transcendence that we may approach as human beings in search of all there is to know about the non-violent world of the true non-violent God (Girard, 1987, pp. 235–236). We can see this difference in Girard's discussion on the absolute difference between the Logos of Heraclitus (transcendent violence)[2] and the Logos of John (transcendent love).[3] It is worth quoting at length what Girard and his interlocutor Jean-Michel Oughourlian have to say about this distinction:

> JMO: You are trying to demonstrate the emptiness of all the differences human beings respect, and you are seeking for one single distinction: the absolute distinction between the Logos of violence, *which is not*, and the Logos of love, *which is*.
>
> RG: This revelation comes from the Logos itself. In Christianity, it is expelled once again by the sacrificial reading, which amounts to a return to the Logos of violence. All the same, the Logos is still in the process of revealing itself; if it tolerates being concealed yet another time, this is to put off for just a short while the fullness of its revelation. The Logos of love puts up no resistance; it always allows itself to be expelled by the Logos of violence. But its expulsion is revealed in a more and more obvious fashion, and by the same process the Logos of violence is revealed as what can only exist by expelling the true Logos and feeding upon it in one way or another. (1987, pp. 273–274; emphases added)

This brings up the relation between "what is" and "what is-not," which points toward the major differences between Girard's work on violence and the notion of violence the "thing itself." These differences concern (a) Girard's vision for a non-violent world, which would be brought about through a method that would exorcise violence (or, the question of how one approaches the study of violence outside of the instrumentalist perspective and the productive-destructive distinction, whereby I want to "free" the concept of violence as opposed to exorcise it); (b) Girard's emphasis and reliance on the difference between mythology and the Word of Christ, which would enable the exorcism of violence (or, the question of the relation between violence and language, whereby I want to explore the traversal of perspectives as opposed to separating two absolute perspectives (victim-persecutor) with an abyss); and (c) Girard's positing of a binary opposition between "what is" God's love and a satanic "what is-not," which forms the foundation of Girard's work (or, the question of transcendence, whereby I want to allow the operation of a continuous tension between "what is" and "what is-not" as opposed to an either/or opposition between the two). To present a critique of Girard on these three points and outline how this critique enables a different analytical approach to violence, I first summarize how Girard sees and defends his work throughout *Things Hidden* (1987) (particularly book 1, pp. 3–138) and in *Evolution and Conversion* (2007).

Girard has been criticized for numerous aspects of his method in particular and his hypothesis in general. Two of these criticisms are recurring and prominent: (1) he never engages in field research (all of his "data" is secondary and based on what is considered today to be more or less "classical anthropology," which has come under serious methodological and theoretical attacks), and (2) he unfairly pivots the sacrificial rites to the centre of diverse communities when it is debatable whether or not they are of central import to the communities concerned (i.e., he "brutalizes the data"). Generally speaking, his response to both criticisms is that he cannot carry out field research when the founding moments of these communities have long passed (if not the communities themselves altogether). His goal is not to present detailed representations of the various human groups that appear in his work, but rather to construct a general theory on the origins of culture. His methodology raises so many understandable concerns, he believes, since his hypothesis deals with a founding mechanism that functions by hiding itself or by being misrecognized by those who use it. But Girard claims that the fact that his hypothesis has been shown to be convincing (or at the very least applicable) in so many different cases despite the lack of direct evidence (and hence his reliance on a wide variety of sources and materials) is reason enough to justify its consideration as a hypothesis (Girard, 2007, pp. 143–144, 173–186).

I find his responses valid (which is not to say that I am convinced of his responses) in the sense that he does not (for the most part) claim to really know much about the life, history, texture, intricacy, or detail of the communities he brings up throughout his work; rather, he is interested only in a founding mechanism that he claims is the same in all human societies (Girard, 2007, pp. 171–172). Many would argue that I concede far too much to Girard in not pursuing these lines of critique. But my aim is not to discredit Girard's work in this book, and instead I pursue a different line of criticism to reach a more comprehensive position on the question of violence and transcendence that is central to my argument.

And in that respect, I think that ultimately Girard falls short in his response to one criticism. Girard defines his hypothesis as scientific in the sense that it "combine[s] the maximum of actual uncertainty with the maximum of potential certainty," (Girard, 1986, p. 98), and I think that his work does more or less develop under this credo. I do not doubt his integrity, and I accept his claim that he did not simply interpret the mythologies and sacrificial rites discussed in *Violence and the Sacred* for the purpose of affirming the Judeo-Christian scriptures, but came to the scriptures only later and somewhat apprehensively (Girard, 1987, pp. 176–177, 446–447). However, he does make it clear in several places that he is reading myths and rituals in light of the Gospels. Granted, he is doing so to counter what he claims to be the dominant mode of contemporary analysis and criticism of the Bible – that is, that modern thinking has been obsessively reading the Bible in light of mythology over the last few centuries. In this sense, his reversal is permissible on the grounds that it is critical of what has come to pass as conventional reading of scripture. But the matter is convoluted when he claims that while he has trouble chronologically ordering in importance the different sources and materials that he uses throughout his works, he nevertheless states, "The discovery of the victimary mechanism was really connected with the reading of *Oedipus* and above all with *The Bacchae*. At that time I compared the tragedies with myths and rituals" (Girard, 2007, p. 137). Nevertheless, "the main source of my intuition is the Gospels, which unmask the role of collective foundational murder," and this is clearly the foundational point that no other text reveals for him (Girard, 2007, p. 136).

In his review of *Violence and the Sacred*, Hayden White (1978) convincingly points out the trouble with Girard's approach to these texts. White argues that Girard's reading of texts of literature, mythology, and sacrificial rites is fundamentally based on an inversion of contemporary "enlightened" analysis of these kinds of "fictional" texts. Girard posits these "enlightened" readings as false, and as such his as true. In this Manichaean battle, or because Girard posits his readings in a Manichaean battle with contemporary analysis, Girard must at one point or another ground his reading in an absolute truth if he is to win the fight. I agree with White's assessment here. It is exemplified in the instance where Girard does not only claim that the Logos of John is superior to the Logos of Heraclitus, he asserts that the Logos of John is the true Logos – the Logos of Heraclitus is thus altogether false, pushed behind in Girard's thinking once and for all. Against this Manichaean approach, White speaks of an "atheist and materialist" approach that views a given dialectic as a "real one" (as opposed to simply an apparent one), which "always remains alienated from the truth of being that it is supposed to disclose" (White, 1978, p. 7).

Basically, Girard's hypothesis is non-falsifiable because it mimics the metaphysical/religious systems that it claims to "scientifically" uncover. Girard's "data" is not an objective representation of the cultures and rituals that Girard discusses, but is rather "data" that has already passed through the interpretive grid of classical anthropology. So at best, "Girard's theories tell us more about the 'literature of ethnology' than they do about that 'culture' which is the ethnologist's supposed object of study" (White, 1978, p. 8). White's review was published before Girard's later writings that posit scripture as an absolute centre that explains everything. Nevertheless, White astutely and skilfully points out a recurring and fundamental feature of Girard's writing: his insistence on the existence of an absolute centre that the true interpretation of so-called objective facts, from a neutral standpoint, can help us uncover – an absolute centre that, once uncovered, can explain all of our facts.

Elsewhere, White challenges the notion that a discipline of "history" (or any other discipline concerned with human affairs, for that matter) can be established on a so-called scientific method that works only with objective facts, as opposed to the so-called fiction of literary imagination (White, 1978, pp. 97–98). Incidentally, Girard's work goes far in dispelling this contemptuous view of literature and fiction. But instead of then presenting literature, mythology, and the so-called fictive or mystical side of sacrificial rites as science – as that which good science should try to emulate and prove right, which is Girard's modus operandi – White argues for a more subtle understanding of the "tropes" through which historiography is constructed: that is, the complex ways in which "modes of emplotment" of "data" (e.g., romance or tragedy), "modes of explanation" (e.g., idiographic or mechanistic), and "modes of ideological implication" (e.g., anarchist or radical) combine, intermingle, dissociate within a historical representation of a given event or experience (White, 1978, p. 70). It is this complex interplay that marks the great works of history apart from those that proclaim to deal only with the "facts."

Girard goes far in moving away from an absolute distinction between science and art – he creatively conjoins literary, anthropological, and psychoanalytic texts in presenting us with a new way of understanding certain human experiences (e.g., mimetic behaviour). The problem is that he insists on presenting this creative intersection of different sources as an objective science that is, moreover, grounded in God himself. Every*thing* that Girard explains orbits around an absolute centre that animates the movement of those things he examines (from animal domestication to cannibalism to the television show *Seinfeld*); once this orbital dance is in motion, *every*thing is explained. These two movements feed each other until no-thing can escape the orbit. Ultimately, the main thing that Girard uncovers from scripture, what he mimics from scripture, is the full materialization in his writing of an all-or-nothing ethos that, as White's review suggests, was there all along. Whether he came to scripture first, last, or in between does not matter; that he posits an absolute centre in his texts is of the utmost importance (the most important and foundational of which is his notion of "mimetic desire," but there are a few absolutes operating in Girard's writing). Girard's distinction between mythology and the Word of Christ is essentially the answer to his efforts to secure an absolute ground in his Manichaean battle against mythological thinking in all its forms, particularly its "modern" form. At this point, it is helpful to examine Girard's view of Derrida's deconstruction in order to illuminate the core of the trouble with Girard's hypothesis, which is related to the problems of his method.

In the epigraph at the beginning of this section, Girard most succinctly summarizes his view of Derrida's deconstruction. For Girard, Derrida's work goes far in revealing the nature of the sacred, and in certain respects, the sacrificial nature of rationalist thought (among other things). While Girard does not undertake a direct or sustained analysis of Derrida's work in making these points, Andrew J. McKenna's (1992a) *Violence and Difference* takes on this task. In this book, McKenna (a former student of Girard's) attempts "to render deconstruction intelligible, to translate and secularize it in the sense both of laicizing its vocabulary and of historicizing it – and therefore, via Girard, of anthropologizing it" (McKenna, 1992a, p. 13). Basically, McKenna wants to save deconstruction from its allegedly more nihilistic and self-defeating impulses, and Girard offers the cure. McKenna's sophisticated analysis successfully, I think, highlights the similarities between the two thinkers on a variety of different levels that I need not delve into. Arguably, McKenna's presentation of the similarities between *différance* and the originary, founding victim is the most impressive and convincing of his analysis, and so I will examine just this aspect, as it is also the most fundamental. Moreover, this discussion appears (sometimes in verbatim with the book) in a shorter, more focused format in an article titled "Supplement to Apocalypse" (1992b), and so I will, in addition to his book, cite from this article.

McKenna argues "that the contradictory logic of the sacred, as it originates in a desire of untraceable origin, conforms to the contradictory logic of the supplement which Derrida uncovers in Rousseau: the supplement of an origin which never took place" (1992b, p. 46). While Girard locates the origin in the scapegoat and the cover up in mythology, Derrida introduces the neologism *différance* and through it seeks to upset and unsettle the rationalist cover-up of Rousseau, among others. There are the following basic similarities between *différance* and the originary victim: (a) both refer to a beginning, or a complicity of origins, that has been erased (in Girard, the erasure of the collective murder of an innocent victim; in Derrida, the erasure of an unrepresentable archetrace, or the constitution, via repetition, of a simple origin that erases a non-simple origin *and* the erasure of that erasure); (b) both are generative of a variety of structures, institutions, and rituals, yet both are posited as transcendental in some sense and thus never reduced to specific structures, institutions, rituals; (c) both reveal the pivotal role of substitution, of a deferral that can never name itself; and (d) both thinkers work with these two conceptions in an effort to deconstruct, to uncover, the aforementioned erasures (McKenna, 1992b, pp. 46–62). Thus the mechanism of the surrogate victim in Girard, McKenna asserts, is not an absolute and deterministic foundation, but is rather a conception of a complex originary moment, which does not hide the complexity of the origin: that is, Girard's hypothesis is not just another version of the constituted simple origin that erases the complicity of origins; rather, the hypothesis has as its goal the revelation of something like the complicity of origins. If Derrida neologizes *différance* as the generative force that will always evade and elude us, Girard gives this force a definitive source: the scapegoat, the victim of a real event of collective murder (McKenna, 1992b, pp. 67–72).

Succinctly put, the general and overarching gist of Derrida and Girard's similarity may be found in their exposition and critique of a sacrificial rationality that is operative in ancient and modern thought (e.g., in Girard, the Logos of Heraclitus; in Derrida, the sacrificial nature of Rousseau's expulsion of writing). However, McKenna asserts that unlike Girard, Derrida fails to take his analysis a step further and grasp the sacrificial cycle, and as such the potentiality of a non-sacrificial interpretation or analysis. This is seen as the weakness of Derrida's deconstruction, which is ultimately Derrida's perceived inability to come to terms with the notion of an origin. For Girard, while any given symbolic system may be decentred, it had to have been originally centred first. Girard disagrees with Derrida's notion "that structures are *always already* decentred" (Girard, 2007, p. 108; original emphasis). Without an original centre, which is always first provided to us (i.e., represented) in the form of religion, Girard claims that there cannot arise any form of human ritual or social institutions (2007, pp. 37–38). Moreover, this original centre is indeed a real event of collective murder that is then covered up in myth. For Girard, Derrida skilfully deconstructs the cover-up, but then goes on to assert that basically, all language is a cover-up (all we can have are traces whose "common root" is arche-writing or the arche-trace), while Girard asserts that the traces are indeed evidence of the erasure of real traces to a real event of a founding collective murder (2007, pp. 162–163, 186–188).

I think McKenna and Girard both miss the main point on which Derrida differs from Girard. This difference ought to radically question the notion that Derrida's work simply confirms Girard's hypothesis in philosophy texts, but ultimately fails to grasp the larger anthropological picture (Girard, 1992, pp. 28–30, 39, 42). The crux of the difference can be easily summed up: Derrida (1997a) argues that what is expelled – writing – in Rousseau and others (Saussure, Condillac, etc.) is not innocent. I do not think that one can simply charge Derrida with siding with the persecutor's text in making this claim, since (a) Derrida is still speaking of an expulsion here, and he is certainly not painting this expulsion as a righteous murder, and (b) Derrida never claims that writing is guilty either (I come back to this later in this chapter). Moreover, McKenna and Girard ultimately fail to accord the "force of rupture" what I think is its proper emphasis in Derrida's thought. McKenna especially conflates Derrida's and Girard's "what is-not," and in so doing throws away Derrida's force of rupture (McKenna, 1992a, p. 198). In Derrida, *différance* cannot be asked the question of "What is it?" The question simply does not apply to *différance*. In other words, while I agree on the surface with McKenna's arguments regarding the similarities between *différance* and the originary victim, I do not agree that the difference is that *différance* simply lacks a definite source, which if introduced via Girard can give deconstruction a direction that the movement lacks; rather, I would argue that the entire Derridean conception of a generative force crumbles, or is completely missed, if we ask: What is it?

Because McKenna foundationally sides with Girard, and reads Derrida through Girard, he can see "what is-not" only as the cyclic mythological violence at work – hiding itself from view, building illusions all around us, preventing us from seeing the truth of its mechanism, and finally preventing us from reaching the true beyond: "what is" God's love. In short, McKenna must add to Derrida's undecidables one very decided question: McKenna says that the origin that never took place is only posited as such in mythology, but in fact it has a definite source; so are you with the texts of persecution or are you with the texts of the victim? (McKenna, 1992b, p. 74). This decidable, however, cannot be simply added to Derrida; it effectively defeats Derrida's undecidability and his notion of *différance*.

Put a different way, McKenna and Girard argue that Derrida fails to grasp that there is a non-sacrificial world, a non-sacrificial viewpoint that reveals the working mechanism of the surrogate victim and is capable of destroying this cyclical mechanism. But even in Girard's own thinking, this formulation of sacrificial/non-sacrificial changes somewhat when Girard revises his position on the sacrifice of Christ. Girard asserts that the death of Christ may be called a sacrifice after all but one that is radically different from the form of sacrifice found in "archaic" religions: the latter is "sacrifice as murder," while the former is "sacrifice as the readiness to die in order not to participate in sacrifice as murder" (Girard, 2007, p. 215). In between the two forms is a non-sacrificial space "from which everything could be described from a neutral viewpoint" (Girard, 2007, p. 216). Jesus remains the only one who has shifted from the first archaic form – sacrifice as murder – to the second form – sacrifice as the readiness to die in order not to participate in sacrifice as murder – while humanity remains largely caught in the first. What this means is that the second form, where Jesus is leading, is not a non-sacrificial space since there is still sacrifice in that second form (albeit of a different order from the first). Moreover, Girard gives up the search for "a perfectly non-sacrificial space" from which to speak – that was his goal in both *Violence and the Sacred* and *Things Hidden* (2007, p. 217). That is, he gives up the search for a neutral viewpoint, which White criticized him for, and his rootedness in an absolute truth whose side he speaks from and/or on behalf of (it is not clear to me which it is in Girard, as he seems to vacillate between the two) in his Manichaean battle with the false becomes more explicit, which White argued was there all along despite Girard's claims of neutrality.

Girard's now more explicit reliance on scripture in interpreting mythology and "archaic" religions tightens for him the connection between mythological, cyclical, violent religions and Christianity. The former become precursors to the latter: they are "a prior moment in a progressive revelation that culminates in Christ" (Girard, 2007, pp. 216–217). Although Girard defends himself against charges of linear thinking by claiming that the process he is describing is not linear (i.e., it is a complex story with many regressions, progressions, mutations, etc.), he is at the same time adamant about the fact that the revelation itself is progressive (i.e., there is no doubt that the introduction of the victim's perspective is a moral progression from the persecutor's perspective) (Girard, 2007, p. 219). This answer I think clearly misses the charges directed toward linear thinking, which has always claimed that there are regressions, mutations, and the like; the challenge (among others) is that in linear thinking, things in the past are viewed as mere precursors to the present, and that ultimately, if and when realized, this present is constituted as a progression from, or as superior to, the past. For me, Girard is clearly a linear thinker, and this fits effectively with his Manichaeism.[4]

In place of a non-sacrificial world that he sees as outside of history, Girard shifts his attention and focuses entirely on the absolute historico-politico-religious distinction between the "what is" of Christ and the "what is-not" of Satan. Furthermore, I believe that these shifts go hand in hand in Girard's thinking: the moment "what is-not" becomes satanic is also the moment when Christ or God cannot possibly be associated with a space that begins with "non," is finally the same moment when humanity cannot be asked to walk into a space that begins with "non." Just as there is not a non-sacrificial space, there is not a non-mimetic world. Girard has to speak in his works about a "good" form of mimesis since the opposite of "bad" conflictual mimesis cannot be non-mimetic (2007, p. 225).

In the last chapter of *Evolution and Conversion*, "Modernity, Postmodernity and Beyond," Girard is forced by his interlocutors to discuss more explicitly the mimetic mechanism in the contemporary world, relating it to issues such as globalization, the free market, the 9/11 attacks, First verses Third World politics, and so on.[5] I find the discussion on these issues lacking in many areas and the analysis largely superficial, and to be fair to Girard, he does allude to the fact that he is not in a position to comment on some of these issues. With this caveat in mind, the chapter is yet telling of Girard's self-proclaimed conversion, which further illuminates my criticism of his work. In this book, I found it very difficult to distinguish Girard from a missionary handing out pamphlets to people on the street, and this despite his attempts to thicken the concept of "conversion" (e.g., I do not see how only conversion can counter the notion of an "autonomous self" – Derrida's work, as well as the postcolonial theorists discussed in chapter 3, accomplish this without the need to convert to the Word of Christ; or, I do not see how the claim that Girard's conversion is one of an epistemic nature, concerned first and foremost with a new intellectual and emotional understanding, changes anything about the fact that this new understanding can only be the One of Christ; see Girard, 2007, pp. 44–46, 172–173). His message is reduced to: if you are not with Christ, then you are with Satan, so convert or perish. Girard complains that intellectuals and the academy in general will not consider his hypothesis; but in retrospect, there is a clear reason for this. Only after his explicit proclamations about the absolute choice between the two kingdoms, the absolute truth of the Word of Christ, and so on does it become obvious that there is not a possibility of dialogically engaging with Girard. When he makes his hypothesis the Word of God himself, he is no longer presenting a hypothesis. He shuts down the discussion well before it can begin. You either convert or you perish.

My interest here is not to argue against Girard by highlighting other religious sacrifices that are similar to that of Christ. To do that would be to accept his thesis by engaging in a futile and dead-end game of whose religion is superior. I do not take the far-reaching claims of Girard's work as seriously as he presents them to be, and this especially applies to his later works that assert the pivotal role of scripture. I find his insights into mythology, religion, and violence penetrating and profound, and the manner in which he theorizes violence is vital, especially for our understanding of the very dynamics involved in theorizing violence. But to move from these insights to claims about nothing short of explaining everything that is human and divine is too far of a stretch, to put it mildly. And this is not because I belong to the "unionization of failure" that nihilistically ceases the search for a foundational mechanism or that shies away from being reductive in any sense (Girard, 1987, p. 40), but because I think that his work too easily surrenders to, first, the strong intellectual temptation to give all explanation to violence – to hypostatize violence – and second, the strong intellectual necessity to counteract such a powerfully destructive temptation: a temptation that only God – guarantor of reality and the sole source of absolute love – can allow one to counteract.

This surrender amounts to Girard's effort to exorcise violence by basing his perspective in the absolute non-violent Word of Christ, as I discussed earlier. Such an exorcism, whether grounded in the name of God or some other absolute concept, is an important feature of theorizing and writing violence outside of the instrumentalist perspective that Girard's oeuvre brings to light more than any other thinker for me. And it is certainly a feature that I wish to avoid in my own attempt to theorize and write violence, especially since I am introducing a conception of violence that tries to account for the relationship between violence and transcendence. By avoiding Girard's view of the "non" and of "what is-not" as satanic, I hope to formulate a different way of looking at violence the "thing itself": a way that does not appeal to the sacred for either death or salvation, but rather engages with transcendental thinking.

As alluded to earlier, there are also two positive reasons for bringing up Girard in this book. The first reason is that Girard successfully explains the productive-destructive distinction without falling back on this distinction as an analytical basis for the study of violence. He essentially theorizes the very oscillation between productive and destructive violence and the manner in which violence propagates itself through this oscillation. But having shown that this distinction is a matter of perspective, Girard then goes on to divide the entire spectrum of perspectives into two absolute ones: victim and persecutor. And then he clearly falls on the side of the victim's perspective, and moreover, grounds the victim's perspective in God. I agree that it is important to analyse the persecutor-victim perspectives that almost always accompany the formulation of the productive-destructive distinction (and vice versa), but I do not agree that the victim-persecutor perspectives are separated with an abyss. Rather, analysts must, as I show in chapter 5, explore how these perspectives are traversed in violence and in texts that represent violence.

The second reason for extensively engaging with Girard is that I agree with him that the mimetic dimension of violence is incredibly important, and I think it would be hasty to throw those elements of Girard's thinking away with his overarching message of convert or perish. Instead of positing mimetic desire as the firm ground and foundation of violence, I argue through the Gadamer–Derrida encounter that a mimetic dimension is possible because of a fourth dimension of violence, because of the groundless (Derrida) ground (Gadamer) of violence, of violence the "thing itself," where postures of incommensurability are formed.

II. The Groundless Ground of Violence

In making sense of the fourth dimension through the Gadamer–Derrida encounter, John Caputo's distinction between the metaphysics of presence and the flux serves as a useful starting point. In *Radical Hermeneutics*, Caputo argues that Gadamer falls on the conservative side of Heidegger's work, while Derrida releases Heidegger's radical side (Caputo, 1987, p. 97). Even though Caputo believes Gadamer is insightful in his critique of method, he asserts that *Truth and Method* consistently falls back on a metaphysical notion of truth (which amounts to a metaphysics of presence in the final analysis), despite Gadamer's claims to the contrary (Caputo, 1987, pp. 5–6). For Caputo, Gadamer's notion of the fusion of horizons (particularly his concept of mediation, which for Caputo is concerned with resolving the conflict of interpretations rather than stimulating it, making Gadamer more Hegelian than Heideggerian in Caputo's view) and of the stability and internal unity of tradition (where, implicit in the notion of continuous transformations of meanings in tradition, we always find *a* tradition open to different expressions of its internal unity) ties him to a definition of "truth" that is centred on the notion of presence (Caputo, 1987, pp. 81–82, 111). Such metaphysics of presence achieves its stability, ground, and unshakable foundation by claiming the ability to delineate the being of what is present, or what is absolute and timeless in things.

This, Caputo tells us, is opposed in contemporary Western philosophy (beginning with Nietzsche but also, and more poignantly for Caputo, with Kierkegaard) by the emphasis on movement, by the continuously changing, the non-essence, the unpredictable, and un-confinable: in short, the flux (1987, p. 35). Gadamer, for Caputo, continuously falls back to this metaphysics of rest, reassurance, and stability whenever he faces the flux. Derrida never ceases in his search for the flux in order to upset any resting place one may find in metaphysics (Caputo, 1987, pp. 95–98). Caputo comes to the conclusion that Gadamer's espousal of movement and transformation only appears to be open to the flux, when in fact Gadamer is only looking for ways to avoid the flux and find a resting place in the metaphysics of presence. Succinctly put, if the flux is Socrates, then Gadamer is its Plato, as Gadamer attempts to answer the questions raised by the flux rather than continuously raise them in order to upset the certainty in our ability to understand things (Caputo, 1987, p. 112).

For Caputo, Gadamer is too focused on *what* "truth" is being handed down in tradition and not enough on the event of handing down. In making this point, Caputo uses the example of Heidegger, who was not interested in "the metaphysical conception of the Being of beings but the very coming to pass of the differences … in the diverse metaphysical systems" (Caputo, 1987, p. 104). This coming to pass is the clearing, or the opening, that Heidegger sought to bring to the forefront in order to show not only that every message we receive from the past has an elusive element that opens the message to varying interpretations, but that this elusive space is the space of "truth," and not the content found in the message itself. In other words, dialogue with a classic text ought not be focused on what is true in it, but rather on how the very sayability of what is said is concealed and un-concealed in the message; and this, for Caputo, is an important Heideggerian lesson that is left out of Gadamer's notion of dialogue (1987, pp. 104–107).

I mentioned earlier that Gadamer follows Heidegger in asserting that "truth" is the event of concealment and un-concealment, but Caputo's claim is that Gadamer fails to live up to this notion of "truth," since Gadamer does not draw on this notion to upset and question what is handed down and instead gives this notion of "truth" a structure: Gadamer is basically interested in *what* is viewed as true in a certain tradition, how it is then taken up, transformed, applied to our present condition, and finally presented as true in our tradition (to be) (Caputo, 1987, p. 115).[6]

Derrida, on the other hand, radicalizes the Heideggerian project and asserts that it is not the "truth" of something that makes it amiable to a handing down in tradition (contra metaphysics); it is rather the handing down of tradition that itself makes something "true." But unlike Heidegger, who still ties the elusive space to some original message of Being that comes from pre-Socratic Greek thinking, Caputo argues that Derrida brings to the forefront the work of the sign – Derrida espouses the play of signs, and not their entrapment in some or other original purity or unity of meaning that takes the sting, as it were, out of their transformative bite (Caputo, 1987, pp. 116–119).[7] Or, as Caputo discusses this point in terms of presence and absence, Derrida asserts that the repetition of a sign (its iterability) is the reason the presence of the sign is present and not, as metaphysics would have it, that something is iterable because it is present. This throws off the metaphysical formula of determining "being as presence and repetition as a representation of presence," and in its place we find what Caputo calls Derrida's "grammatological reduction," which is guided by the "principle of the 'constituting value' of nonpresence in virtue of which presence is a function of repetition" (Caputo, 1987, p. 123).

This seemingly does away with transcendence altogether and makes it impossible to speak of any such thing. But as Caputo argues, Derrida is by no means suggesting this. Rather, it is only a notion of absolute transcendence that is discarded in Derrida (Caputo, 1987, p. 129). The transcendental element in Derrida is "what is-not," and "what is-not" is always already part and parcel of "what is." The transcendental element is not a space that we strive toward, and where we achieve total knowledge, for instance, nor is it a space where we recover an original totality; rather, the transcendental element is what is always beyond totality's reach, its other, that "not" that keeps us moving (Caputo, 1987, p. 130). The bringing forth of the "not" – that productive element of absence – is the work of the sign. Signifiers are not merely communicative instruments that transmit certain meanings, but they are the unpredictable and transformative elements in dialogue since they do the work of objectification, repetition, making present, and as such of putting the absent (which is the very condition of possibility of the present) into play (Caputo, 1987, pp. 132–133): in short, "the work of signs is the work of place taking" (Caputo, 1987, p. 135). Thus the emancipation of the sign is the letting of its work be. It is to avoid the centralization of meaning that ties the signs to a larger whole that swallows them, and instead open up the infinite potential to realign signs, join disparate ones together, separate harmonious signs, and create the new (Caputo, 1987, pp. 149–152). Accomplishing this is the work of deconstruction. A brief discussion on Derrida's deconstruction and the pivotal notion of *différance* can better illustrate the transcendental element in Derrida.

Derrida's deconstruction moves with the tune of the heterogeneity and alterity already there within a text, a tradition, a law, etcetera. Deconstruction puts into play, or releases, the relation to the "other" that can never allow any totalizing effort the complete closure of itself that it seeks (Derrida, 1997b, pp. 8–9). The other, in Derrida, concerns what is different in a culture, an identity, a self, a language, etc., from *itself* (1997b, p. 13). So the other is not only, for instance, a racialized or gendered other, but what is deferred and differentiated in any claim to presence, or *différance*.

If deconstruction is at all capable of opening up new possibilities in the free play of signs, it is through *différance*. Basically, deconstruction is an inauguration that highlights the tension (not the mixture) between the past, present, and future, and *différance* is its passageway to the new (Derrida, 1997a [1967], pp. 66–67). Caputo tells us that *différance*, like its "sur-name" (or allegory) Plato's *khôra*, is that which "receives all and becomes none of what it receives" (Caputo, 1997, p. 95). Caputo asserts that *différance* is the receptacle par excellence: it is place itself – not *a* place *of* something (this is what leads into binary oppositions of all sorts), but place; or rather, place of non-place since it cannot be *something*. It is form only when it takes the form of what is inscribed in it; it is locatable only when something finds itself in it: it is "the formation of form" but never form itself (Derrida, 1997a, p. 63). To deconstruct is to set *différance* in motion, or rather to move according to that motion, and this can open us to alterity, heterogeneity, and dissociation: in short, to the possibility of the impossible (Caputo, 1997, pp. 96–99). But *différance* is itself "indeconstructible," because it is-not.

In this sense, *différance* has a transcendental "structure," which can be referred to as a quasi-essential condition (the essence of non-essence), and this is different than renouncing the transcendental altogether and thus taking a hyper-essential position (the essence of negativity) (Caputo, 1997, pp. 102–103).[8] Derrida's deconstruction, then, does not aspire to solve an enigma or aporia when one is encountered, nor does it strive to avoid an aporia or move away from it, but as Derrida describes it, the point here is to move *"according to* another thinking of the aporia … 'according to the aporia'" (Derrida, 1993, p. 13; original emphasis). Put differently, the point is to release what is in every aporia, *différance.*

In consistently going back to the productivity of "what is-not," Derrida not only faces the flux, but he dwells in it. Whenever a statement is made to assert the being of what is present, Derrida sinks the statement into the abyss, into the flux, and laughs at any such attempt. But Derrida is not the perennial troublemaker who simply wants to mock us. He is rather – and this is why Derrida is so central to Caputo's project of radical hermeneutics – infinitely attempting to bring philosophy back to what Caputo constantly refers to as the "original difficulty of life." To instigate thought where it has gone stale; to move thinkers when they have become stagnant; to shake our positions when they become too rigid; and to energize whoever succumbs to fatigue – that, for Caputo, is what Derrida's work engenders. Ultimately, this philosophy (contrary to the common charge of disinterestedness and unethicality often directed against Derrida) is an ethic, or philosophy and ethics are melded into one practice of deconstruction (see Critchley, 1999, for a detailed analysis of the ethics of deconstruction and its limits, particularly the limits of moving from ethics to politics). And this practice of deconstruction relies on dwelling in the flux, where the "thing itself" is forever elusive (Caputo, 1987, pp. 191–192, 276).

Caputo's radical hermeneutics is basically an effort to open up Derrida onto Heidegger and Heidegger onto Derrida. He is not so much aiming to follow Derrida into the flux (to dwell in it), and neither does he want to follow Heidegger in simply opening up a window through which we can view the flux, in the sense of looking at it from a distance with a meditative gesture. Rather, he wants to "cope with the flux": to open it, walk near it perhaps, but eventually leave it behind, only to come back to it once again, and so on. There is great value and promise in this ethical stance, but I want to point out that it does ultimately book its return ticket from the flux before ever going there, and more so, it knows its final destination – the "original difficulty of life" – before ever moving, hence its coping gesture and Caputo's emphasis on the *"readiness* to be shaken" and not on the shaking itself (1987, p. 146; emphasis added).

In a sense, the dialogical analytic proceeds on a somewhat similar path in its study of violence in general and the fourth dimension in particular, mainly because this kind of flux and incessant movement is inherent to violence. Caputo is helpful in this respect, but the dialogical analytic is different from Caputo's approach to the flux in three important ways. First, while speaking with violence is similar to Caputo's notion of dwelling in the flux, I draw more on Gadamer for the simple reason that Gadamer explains the process of the stabilization of things while still attending to their elusiveness and transformative element, better than Caputo gives him credit for. Or rather, Caputo derides Gadamer because he raises the process of stabilization to a central place in his philosophical hermeneutics. And while I do not centralize this process of stabilization in my approach, I do not ignore it either, as does Caputo. Second, I am not at all interested in Caputo's notion of booking one's return from the flux before journeying "there," not necessarily because such a notion is not "radical" enough, but because of its instrumental view of the flux.[9] The reason, I think, Derrida's work is so powerful and difficult is that the flux gains an epistemological status in it. Derrida raises himself to the ultimate challenge of the flux, or of the aporia: to hear according to the aporia, to "experience the aporia," not simply for the sake of shaking our stable grounds, as if it could be visited at any time so as to provide us with this service, which would constitute an attempt to overcome the aporia that, according to Derrida, would be just as much an escape from the aporia as an attempt to stop at it (Derrida, 1993, p. 32). This shaking is indeed the effect of the challenge that Derrida undertook in his work: he dwelled in the aporia with a gesture of a chase – a chase after the mystery of life, not its original difficulty, which is perhaps a more Heideggerian/Kierkegaardian notion. Derrida's chase moves toward a place of non-place, or the groundless ground. Thus, speaking with violence is in a sense marked by this chase toward the mysterious side of violence, to the groundless ground of violence.

This brings up the third crucial difference. Since we are dealing with a groundless ground, it seems misguided to pursue this path further with the language of the flux. The latter term is meant to highlight the incessant movement of the space that is not metaphysics. And while such incessant movement is a crucial feature of the groundless ground of violence, the flux highlights only the "groundless" and does not account for how it is a "ground." The groundless is not simply the negation of ground in groundless ground, but its paradoxical companion. It is this aporia that we must think with. Instead of flux, I shift towards what, outside a few select philosophical circles, is perhaps an antiquated term, one that can account for stabilization and the flux, the ground and the groundless: the "thing itself."

III. To the "Thing Itself"

The warning that Plato entrusts to the Idea is therefore that *sayability itself remains unsaid in what is said and in that about which something is said, that knowability itself is lost in what is known and in that about which something is known.*
　　　　　　　　　　–Giorgio Agamben, "The Thing Itself" (original emphases)

I am not about to attempt a recovery of the early twentieth-century call emanating from the school of phenomenology, "to the things themselves." There is of course a certain affinity to this call in this work, since I am drawing on thinkers who have been heavily influenced by this school of thought, or at the very least who have extensively engaged with it. But I am by no means going back behind or beyond language and toward the immediacy of the thing (by way of pure immanence or pure transcendence, respectively). In his discussions on Derrida and Plato, Giorgio Agamben shows a different way of looking at the call "to the thing itself." For Agamben, *différance* is not something that can be named, but this does not mean that *différance* refers to something unnameable. It simply points us toward the limits of language, which is the inability to name naming itself (Agamben, 1999b [1990], pp. 209–211). But it is precisely this inability that lays the ground of possibility for naming. That is, if it is possible to name a thing, it is only because the thing itself cannot be named (Agamben, 1999b, pp. 216–219), and it is in this sense that "the thing itself, while in some way transcending language, is nevertheless possible only in language and by virtue of language: precisely the thing of language" (Agamben, 1999a [1984], p. 31).[10] The thing itself is not an obscure object that cannot be captured by language; it is rather the very condition that makes an object knowable: "the thing itself is not a thing; it is the very sayability, the very openness at issue in language" (Agamben, 1999a, p. 35).

It is worth directly examining Derrida's *Of Grammatology* in order to take a further step from Agamben's piece, which will help justify why I link this framing of the "thing itself" to violence.[11] This link is not Derrida's main goal in that work. At the very least it is not what has attracted the most attention in the numerous commentaries and analyses of this work. Nevertheless, it remains an important one since it is directly linked to what I understand as the impetus of the work, which mainly involves a counter to the classical notion (as found mainly, albeit with some differences, in Ferdinand de Saussure, Jean-Jacques Rousseau, and Claude Lévi-Strauss) that the introduction of writing is, first and foremost, a violent episode in the history of language. Derrida wants to counter the notion that writing is a violence that distorts the natural form of human communication, which is speech. In countering this notion, Derrida does not seek to prove the "innocence" of writing; rather, he is concerned with "showing why the violence of writing does not *befall* an innocent language," where he asserts, "There is an originary violence of writing because language is first ... writing" (Derrida, 1997a, p. 37; original emphasis). Put differently, Derrida is interested in asking (particularly in the chapter titled "The Violence of the Letter," which sort of bridges the two parts of *Of Grammatology*): "What links writing to violence? What must violence be in order for something in it to be equivalent to the operation of the trace?" (1997a, p. 101).

In addressing this question, Derrida does away with absolute transcendence, or as he calls it in *Of Grammatology*, the "transcendental signified, which, at one time or another, would place a reassuring end to the reference from sign to sign" (1997a, p. 49). He moves the discussion from a thing itself that may be luminous in its presence (which, if reached, would put an end to the indefiniteness of reference) to a thing itself that is a sign (Derrida, 1997a, pp. 49–50). Derrida thus dispels notions of the "natural," "pure," and "untouched" voice of language (speech) that was supposedly disrupted by the violence of writing, since the voice of language (whether that voice was believed to have come to us from God or Nature) is always already a sign and not a revelation of the thing itself (1997a, pp. 56–57, 70–73, 158–159).[12] Or the "trace" is all there is at the origin of writing. The "trace," or "arche-writing,"[13] "is" writing in general, or "is" the "common root" of our narrow conceptions of speech and writing (graphic, phonic, etc.). But since arche-writing is the "complicity of origins" (i.e., the complicity or complex intertwinement of various movements of law, science, religion, politics, economy, etc.), arche-writing comes to be seen in Derrida as a "certain nonorigin": it is-not. The question of "What is it?" does not apply to arche-writing (Derrida, 1997a, pp. 74–75, 92–93). Arche-writing "is" a "common root, which is not a root but the concealment of the origin and which is not common because it does not amount to the same thing except with the unmonotonous insistence of difference," and as such, and like its other name *différance*, arche-writing "is" itself "unnameable" (Derrida, 1997a, p. 93).

Worthy of note here is that it may well be the case, as Christopher Wise argues, that Derrida's conception of the "trace" and "arche-writing" is "so deeply enmeshed in Jewish theology" that it cannot speak to different conceptions of the trace that can be found in Islamic and Christian theologies (Wise, 2009, p. 43). It is also likely the case that Derrida's conception is not purely Jewish and that there are in fact clear "structural affinities between deconstructive, Judaic, ancient Egyptian, and current West African concepts of the trace" (Wise, 2009, p. 173). The purpose of my discussion here is not to present a full account of the trace as such, but to highlight that in stressing the link between violence and writing, rather than positing the so-called violence of writing as an exterior force that threatens language and speech, Derrida effectively highlights "the originary violence of a language which is always already a writing" (1997a, p. 106). In Derrida, "proper name/naming" is impossible in the sense of the name being proper to what the thing is. Rather, the name is already the "obliteration" of such a notion of "proper to what a thing is" (Derrida, 1997a, pp. 109–110). Hence, there is no pure or innocent vocative gesture that is violently destroyed by writing, since what the likes of Rousseau and Lévi-Strauss posit as the violence of writing is indeed the originary unity of violence and writing, which a language always already is:

> To name, to give names that it will on occasion be forbidden to pronounce, such is the originary violence of language which consists in inscribing within a difference, in classifying, in suspending the vocative absolute. To think the unique *within* the system, to inscribe it there, such is the gesture of the arche-writing: arche-violence, loss of the proper, of absolute proximity, of self-presence, in truth the loss of what has never taken place, of a self-presence which has never been given but only dreamed of and always already split, repeated, incapable of appearing to itself except in its own disappearance. (Derrida, 1997a, p. 112; original emphasis)[14]

Out of this arche-violence, a second violence emerges that prohibits the unveiling of the obliteration of the proper name (e.g., moral codes of conduct), and if the prohibition is transgressed, there arises the possibility of releasing a third violence, which we commonly know as punishment, war, etcetera (Derrida, 1997a, p. 112). In Derrida, these three kinds of violence are not separated along an axis of interiority/exteriority. So while there are distinctions to be made between the three, the space in-between is not an abyss that separates one from the other; rather, the three intermingle together within a "space" that can neither absolutely separate nor conjoin them.

Arche-violence (the first kind of violence) cannot be posited as something that is exterior or interior to the prohibition (second kind of violence) or to this thing we commonly call violence (third kind of violence). Rather, I read Derrida as positing arche-violence as that which is always other to this thing called violence. An "othering," as it were, that is accomplished by a rupture that is always already there in the prohibition, which forbids naming the obliteration of the "proper" that has never taken place. In other words, the three kinds of violence do not reside or even operate at different vertical levels; rather, they are seen as different dimensions of the same phenomenon, and this is the key point that I want to underscore. Now, I cannot simply borrow Derrida's three kinds of violence without translating them into terms that are more amenable to the dialogical analytic of this book, because (a) I divide Derrida's second kind into two dimensions (linguistic and mimetic) that I believe better capture the complex relationship between violence and language, (b) I add certain Gadamerian elements into these terms, namely to "arche-violence," which will be translated into violence the "thing itself," and (c) I avoid the language of "different kinds" of violence, since such language may lead to unnecessary misunderstandings regarding the dimensional outlook (as opposed to a level-oriented outlook) that the dialogical analytic espouses. In fact, Derrida's argument points out precisely how the ever-elusive arche-violence is interlinked with what we commonly call violence. His work allows for the argument that the most elusive fourth dimension is intricately connected with the three other dimensions this book has already outlined. It is crucial that the fourth dimension not be viewed as a purely abstract violence, because if it is viewed as such, then it can quickly turn into a present thing-in-itself – a God of violence that, unseen and unheard, controls human affairs from a transcendent distance.

In Derrida, there is no "real" thing called violence that exists on its own, in and of itself, distinct from language.[15] Language and violence are not two separate entities that take shape independently of one another, but they are interlinked in two senses. The first sense involves the notion that language and violence are linked in the very institution of language, or the violence of language. For Derrida, violence is not defeated by language, although "speech is doubtless the first defeat of violence" (Derrida, 1978 [1964], p. 117).[16] That is, violence does not exist before language, outside of language, in a relation of before/after, interiority/exteriority; rather, in the institution of language, violence becomes possible at the same time that the possibility of the defeat of violence first emerges. But language cannot be said to be the realm of non-violence, since it must continuously use violence (in the sense that the institution of language is always already violent with the obliteration of the "proper" name) to evade that all-encompassing dark and destructive violence (i.e., "the violence of primitive and prelogical silence"; Derrida, 1978, p. 130). Thus, violence always appears with articulation to evade the worst of all violences (Derrida, 1978, pp. 147–148). This seemingly points to a sphere of violence of pure madness and nonsense that is akin to the one operative in Das. But Derrida, I think, dispels such an idea with the second sense in which violence and language are interlinked.

The second sense involves the impossibility of a violence before the violence of language – that is, the impossibility of arche-violence, which is an impossibility that makes language possible (Derrida, 1978, p. 125).[17] Arche-violence makes language possible because it is the irreducible violence of naming, the obliteration of the "proper" that has never taken place (Derrida, 1978, pp. 128–129). Arche-violence cannot be known because it is indifferent to what is known, but it is the very thing of (un)knowability. Thus, the worst of all violences is-not, but in a productive sense. It is certainly not pure madness as it is in Das.

What can be surmised from these two senses in particular, and Derrida's three kinds of violence in general, is that it is indeed virtually impossible for the definition of violence to hold in one firm place, and this is because violence always has its "other" that unsettles whatever definition we may give it. Derrida's three kinds of violence indeed show this because, at bottom, they undercut the very idea of a typology. They are interlinked in a manner whereby the first kind both enables and unsettles the second and third kinds: the first kind, arche-violence, "is" unnameable violence that makes naming possible; the second kind is the violence of naming in the sense of the obliteration of the contingent nature of naming and in the sense of the obliteration of a "proper" that has never taken place; the third kind arises out of the transgression of the second kind and is the thing we commonly call violence. So Derrida shows that the definition of violence that is operative in the discourses and events of/on/about violence never operates alone, and is always already enabled by the first "kind" of violence and can be unsettled by it through an examination of the second "kind."

This is the philosophical basis upon which the dialogical analytic operates. It allows the dialogical analytic to link the fourth dimension of violence back into the other dimensions. The fourth dimension is akin to Derrida's first kind of violence, where violence the "thing itself" remains ever elusive yet forms the condition of possibility and impossibility for the other three dimensions.[18] Four-dimensional violence does not constitute or refer to four levels of ascending abstraction or descending concreteness. The four dimensions had to be presented in this gradual way for the sake of clarity. But in specific violent events and contexts, the four dimensions are intractably interlinked and simultaneously operative in any given context.

Now, this incessant shaking of any definition of violence is not a self-defeating exercise that simply takes the ground from under the feet of the analysis before the ground is even set: the point, rather, is to work with a groundless ground from the outset and let the shaking of the ground take place before it takes place anyway. Whatever definition scholars give violence must be wedded to violence the "thing itself" from the outset – to the four-dimensional outlook in which this definition always already belongs. There is one more question left: Why use violence the "thing itself," and not the flux, or arche-violence?

In my view, Gadamer and Derrida are not very different in what they aim toward: the "thing itself." But they are very different in how they go about it. I do not believe that I can definitively claim that either succeeds in his way, and I do not believe that if I select the best of each way, I will find the "right" way.[19] The "thing itself" is nowhere – groundless ground – and as such there is no way to it. Both Gadamer and Derrida strive toward this groundless ground and away from the metaphysics of presence, but they face two different directions: Gadamer faces the direction of dialogue, whereas Derrida faces the direction of deconstruction. Gadamer captures this difference when he states,

> It seems to me that, along with Heidegger's own efforts to leave behind "the language of metaphysics" ... two other paths exist and have in fact been taken in efforts to overcome the ontological self-domestication belonging to dialectic and move into the open. One is the path from dialectic back to dialogue, back to conversation. This the way I myself have attempted to travel in my philosophical hermeneutics. The other is the way shown primarily by Derrida, the path of deconstruction. On this path, the awakening of a meaning hidden in the life and liveliness of conversation is not an issue. Rather, it is in an ontological concept of *écriture* – not idle chatter nor even true conversation but the background network of meaning-relations lying at the basis of all speech – that the very integrity of sense as such is to be dissolved, thereby accomplishing the authentic shattering of metaphysics. (1989b [1986], p. 109)

The "thing itself," in its absence, makes presence possible. The "thing itself" is that transcendental element always beyond our reach, at the same time that it is-not – it is the opening that is itself never open (Derrida, 1973, p. 104). What I take from the Gadamer–Derrida encounter is then this: the "thing itself" is beyond reach (in the sense of, it is forever *over-there*), at the same time that it is what summons *us* to dialogue, revealing our communion (Gadamer); the "thing itself" is beyond reach (in the sense of, it *is-not*), at the same time that it "is" to the extent that we reach for it, mark it, repeat it, cut it off as it cuts us off (Derrida).

This is precisely what is at issue in exploring this thing called violence. Das is correct in her claim that violence always has an unspeakable or inexpressible sphere, which is her positive sense of the limitations of language vis-à-vis violence. But unlike Das/Wittgenstein, I will not posit a sphere of violence in the negative sense of the limitations of language vis-à-vis violence and then pass this sphere over in silence, for my claim is that the sphere where language and violence are most difficult to imagine is violence the "thing itself" – the very (un)knowability of violence. To speak with violence is to unleash this very (un)knowability.

Thus the assumption here is that the violence proclaimed and employed is the thing called violence. And to this thing, there is its other, which makes it impossible for anyone to claim the final word on this thing called violence; this other is violence the "thing itself." The former is "knowable" violence; the latter is incalculable, non-knowledge (in the sense of "we do not know" and not in the sense of possibly knowing something that is called non-knowledge), which makes knowledge of the former possible at the same time that it makes it impossible.[20] And this articulation of the matter opens the door for an analysis that explores a perpetrator of violence who acts without knowing what one knows in knowing, (not)knowing. The more Gadamerian part of the statement emphasizes the stabilization of things as things that summon us to dialogue at the same time that things remain elusive (since we still do not know everything we know when we know a thing); the more Derridean part adds a kind of mysterious element that is beyond language at the same time that it is the very thing of language. This articulation of the fourth dimension opens up a significant area of study where the forging of "enemy-siblings" as "enemy-siblings" takes place. "What is-not" begins to show postures of incommensurability that are crucial to understanding the nature of the communion between enemy-siblings. The dash in between these two terms takes on profound importance when this fourth dimension is taken into account since we are now directly confronted with the question of how the dash is/continues to be forged. To properly explain these postures of incommensurability, a further elaboration is first needed to show how the four-dimensional outlook does not create a distinction between a founding and continuing violence, without at the same time ignoring the uniqueness of these moments. This is important because in place of an absolute distinction between founding and continuations is found the formation of postures that demand the release of violence.

IV. The Formation of Postures

Like the political institutions historically preceding it, the state is a relation of men dominating men, a relation supported by means of legitimate (i.e. considered to be legitimate) violence. If the state is to exist, the dominated must obey the authority claimed by the powers that be.

–Max Weber, Politics as a Vocation

Humanity does not gradually progress from combat to combat until it arrives at universal reciprocity, where the rule of law finally replaces warfare; humanity installs each of its violences in a system of rules and thus proceeds from domination to domination.

–Michel Foucault, Language, Counter-Memory, Practice

As I asserted in chapter 3, the question of the representation of violence is always entangled in the issue of the (un)knowability of violence. In other words, if, as I claim, violence escapes the signification of those who proclaim and employ violence *as well as* those who attempt to (re)present violence, then what is precisely the nature of the relationship between this (un)knowability of violence and representation? To address this question, I first examine how it is dealt with in Taussig, which brings us back to Das in some respects. I argue that the question of (un)knowability relates for both Das and Taussig to the distinction between founding and continuing violence.

A. Representation and (Un)knowability

To examine how Taussig deals with the question of (un)knowability, let us move backwards from his previously discussed work. One of the impetuses underlying Taussig's understanding of mimesis/alterity began to form in *Shamanism, Colonialism, and the Wild Man* (1987).[21] In that work, Taussig explores the representations of violence in the colonial setting of the rubber industry in South America. The problem that strikes Taussig here is not that of the difficulty one encounters in representing violence, but of the manner in which this difficulty, or "the epistemic murk of the space of death," plays an integral role in the production, sustenance, and continuation of violence within these colonial settings (Taussig, 1987, pp. 127–128). Colonial fantasies, fantastic tales of "Indian savagery," fear of the jungle, and the capitalist fetishization of commodities all combine to create a culture of terror where outrageous violent acts are committed and ruler and ruled are consumed by fear. Efforts to represent violence contribute in one way or another to this culture of terror that continuously nourishes itself on representations and counter-representations of violence – a culture of terror that is itself part and parcel of the violent acts of the death squads, of the torture and killing of the so-called savage.

In addition to the fantastic tales and fantasies of the colonialists, Taussig identifies two main modes of official representation through which this violence is represented: banality and melodrama (both belonging to a liberal politics that neatly compartmentalizes the world – i.e., neatly separates good from evil, war from rebellion, politics from violence, and so on). In different ways, both modes pose as a counter-discourse to the savagery of the killing and torture, but are nonetheless complicit with what they oppose since both represent the violence as an unrepresentable terror, without paying any attention to the productive dimension of such representations to the violent acts themselves. By positing the violence as unrepresentable (not in the sense of not presenting the gruesome details of the violence, but in the sense of positing this violence as inhuman and nonsensical), the modes of liberal banality and melodrama look past the violence and treat it as a mere symptom of underlying puzzles and causes that may be solved much like a physician cures a disease, essentially ignoring the violence or even excusing it.[22] Put differently, akin to the instrumentalist perspective (and, in certain respects, much like the more contemporary global discourses of "liberal peace," which, for a prominent example, Mark Duffield, 2001, effectively critiques), these liberal discourses in the colonial setting first posit the violence as unrepresentable, and then explain it through more comprehensible concepts or paradigms, such as liberal capitalism, in order to transform what they first posit as unknowable into a knowable.[23] Both modes of representation essentially succumb to the ever-prevalent temptation to "insist on the distinction between reality and depictions of it. But the disturbing thing is that the reality seeped through the pores of the depiction and by means of such seepage continued what such depictions were meant only to be about" (Taussig, 1987, p. 133).

Once again, mimesis here is not a mere a copy of the thing; rather, "the magic of mimesis lies in the transformation wrought on reality by rendering its image" (Taussig, 1987, p. 134). In the image of the "savage

Indian," the colonialists mimicked their savagery: they engaged in savagery toward the natives in accordance with their imagery of the "savage Indian." Taussig's goal of a counter-representation, of a counter-discourse, rests then on the ability of the anthropologist to understand the counter-representation already found in the discourse of the natives – in this case, in the culture, discourse, and practices of healing, where "the healer desensationalizes terror so that the mysterious side of the mysterious (to adopt Benjamin's formula) is indeed denied by an optic that perceives the everyday as impenetrable, the impenetrable as everyday" (Taussig, 1987, p. 135).

It would be erroneous to claim that Taussig's approach is the same as that of Das's ethnographies, but we are nonetheless and in some important ways back to Das at this point. In her discussion on the "magical" and "rational" forms of the state, Das distances herself from Taussig's work by claiming a more concrete view of the spectacular and the magical as she observes such practices in the routines of everyday life (as opposed to spectacular productions in the form of state rituals, for example) (Das, 2007, pp. 163–164). However, I do not see a major difference between the last quote from Taussig above and what Das found in the healing practices of the everyday (e.g., the "gesture of mourning"). Indeed, there is a great deal of similarity in terms of where each locates this healing (the everyday and the local), as well as where they locate that against which this healing is juxtaposed: "the mysterious side of the mysterious." Das is probably correct in her claim of distance from Taussig's approach, which is perhaps more inclined to keep this mysterious, abstract, and in a sense transcendental optic in play throughout the analysis than to attempt to speak primarily from the optic of the everyday. Regardless, both thinkers illuminate a crucial point: when world-annihilating violence or unrepresentable violence "ends" (according to state and liberal discourses), it does not truly end but moves, seeps into the everyday in a variety of localized ways, and this suggests that we should analyse a founding (not original) and a continuing violence.

There are two general forms of this seepage: the first form reintroduces, re-stimulates, reignites the founding violence; the second works toward healing. Both forms operate on the notion that the founding violence is unknowable, although in different respects. So, in Taussig, the first form is that of the two modes of official representation; in Das, it is the language of rumour or the legitimating discourse of the state. In Taussig, the second form is that of magical healing practices; in Das, it is the routines of everyday life, as in mourning practices, for instance, or the recovery of damaged everyday relationships. Since each thinker fully understands how state discourse or discourses of liberal capitalism make violence knowable in a manner that feeds the oppressive and violent first form, Das and Taussig instead tend to focus on the optic that is fundamentally different in its approach toward (un)knowable violence. The difference is that in the second healing form, the unknowability of violence is dealt with as an unknowable, an absence, that must not be breached but at the same time must not be ignored as something that is unknowable, is absent. This is in contrast to the first form, where the unknowability of violence is approached as a task in which certain words may indeed describe the founding violence as it is – for example, words, which free rioters from authorship, being circulated as if they were absolute and absolutely correct in their description of a founding violence, which consequently allows rioters to act without knowing what they are actually acting; or liberal discourses claiming to solve the symptoms of violence much like a physician cures a disease.

One of the important points here is that both forms and the founding violence are connected. This is the point that distances both thinkers from Girard, who argues that there is a connection between these forms and the founding violence only in cyclical mythological thinking, and that there exists an absolute healing form that lies in wait outside of this connection, ready to break it and create something altogether new. The unknowability of violence in Girard is a kind of ruse that violence plays on us in its effort to continue itself (violence to end violence). In Girard, the founding violence, or rather original violence, is knowable – it is the murder of a surrogate victim that the Word of Christ has revealed for us, and that which only mythology wants to render as unknowable.

I have stated my reasons for not following Girard in this direction, but when he is used as a counter-position to Das and Taussig, a challenge is raised against their approach of maintaining a safe distance from the unknowable violence, and that challenge is: On what basis should we simply accept an unknowable violence as a sort of brute fact in the first place? Even if their approach is directed toward healing, why should a founding violence be approached as something that is unknowable? What if (and this question now moves beyond Girard, Das, and Taussig) what is at issue is the (un)knowability of violence, and not violence as unknowable or violence as knowable? Or, what is perhaps a more fruitful posing of the matter: How could we formulate the (un)knowability of violence in terms that do not tie us to the idea that violence is unique in its (un)knowability and/or that it exists as an unknowable?

Das explores, in the everyday, what it means to speak of a founding violence that is absent, and she convincingly shows how this is indeed a question that is dealt with in the everyday; but in this, the absence of founding violence is not breached, and "walls" are erected around it in order to protect us from its destructive force. Even if this allows for healing, and I do not doubt that it does, why cannot the "walls" be breached? Are they around "us"? They are not in Das, since she is speaking of a founding violence that has seeped into us (again, following Wittgenstein, there is not a radical distinction between subject and world in Das); so the "walls" are in us, we build them around a founding violence that is also already within us; *but why are there walls around an "it" that is?* Instead of following Das's line of questioning here, I want to ask and explore in the dialogical analytic: What does it mean to speak with violence that "is" and "is-not"?

Bringing the discussion back to perpetrators of violent acts, I agree that in a certain sense, perpetrators of violence act without knowing what they are acting (à la Das). This is indeed a recurring statement throughout history on humanity's misrecognition and misunderstanding of its violent acts, perhaps most famously in the biblical phrase "Father, forgive them; for they know not what they do" (Lk. 23:34). But what this misses is the way in which this statement itself prevents us from following violence into its third and fourth dimensions. The dialogical analytic must account for the knowledge we have, or that we use, as human beings, about that which transcends us, in a manner that does not treat transcendental knowledge as if it is truly transcendent, as if it is a Subject as opposed to a subject matter. Yet I maintain that there is a transcendental element of knowledge that is indeed beyond our reach in the Gadamerian sense. And what this accomplishes is an analytic that accounts for the knowledge we have, or that we use, as human beings, about that which transcends us, in a manner that does not treat, as Girard does, transcendental knowledge as if it is truly divine (or as if it is transcendent, as if it is a Subject as opposed to a subject matter).

Earlier I made the case as to how this "beyond our reach" can be viewed via the Gadamer–Derrida encounter. I suggested the combination of two senses of beyond our reach ("over-there," and it "is-not") in an admittedly awkward sentence that states the modus operandi of the dialogical analytic: to examine and analyse a perpetrator of violence who acts without knowing what one knows in knowing, (not)knowing. And as a guide to this sentence is a certain formulation of violence the "thing itself," as opposed to an originary, unknowable or knowable violence (depending on whose perspective) that forms the basis of the above sentence from scripture.

When I speak of violence a "thing itself," I reiterate, I am not referring to a mystical force that rules human affairs from a distance through violent acts and events. While the following quote was posited in quite a different context and for different purposes, I think White's words capture precisely what I am positing here:

> But the word here referred to is not the word of Scripture; it is not a sacred word, but the word desacralized, returned to the order of things in which it has a place as one *thing* among many. The result of the desacralization of the word is to destroy the impulse to see eternal hierarchies in the order of things. Once language is freed from the task of representing the world of things, the world of things disposes itself before consciousness as precisely what it was all along: a plenum of *mere* things, no one of which can lay claim to privileged status with respect to any other. (White, 1978, p. 250; original emphases)[24]

Not only language, but also violence is posited in my approach as just another "mere" thing. Or, back to Gadamer's terminology, as just another "subject matter." This is the meaning of a desacralized word, and not, as Girard would have, a capitulation in the face of a wondrous and fear-inducing thing called violence. The only part that I must add to White's quote is that in my approach the desacralized word does not do away with the element of transcendence, as I have repeated ad nauseam. If I have spent more time discussing transcendence, it is only because transcendence has been under attack in much of contemporary critical thought. But I am far from proposing an approach that is built solely on a notion of transcendence; rather, I simply wish to put the idea back into play with the notion of immanence. It is not a question of either/or; in the Derridean spirit, my goal is to keep the tension open analytically, just as Derrida had formulated the matter in "Force of Law." Before delving into Derrida's text, I first briefly examine Pierre Bourdieu's sociological framing of the connection between founding and continuing violence, which sets the stage for an analysis of deep postures as opposed to a fixation on locating an originary point of violence. So before revisiting Derrida's deconstruction of a firm distinction across moments of violence, I want to prepare through Bourdieu the piece (deep dispositions) that will take the place of such distinctions.

B. Symbolic/Brutal Violence and the Operation of Dispositions

Pierre Bourdieu's work on "symbolic violence" offers a sociological framework for understanding the interconnections between the two main moments of violence, laying out a path that, instead of fixating on neatly categorizing the two moments of violence, directs toward an analysis of deep dispositions that are not necessarily directly observable. Similar to Max Weber's agreement with Trotsky's statement that "every state is founded on force" (Weber, 1958a, p. 78), Bourdieu first positions the founding of the state in violence and highlights, just as Weber did, that the question of the state's legitimacy is always bound up with the use of violence. But more crucial for Bourdieu than it was for Weber was the idea of symbolic violence, which refers to the implicit means through which the state aims to "secure doxic submission to the established order" (Bourdieu, 2000, p. 178), wherein the dominated consent to their domination by perceiving their actions as if they stemmed from their own natural inclinations (Bourdieu, 2000, p. 169). The state perpetuates certain relations of domination through a symbolic violence that forces the dominated to perceive and evaluate themselves and their situation through the use of "instruments of knowledge" that are shared by the dominator and dominated (Bourdieu, 2000, pp. 170, 175). The dominated and dominator are entrenched in their relations of domination by their unknown consent: they do not know – and do not want to know (Bourdieu, 2000, p. 192) – that what they speak or feel, or how they act, is not at all natural, but rather works to perpetuate relations of domination by having the dominated continuously (re)make these relations (Bourdieu, 2000, pp. 172–176, 206).

Thus in Bourdieu the manner of our communication – our categories of representation – is at the heart of the problem of domination. He claims that when agents are "endowed with the same cognitive schemes and inclined to communicate and consequently to recognize each other as legitimate interlocutors, equal in honour, to agree to talk," then we have a form of communication that "converts brute power relations, which are always uncertain and liable to be suspended, into durable relations of symbolic power through which a person is bound and feels bound" (Bourdieu, 2000, p. 199). It is in such communication that agents are bound with one another in a stable and long-standing fashion. Symbolic violence ensures this by closing off the terms of communication in one direction or another (Bourdieu, 2000, p. 200). The misrecognition of this process as "natural" is the very weapon that the symbolic order launches to protect itself.

Reflexive sociology denaturalizes such categorizations and then seeks to retrain agents for a subversive way of thinking, perceiving, and acting (Bourdieu, 2000, p. 188). So rather than ignore the misrecognitions of the agents (thereby transgressing the misrecognition in a scholastic fashion), and rather than dwell solely in them (thereby bowing before their symbolic violence), Bourdieu's reflexive sociology focuses almost exclusively on symbolic violence by using the misrecognitions of the agents in order to explore how and why they cast as unknown the nature of the game that is being played in the social field and the fact of their playing it, which always remains un-thought by the agents (Adams, 2006, pp. 514–516; Croce, 2015, p. 331). The agents do not recognize the actual mechanisms that guide their action and behaviour in any given field (the family, school, the workplace, the state); the task of the sociologist is to first discover these mechanisms (not by claiming an objectivist viewpoint that is beyond the agents who do not know any better but through a direct engagement with the agents and their practices), and second to aid in the critical task of transforming them (Croce, 2015, p. 343).

Bourdieu captures two important points here that have been extensively written about across the social sciences. First, his work illuminates how "natural" feelings, beliefs, opinions, statements are not all intrinsic to "who we are" but are rather indicative of the deep dispositions (i.e., "habitus") to which we belong and in which we act, say, feel. For Bourdieu, habitus is basically a unifying disposition (or incorporating structure) that cannot be directly observed but that is made observable in the effects it generates (agents' tastes, opinions, hobbies, and so on); habitus is also to be understood as a structuring structure that is itself structurable (Bourdieu, 1990, p. 53; Bourdieu, 1998, pp. 6–9), which means that even though it is unifying, habitus is not a fixed/ static object or deterministic system (Croce, 2015, p. 330) but rather a flexible and sometimes contradictory set of structuring structures (as in the colonial setting in Algeria, from which Bourdieu's observations and theory first emerged) (Laurier Decoteau, 2013, pp. 280–282). I need not delve into here the various ways in which Bourdieu theorized the operation of habituses – their dysfunctions, lags, smooth functioning, and so on – since I simply want to highlight how he situated these deep dispositions vis-à-vis symbolic/brutal violence.

This leads to the second point, where Bourdieu's work highlights that what passes as what would conventionally be called and recognized as peaceful dialogue ("same cognitive schemes," "to recognize each other as legitimate interlocutors," "to agree to talk") is intricately connected to the sustenance of relations of domination born in violence. What Bourdieu does not emphasize enough, as Karl von Holdt suggests in the case of postcolonial contexts, is that symbolic violence can never give absolute stability to any given order, since "the making of order contains also tendencies towards the unraveling of order" (von Holdt, 2012, p. 128). The latter statement is indeed not restricted to postcolonial orders; as was discussed through Foucault in chapter 1, violence can create, maintain, and/or reconfigure relations of domination, both making and unmaking orders. Going a step further, I want to ask: Is any given order able to bound people together in relations of domination only because of a fundamental partnership between peaceful dialogue and what I call violent dialogue? Does peaceful dialogue substitute for what violent dialogue could not speak?

Bourdieu already directs this line of questioning in the affirmative, wherein he suggests that what passes as "peaceful dialogue" is indeed a different species of violence; that is, Bourdieu's symbolic violence, though distinct from brutish violence, is yet connected to it in that it continues the relations of domination established through the founding violence of the state. But to focus on symbolic violence at the expense of brutal relations (á la Bourdieu) is to miss the deep entanglement of violent and peaceful dialogue: it is to miss the manner in which deep postures that are forged in violence themselves provide meaning to the words of so-called peaceful dialogue, which can then (to go back to Foucault) ensure the continuation of certain relations of domination at the same time that these postures form the seeds of a reconfiguration of relations of domination, of their violent overthrow. Therefore, not only does the formation of certain postures in and through violence signal the workings of deep dispositions from which we speak, feel, act, but these postures are furthermore formed and forged in such a way as to demand the release of violence. This is why it is not enough to focus on the "misrecognition," which highlights the "tacit battle" in the symbolic order at the expense of the "brutish battle," ignoring the latter's important role in giving a specific force the power of knowing and in simultaneously forming the seeds of its overthrow – in other words, such a focus does not sufficiently speak to the intimate and intricate connections between brutish and symbolic violence and the ways in which violence the "thing itself" explains and reveals those connections as opposed to tracing them through power per se. So the analytical point here is this: to give the brutish battle, to give violence, its direct analytical attention, we must follow not just the misrecognition of the agents, but that which evades them because it cannot be captured, neither by agents nor by the analyst – that is, violence the "thing itself."

In critiquing (albeit lightly) misrecognition, I do not suggest here that Bourdieu is guilty of positing for the sociologist a superior, objective viewpoint from which they discover a reality that the agents cannot see. I indeed agree with Mariano Croce's (2015) excellent defence of Bourdieu's theory against charges of "objectivism" – charges that assert that despite his intentions, Bourdieu reverts to a self-affirming theoretical model that cannot be corroborated by or even made relatable to social agents. In contrasting Bourdieu's "habitus" with Wittgenstein's "rule-following" and in showing the links between them on the crucial point of how agents continuously engage with rules and practices (sometimes affirming them, other times renegotiating them or transforming them), Croce illustrates how Bourdieu's theory and methodology denaturalizes a reified social space through "an ongoing collaboration between theory and the agents on the fields" (2015, p. 343). Like Wittgenstein, Bourdieu's methodology thus helps "social agents free current accounts of practices from the yoke of reification so as to favor the emergence of alternatives" that may challenge the indeed transient status quo (Croce, 2015, p. 343). Again, I do not think that this approach lacks value; just as I greatly value Das's approach of learning from the victims of violence to formulate theoretical insights into the operation of state violence, I find significant transformative and progressive potential in Bourdieu's efforts. But instead of focusing on misrecognition and its concomitant therapeutic approach (which is, for me, what Wittgenstein/Das/Bourdieu leave us with), important and valuable as this approach is, I agree with Kögler's claim that Bourdieu's analytical tools are limited in that they can raise the agents' consciousness of power (and therefore their potential to transgress that power), but cannot speak to the transformative element of our very understanding of the concept of power that occurs by virtue of the analysts' dialogue with social agents, which revealed the operation of this power in the social world in the first place (Kögler, 1999, pp. 225–226). Phrased differently, highlighting the transformative process of dialogue underscores the subject matter and its elusiveness as opposed to whether or not the agents recognize the full scope of their actions, beliefs, and practices. I am not denying that this misrecognition, or "errancy" as Daniel Monk (2002) puts it (I come back to Monk in the last chapter), takes place. As previously discussed, the hermeneutic principle that asserts the failure of the agents to fully comprehend "all of what they know when they know" is underscoring a kind of misrecognition on the part of the agents. But in Gadamer's philosophical hermeneutics, the misrecognition is not primarily viewed in terms of power relationships that prohibit the agents from full comprehension, as is the case in Bourdieu (and as is the case in Mouffe, 2005, pp. 60–79, who draws on Wittgenstein's emphasis on "rule-following" as opposed to interpretation in order to highlight the operation of hegemonic social relations); rather, the subject matter itself always prohibits full comprehension by virtue of its elusive character (also see Kögler, 1999), and this, as I have argued from the beginning, is very much the case with violence.

So instead of misrecognition, it is critical to emphasize what always evades recognition, to go back to Gadamer (whom Kögler, 1999, prefers over Bourdieu as well), which is the evasiveness of the subject matter. This does not mean that we ignore how power practices/structures limit what we see, know, understand, and believe (to go back to Kögler's intervention into hermeneutics that was discussed in the introduction); rather, it means that in addition to focusing on limitations imposed in/through/of power, we must first and foremost *emphasize the limitations of our very ability to understand violence.* The agents' views and actions, always short of capturing the subject matter, can be followed to launch us into a dialogue over the subject matter of violence, allowing the analyst to chase the elusiveness of violence the "thing itself" in the very dimension where it cannot ever be directly seen but is observable through its effects. These effects can be gleaned in the very inability of the agents to (a) capture violence, give a name to what is nameless, and (b) understand their very transformation by the subject matter of violence, by violence the "thing itself."

To further elaborate these points, and indeed extrapolate from what has been asserted so far, we need to go back to Derrida. Specifically, Derrida's "Force of Law" reveals that the formation of the categories of representation that perpetuate any given configuration of relations of domination is invariably connected to the founding violence that could not present itself, and as such it always already contains the seeds of a violent overthrow of this violent founding. And while this, at its most basic form, looks like the proverbial cycle of violence, it is more than that. A closer examination reveals that the formation of certain deep postures, and not the cyclical exchange of violence itself, is what ensures the propagation of violence.

C. Presence/Non-presence and the Propagation of Violence

In "Force of Law," Derrida builds on Walter Benjamin's "Critique of Violence." Benjamin asserts that there are two types of violence: a "mythic" violence, which is "lawmaking," and a "divine" violence, which is "law-destroying" (Benjamin, 2004 [1921], p. 249). Benjamin is advocating divine violence so as to counter mythic violence. His intent is to critique legal violence by way of the "philosophy" of its history.[25] He basically refers to "pernicious" law-making and law-preserving violence when he speaks of mythic violence (Benjamin, 2004, p. 252). When law-preserving violence becomes too overbearing, it destroys its own law-making abilities, and is then replaced by a new law-making violence, which then begins the cycle of mythic violence once more.

Divine violence, on the other hand, is revolutionary "sovereign" violence (Benjamin, 2004, p. 252). This violence can come in the form of "educative power," which is marked by the "expiating moment … that strikes without bloodshed, and … by the absence of all lawmaking" (Benjamin, 2004, p. 250). The difficulty we face in understanding divine violence – "unalloyed violence" – is that it can almost never be seen (Benjamin, 2004, p. 252).[26] It expiates us without us ever knowing it. Only mythic violence is visible and easy to point to, for it merely punishes; it makes laws and preserves them. Divine violence, on the other hand, only expiates us and thus leaves its mark on us without threat or warning; it simply happens, and it never makes laws that may govern us (i.e., it never produces a contract). Benjamin believes that divine violence can break the cycle of mythic violence. Just as God defeated the mythic in every other realm, so will God defeat the mythic in the sphere of violence and bring about the superior ideal of the divine (Benjamin, 2004, pp. 244–252).[27]

Derrida argues that implicit in Benjamin's distinction is an opposition between Greek mythology (the mythic) and Jewish messianism (the divine) (Derrida, 2002 [1990], p. 265), which Benjamin utilizes to tackle the difficult relationship between law and violence. This is indeed the main reason why Girard admired the work of Benjamin, although obviously Girard moves beyond Jewish messianism in his work, and he does so in three senses. First, in Girard the divine does not accept sacrifice, but rather acts in a manner that is completely outside the realm of sacrificial societies (the earlier Girard) or uses sacrifice as a way to refute the sacrificial order once and for all (the later Girard). In the second related sense, the true divine in Girard has nothing to do with violence, even if we say that the violence of the divine "strikes without bloodshed." And third, the law is problematic for Girard because it is unable to control and contain violence enough, and not just because it continues violence as it contains it. These three differences point us toward Girard's two governing horizons: one is a horizon where violence reigns supreme and lies at the basis of all social/cultural/political formations (the mythic); the second horizon is a realm of divine love and absolute non-violence (the divine).

I wish to avoid not only an analysis that would move into either of the two extreme horizons, but also an analysis that would situate itself in-between them as if they were truly separated by an abyss. Moreover, while Taussig and Das do indeed challenge the Girardian idea of two extremes by showing the continuum between a founding and continuing violence, they do so by maintaining a certain distinction between them (since the founding violence is posited *as* an unknowable that *is* distinct from the continuing violence). The move beyond Girardian absolutes and Das/Taussig's distinctions of violence is made possible by Derrida's reading of Benjamin, and his argument on the force of law.

Derrida theorizes in "Force of Law" the question of the law's "enforce-ability" through justice (2002, pp. 231–233). Derrida first posits justice as the incalculable and un-presentable opposite of calculable, determined law (2002, pp. 244, 250; also see Agamben, 2005 [1999], pp. 18–19). At the heart of the matter is the manner in which justice can be periodi-cally taken up to unbalance the legitimacy of the law.[28] Derrida poses the question of how we are to "distinguish between the force of law ... of a legitimate power and the allegedly originary violence that must have established this authority and that could not itself have autho-rized itself by any anterior legitimacy" (2002, p. 234). Derrida suggests that the founding of the law is beyond (in)validation from past/pres-ent categories of just/unjust (which such founding annihilates) and has yet to formulate the categories of justice that will render the founding moment "just" (i.e., its justice is "to-come") (2002, p. 241).[29]

For Derrida, the law is not the servant of force, and neither is force the servant of the law, but this founding moment gives birth to a "law that would maintain a more internal, more complex relation to what one calls force, power or violence" (2002, p. 241). Violence, then, is not exterior to law but is indeed the very force that founds law and is then used to preserve it. If there is an order between the two, it is not settled, and the two continuously change positions (Derrida, 2002, p. 268).

The complexity of this relation brings us back to Derrida's original opposition between justice and law, for he argues that

> everything would still be simple if this distinction between justice and law were a true distinction, an opposition the functioning of which was logically regulated and masterable. But it turns out that law claims to exercise itself in the name of justice and that justice demands for itself that it be established in the name of a law that must be put to work ... (constituted and applied) by force "enforced." (Derrida, 2002, pp. 250–251)

So justice is never resolved or attained, and all the founding of law can do is defer the question of justice. The founding of law can assert itself as just only through the continued affirmation of its legality (i.e., this ruling is just because it followed the legal system), but never on the grounds of an absolute justice (i.e., it cannot be absolutely guaranteed on something other than itself) (Derrida, 2002, pp. 252–253):

> This moment of suspense, this *epokhē*, this founding or revolutionary moment of law is, in law, an instance of nonlaw.... But it is also the whole history of law. *This moment always takes place and never takes place in a presence.* It is the moment in which the foundation of law remains suspended in the void or over the abyss, suspended by a pure performative act that would

> not have to answer to or before anyone. (Derrida, 2002, pp. 269–270; original emphasis)

This is why justice (always to-come, always making it possible to unsettle the legitimacy of the law) "opens up to the *avenir* the transformation, the recasting or refounding ... of law and politics" (Derrida, 2002, p. 257).[30] Consequently, justice dances, as it were, with law through violence, which constantly (de)stabilizes the law through its other, justice.

There is here an interesting formulation of the relationship between restricted, mythic violence (seen in Derrida as the legality of the law – presence in law-preserving/making form) and unbound, divine violence (seen as the justice of the law – non-presence of a violence that founds the legitimacy of the law), which leaves us with two schemes. In the first scheme of restricted violence, we are certain of our justice in law only because of the uncertainty of what lurks in it (i.e., legality is the only certain means/grounds of justification because we cannot grasp justice), leaving us with "decidable knowledge and certainty in a realm that *structurally remains that of the undecidable*" (Derrida, 2002, p. 291; original emphasis). In the second scheme of divine violence, Derrida does not accord the divine the immunity Benjamin posited for it, and it no longer occupies a superior position that is of a different species from mythic violence (Derrida, 2002, pp. 272–274). Derrida offers different reasons for this, but the main one is that Benjamin's attempt to speak of a divine violence that leaves no trace fails because its lack of presence in a contract (for it does not make laws, according to Benjamin) is nevertheless "represented by the supplement of a substitute," which in itself contributes to the degeneration of an originary purely expiating violence (Derrida, 2002, p. 282). If Benjamin's divine violence does not produce the contract (whose non-production is a necessary element of divine violence in Benjamin), then something else will do so in its place. And this something else is the representation of the founding violence in law-preserving/making form: "destined from the start to be repeated, preserved, reinstituted" (Derrida, 2002, p. 290). The scheme for divine violence in Derrida is thus "decision (just, historical, political, and so on), justice beyond law and the state, but *without decidable knowledge*" (2002, p. 291; original emphasis).

In Derrida, these schemata meet – or, they will always have already met.[31] We thus can no longer imagine that a divine violence exists as a non-cyclical force that can break the cycle of mythic violence from the outside, as it were. The two schemes are rather interconnected, and they will always meet. The nature of this meeting suggests that the divine, in transcendence, offers no guarantees of pure expiation (á la Benjamin), but is a temporary moment in a larger picture of continuous movement between the schemata. Violence (divine and transcendent) as a "thing itself" does not enjoy immunity from violence as a practice (mythic and immanent). The undecidability of divine violence meets the decidability of mythic violence, gaining form in a certain representation (immanent/mythic – law-preserving/making) of an uncertain non-presence that is incapable of presenting itself (transcendent/divine – law-founding). Crucial here is that there is no longer in Derrida a founding violence that we can point to or know – that is, there is not in Derrida an unknowable or knowable founding violence that *is* (as in the cases of Taussig and Das); rather, we find a complex interplay between presence and absence, or *différance*. And just like Derrida's *différance*, I propose that violence the "thing itself"

> is to be heard in the openness of an unheard-of question that opens neither upon knowledge nor upon some nonknowledge which is a knowledge to come. In the openness of this question *we no longer know*. This does not mean that we know nothing but that we are beyond absolute knowledge ... approaching that on the basis of which its closure is announced and decided. (Derrida, 1973, p. 103; original emphasis)

In his essay "Différance," Derrida admits that his discussion of *différance* (which he claims is neither a word nor a concept) may sometimes be indiscernible from negative theology (Derrida, 1973, p. 134). But he is adamant that *différance* does not denote anything theological. Negative theology posits God as an ineffable being that is beyond our categories of knowledge, but it nonetheless gives this ineffable being a name – God – by which it approaches this being as if *it is*; *différance* simply does not belong to categories of essence, presence, or existence at all, but rather "opens up the very space in which onto-theology – philosophy – produces its system and its history" (Derrida, 1973, pp. 134–135). *Différance* produces differences, not in the sense of conscious or active production but in the sense of leading to effects of difference from the movement of play (Derrida, 1973, pp. 140–141).

Différance is "the movement by which language ... becomes 'historically' constituted as a fabric of differences" (Derrida, 1973, p. 141), but *différance* does not "constitute" or "produce" a being-present (Derrida, 1973, p. 145). Presence, what is being-present-to-itself, is forever differed in the movement of *différance*: "If the diverted presentation continues to be somehow definitively and irreducibly withheld, this is not because a particular present remains hidden or absent, but because *différance* holds us in a relation with what exceeds ... *the alternative of presence or absence*" (Derrida, 1973, p. 151; emphasis added). Unlike the transcendent in theology, *différance*, first and foremost, is-not: "It commands nothing, rules over nothing, and nowhere does it exercise any authority" (Derrida, 1973, p. 153). *Différance* is-not a unique or master word that refers to something that is ineffable, but the affirmation of the impossibility of any such mastery and of anything that is masterful (Derrida, 1973, pp. 159–160).

Likewise, violence the "thing itself" does not denote an original or founding violence, does not denote a continuing violence, and finally does not denote a divine violence that *is*. Violence the "thing itself" is no-thing at all or "is-not," and "is" "over-there" in acts of violence and representations of violence, escaping us the more we reach for "it." Crucially, this manoeuvre through Derrida I believe deals with the danger of hypostatization – of conceding to violence all explanations of human life – which Hans Joas warns about and which, as I claim in chapter 1, Joas fails to effectively deal with. By bringing to the forefront the element of (un)knowability, I am shifting the emphasis from a view of violence as a fixed and sealed occurrence that determines various social and political relations/institutions/formations, and instead examining how the (un)knowability of violence reveals and makes possible a dynamic of violent dialogue. In other words, violence the "thing itself" avoids hypostatization because in a sense it "is-not" – like *différance*, it does not refer to a master sign and indeed undercuts the idea of anything masterful. Rather, violence the "thing itself" points out and guides the analysis toward a dynamic of violent dialogue that can be traced in specific acts/representations of violence. The guide, then, is ever elastic so as not to constitute a Godly figure, but not so elastic (since the analyst must follow and trace its movement) so as to appear anywhere, everywhere, and nowhere simultaneously. That which escapes representation is not an abstract and absent presence or a present absence, but is "the alternative of presence or absence," as Derrida puts it above.

Violence the "thing itself" is impossible to observe, because in the enactment of violence, words falter and dissipate, and we become speechless. But it is precisely in this dimension that deep postures are formed, and while they cannot be represented, while they constitute the uncertain non-presence that cannot represent itself, they can be observed in that which substitutes for the incommunicable and the unrepresentable. There are two main substitutions here. One is the substitution of violent dialogue for postures of incommensurability, and the other is the substitution of peaceful dialogue for violent dialogue (and vice versa). Thus, violent dialogue substitutes (in acts of violence that communicate meanings) for the uncertain non-presence of postures of incommensurability; at the same time, because of the dimensional operation of violence where the elusiveness of violence does not end with that substitution and violence continues to escape and elude our ability to comprehend or know all of the meanings that are communicated, then peaceful dialogue substitutes for what violent dialogue could not speak, just as violent dialogue reciprocally substitutes for the absence of written/verbal exchange (which I argued in chapter 3). The substitutions are not to be confused with separations of violence across species and subspecies – what passes as peaceful dialogue carries with it elements of violence the "thing itself," what is constituted through violent dialogue carries with it elements of peaceful dialogue, and so on. The substitutions, we must remember from Derrida, are always inherently incomplete and constitute a *movement* – hence the continuous propagation of substitutions as the different dimensions persistently link up with one another.

When the dialogical analytic chases the fourth dimension of violence, it is for the sake of discovering not the impossible identity of violence itself, but the very thing that makes violence knowable. The formation of postures, which takes place in this fourth dimension, cannot be proven theoretically, or directly in observation, for that matter. The operation of such postures, however, can be observed by following the substitutions, and social scientists can begin to piece these postures together through a direct observation of their effects (and it is precisely in this sense that my approach borrows from Bourdieu's theory of dispositions) – effects such as the formation of enemy-siblings.

In chapter 1, I argued that we must shift the analytical gaze away from enmity per se and toward violence, the result being a focus on the formation of enemy-siblings, which I outlined in chapter 3. The full consequences of this shift can now be more clearly stated. Schmitt, Bernstein, and others assert that the dehumanization of the enemy as an absolute "other" who must be annihilated clearly carries dangerous consequences. I agreed with some of the practical solutions offered by thinkers who are concerned about humanizing "others" and avoiding the destructive violence of absolutist thinking. But I also indicated that analytically speaking, something is missing in those explanations, which I can now state concerns the manner in which enemy-siblings come to share deep postures and how those postures continue to shape and form enemy-siblings as enemy-siblings. At this point of the argument, I think that this missing piece can be best gleaned through Mouffe's (2005) distinction between the "enemy" and the "adversary," which centres on the question of a shared symbolic space. Mouffe shares with the likes of Bernstein a concern over the dehumanization of the enemy, but she also asserts that Schmitt was not entirely wrong to stress the importance of a friend/enemy distinction (Mouffe, 2005, pp. 38–42, 44). For Mouffe, the logic of the political is antagonism, and to follow the liberal tradition (among others) of downplaying conflict and emphasizing consensus is to betray the very nature of the political (Mouffe, 2005, pp. 17–35). There is no avoiding the construction of an enemy in an antagonistic relation, because that would mean the death of the political. This death would not signal the end of conflict and antagonism. Rather, in claiming to have reconciled all conflicts under the banner of a rational (neo)liberal consensus, (neo)liberal democracy closes down the ability of social actors to politically express and potentially resolve antagonistic relations in their favour. Instead of reconciliation, such models simply direct the antagonism toward a dangerously violent and highly destructive path (Mouffe, 2005, pp. 13, 31; Mouffe, 2013, pp. 120–122).

Thus for Mouffe, we must distinguish between two kinds of antagonism. The first concerns a confrontation with an enemy with whom we do not share any common symbolic space; the second concerns an "agonism" with an adversary – "friendly enemies … who are friends because they share a common symbolic space but also enemies because they want to organize this common symbolic space in a different way" (Mouffe, 2005, p. 13; also see Mouffe, 2005, pp. 108–128). Mouffe clearly favours the second kind of antagonism as a model for radical democracy, where adversaries engage in a real confrontation (not merely a competition) whose democratic rules and procedures are agreed upon but also in which one or more of the sides involved would be defeated since no reconciliation between their interests/vision is possible (Mouffe, 2013, pp. 8–9).[32] I endorse much of Mouffe's model, particularly as it unfolds within a democratic system such as Canada, for example (although some Indigenous perspectives might not find such a model useful in their struggle against the Canadian settler-colonial state – e.g., Simpson, 2014). But what distinguishes absolute enmity is not the absence of a common symbolic violence, as Mouffe suggests; it is rather the presence of a hidden common symbolic violence that I call a violent communion. Thus, while on the surface, positions between such enemies seem to be incommensurable (in Mouffe's terms, do not share a common basis), they are paradoxically produced as such through *shared and common* postures of incommensurability.

What the analyst must therefore seek to investigate in violent acts is precisely how a complex interaction of enemy-siblings reveals postures of incommensurability that continuously produce incommensurable positions across a spectrum of time and space. What is crucial is not only that the positions of the sides engaged in violence are incommensurable – what is highlighted in this analysis is that the sides' postures of incommensurability, which are made and remade in violence, are really at the heart of the violent communion since they will very likely continue to produce incommensurable positions. Through violence, not only are instrumental goals achieved, but postures are made and remade, communicated and formative of a communion between the sides as enemy-siblings. To change the postures of this violent communion, no political process that simply proclaims to counter violence can succeed – what is needed first and foremost is a deeper understanding of these postures, of the violence they continuously (re)create and that constantly (re)creates them.

To reiterate, this work does not propose a theoretical solution to the problem of violence, because none exists. The effort to counter violence can be undertaken only in the specificity of a given context. But to do so effectively, then we must first properly understand violence, to the best of our abilities and working within the limits that we face in our efforts to understand it. Toward this end, this book offers a set of theoretical tools that can be useful for the study of violence. And while I cannot put them to use for a detailed and sustained analysis of a specific case, I can, for the purposes of further elucidating the book's major theoretical assertions, but not for a substantiation of the theory, present a brief example of how to proceed in a dialogical analysis of violence.

Chapter 5's analysis will not cover all of the theoretical materials presented in this book, but will be undertaken in order to better delineate the analytical space that this book is trying to open up for future analysis. I conclude this book then by re-engaging with Said's mode of representation along with Benny Morris's mode of representation of the 1948 war in Palestine/Israel. I chose these two thinkers because there is an interesting common theme in their works, which concerns the traversal of the victim-persecutor perspectives. Rather than present the two perspectives as absolute opposites, they each, through different methods of traversal, unsettle these perspectives in their explanation of violence. Understanding their differences on this crucial theme can bring to light precisely how violence moves in the mimetic dimension, and indeed reveals a fourth dimension.

It is indeed easier to find the dynamic of violent dialogue in texts that promote and/or participate in violence (see Ayyash, 2010a, for my analysis of Hamas's original "Covenant" and Israel's "terrorist laws"), but my hope here is that if I can show how violent dialogue operates in complex writings that attempt to counter violence by either following through with its instrumental logic (Morris) or by challenging violence through justice (Said), the overall case I am making for four-dimensional violence will be more convincing. To properly situate my analysis, I engage with Daniel Monk's work in the first step of chapter 5 since his analysis of monuments and violence in Palestine/Israel covers some of the features of violence I have outlined in this book, at the same time that his work challenges an attempt like mine to posit a fourth dimension of violence.

5 A Dialogical Analysis of the Representation of Violence: The Case of Palestine/Israel

As the ship carrying Ben-Gurion docked off Jaffa, "the harbor was suddenly filled with skiffs, and Arabs clambered up the sides of our ship. The shouting and shoving were awful." Porters carried the young Ben-Gurion to a skiff and then from the skiff to dry ground. He literally arrived in the Promised Land on the back of an Arab.

–Benny Morris, Righteous Victims

For those who challenge all this and call it utopian or unrealistic, my answer is a simple one: show me what else is available today. Show me a scheme for separation that isn't based on abridged memory, continued injustice, unmitigated conflict, apartheid. There just isn't one, hence the value of what I've tried to outline here.

–Edward Said, "Afterword: The Consequences of 1948"

On 16 September 1996, Israeli prime minister Benjamin Netanyahu ordered the opening of an "archaeological tunnel" near the Western Wall and al-Aqsa Mosque. Following the order, protests ensued and around seventy Palestinian protestors were killed in their confrontation with Israeli forces. Daniel B. Monk (2002) perceptively points out three points of "tacit consensus" or agreement between seemingly opposed Palestinian and Israeli interpretations of these violent events. First, the interpreters, in their view of the tunnel as that which begets violence, agree in "the presumption that in architecture a political reality presents itself to view directly and without mediation" (Monk, 2002, pp. 2–3). Second, they agree "that the monument is a fuse with which one can ignite a human bomb" (Monk, 2002, p. 3). And third, they agree "that the immediacy of their political situation is confirmed in architecture's *representation*" (Monk, 2002, p. 3, original emphasis). Over the course of the conflict, the notion that the other side uses architecture to advance its interests has become seamlessly accepted as the manifestation of political reality and as the reason behind the outbreak of violence (Monk, 2002, pp. 54, 70, 119).

For Monk, the only difference between Palestinian and Israeli interpretations concerns the question of who sets the trigger for violence, but on a fundamental level, we find shared positions. The tacit agreements between the sides, which render invisible the inadequacy of adequating the immediacy of architecture with political reality, point "to a conflict unable to account for itself to itself" (Monk, 2002, pp. 5, 126). That the sacred monuments in Jerusalem have come to constitute so dominant a place in the interpretations of this conflict – that architecture has become one of the "atoms" of this conflict – is precisely what needs to be questioned and challenged (Monk, 2002, p. 4). For Monk, the belief "that an organic relation between monuments and violence explains this conflict and as such demands no explanation" is not only inadequate but also plays a role in perpetuating the conflict (Monk, 2002, p. 131).

Although Monk operates from a different interpretive and theoretical tradition, which is perhaps more heavily influenced by post-structuralism and is oriented by an Adornian negative dialectics, there are a few important similarities between four-dimensional violence and Monk's arguments. His work (a) interrogates the instrumental uses that actors and interpreters make of mass violence in advancing their ideological positions and strategic interests (similar to the first dimension); (b) captures the tacit agreements between the sides within a sea of seemingly irreconcilable difference and enmity (similar, in some respects, to the third dimension); (c) articulates as an obstacle to peace and reconciliation the inability of the conflict "to account for itself to itself" (similar to the dialogical analytic's emphasis on the need to directly gaze at and account for violence, and taking seriously the implications of not doing so); and (d) highlights the contestation over the naming of violence as integral to our understanding of the violence (similar to the dialogical analytic's emphasis on the seepage of the object of representation into the representations of violence).

These similarities can all be seen when, in his analysis of representations, Monk argues that the British, Zionist, and Palestinian invocations of the opposition between "pogrom" (which involves the rioters, who are instruments of the elite) and "cataclysm" (which involves the mobs, who are instruments of nature) constantly repeat the "conflict over the name of violence" (Monk, 2002, p. 76). In this repetition, the sides agree that the figuration of mass violence rests on the pogrom-cataclysm opposition, and simply disagree on who fits under which category. Monk argues that the two names are indeed interchangeable in the various texts he analyses and suggests that this interchangeability "has guaranteed their inclusion within a series of other recognizable geopolitical oppositions" (2002, p. 77) – Monk thus claims that

> in the history of Palestine and Israel, the "cataclysm" and the "pogrom" may appear, and have appeared, as the refractions ... of larger confrontations between metropole and periphery, colonizer and colonized, and between East and West – in short, between identities that are themselves allegorical, structurally interdependent, and driven to contrariety. (2002, pp. 77–78)

The actors and interpreters of the conflict fail to recognize the interchangeability of the two names – particularly in how the two names privilege, in their textual deployment, "mass violence as the vehicle of a historical transformation" (Monk, 2002, p. 79). Moreover, in emphasizing the instrumental position of the masses within the cataclysm and the pogrom, dominant historiography posits the participants in the violence as lacking agency and denies them the ability to guide and lead change. Therefore, "the historiography of Israel and Palestine's violence effaces what it represents and annuls what it privileges" (Monk, 2002, p. 79), and in the process, such conceptual paradigms come to normalize the violence and as such contribute to its continuations. Like Monk, the dialogical analytic seeks to counter the view of the participants as mindless masses who commit violence, emphasize the "structurally interdependent" character of the "enemies" as enemy-siblings, and highlight that the sides agree on more than they disagree on but that their agreement is structured in such a way so as to drive them to "contrariety."

The latter similarity is where we also find a difference. I posited postures of incommensurability as deep dispositions that demand the release of violence, which is in some ways similar to the idea of identities *being driven* to contrariety. But in Monk, it is not clear how they come to be driven to contrariety, and at the very least, the drive is not directly linked back to violence itself. What this points to is a difference surrounding the question of the (un)knowability of violence. Instead of an emphasis on the elusiveness of violence, Monk understands this limitation of understanding, in light of his critical engagement with Gayatri Spivak's work, as "errancy" (Monk, 2002, p. 80). For Monk the alternative to the inability of the conflict to "account for itself to itself" is to reveal how historiography fails to express the immediacy of the conflict – or to privilege "the nonidentity that pervades each claim for the identity of history and its designated instantiations" (Monk, 2002, p. 131) – insisting throughout, though, that one cannot look at this "nonidentity" as the mark of what is true or authentic or real immediacy. The latter point directs Monk toward an important conclusion:

> A historiography of immediacy cannot culminate in transcendental perspective, as if in moving between the positions/accusations potentiated in monuments' inadequacy to the adequacy they represent, one is somehow deposited outside the conflict and above the fray.... A historiography of this conflict's logic of manifestations cannot offer anyone consolation in the certainty that language will always be the language of "false escapes" or, in other words, that when one points to the element of nonidentity that exerts itself from within claims for architecture's identity with history, one directly points to freedom in the play of language. Here, as indeterminacy takes solace in its own idea, it reverts to mere contingency. It begins to serve other ends. (2002, pp. 131–132)

Instead of a search for a redemptive path through the inadequacy of current historiography, Monk asserts that we must acknowledge "that the promise of another, reconciled existence survives in our failure to articulate the impossibility of reconciling in this one" (2002, p. 132).

With the point on not equating non-identity with truth or immediacy, I agree, and I go back to Gadamer's point here that what escapes language is not the full truth or correct account of the thing, since the thing will always evade any total, full, or correct description in language. Therefore, I agree that we ought not to *mark the escape as an errancy that can be corrected by that which gives us the means to follow the escape.* I also share the need to remain vigilant against the possibility that a focus on the errancy, or as I prefer, the elusiveness of violence, could lead to an escape from, or worse, a blindness to, the ways in which our false sense of freedom from the messiness of the conflict (our transcendence of it) can be used for instrumental purposes by actors and/or conceptual paradigms that benefit from and continue the status quo. I share Monk's sensitivity to this possibility, but I do not believe that it is the only path toward which an emphasis on the elusiveness of violence can lead. In other words, and following Gadamer, I believe that beyond the limits of language is not necessarily the free play of language, but rather a continuous and constant chase after an elusive thing we call violence. And following Derrida, the free play of the sign should never be associated with a free or reconciled alternative to the status quo, but simply with an opening toward the infinite configuration and reconfiguration of signs that *may* open up alternative ways of being (again, the element of potentiality is crucial in Derrida and indeed Gadamer as well). Hence, I would never claim that the dialogical analytic offers a foolproof defence against the possibility of being used in unforeseen and undesirable ways whereby it "begins to serve other ends," as Monk puts it. But I am not sure that any scholarly attempt is immune to this possibility. But more to the point of where there is a difference from Monk, I think that there is a transformative potential to our understanding of violence when we chase it in its elusiveness – when we chase violence into hidden dimensions that I argue better explain violence and that can perhaps open up an opportunity for a more complete – not fully accurate, sufficient, or immediate, but simply more complete – accounting of the conflict. The elusiveness of violence in the fourth dimension is not necessarily an escape from the messiness of the case, because it must be linked back to the other observable dimensions – as that which both enables and unsettles them. The analysis in this chapter will indeed highlight some of the same insights as does Monk in accordance with the similarities listed above, but I also hope that it will show how an additional emphasis on the elusiveness of violence can add to our understanding of the violence in this case, wherein we point out not only the limitations or failures of representations, but also the hidden ways in which they come to be constituted in and through postures that demand the release of violence.

Needless to say, I cannot in this analysis discuss the Israeli–Palestinian conflict as a whole or cover all of its different aspects, and my analysis will be much more limited than Monk's wide-ranging and sustained analysis. Instead of examining as does Monk actors in, and interpreters of, the conflict, I focus only on two different and prominent kinds of scholarly representations of violence in the Israeli–Palestinian struggle as found in (a) the objectivist/instrumentalist work of Benny Morris and (b) the critical work of Edward Said. To go back to Kögler from the book's introduction, I will focus on the structure of preunderstanding that is found in these works, taking into account life history/experience, the symbolic order through which they understand violence (or, their mode of representation), and the power practices/structures that limit what can be said, understood, known. In this analysis, I show the manner in which violence the "thing itself" escapes these two representations of violence, and I begin to outline how the dynamic of violent dialogue reveals a certain kind of communion between the two sides (although not specifically between the two sets of texts), which is missed by both representations, albeit differently.

Before proceeding, there are two sources of justification for my choice of authors. First, these are certainly two very prominent and important thinkers in this broad field of study. One cannot undertake a serious analysis of the Palestinian–Israeli struggle without, at one point or another, having read and analysed (directly or indirectly) these two scholars. Thus, it makes sense that if one is to focus the analysis on one or two sources, then these scholars should be those sources. Second, the works of these scholars do not constitute the proverbial "straw person" that makes for an easy or straightforward analysis. It is indeed difficult to follow violence the "thing itself" and make the case for a dynamic of violent dialogue in these thinkers' writings. In Morris, it may seem simpler to follow violence the "thing itself" because he adopts an instrumentalist perspective and operates on a distinction between "legitimate/productive" and "illegitimate/destructive" violence, but this task is made more complex because Morris traverses the victim-persecutor perspective in a complex manner and shatters many of the deeply held mystifications of the Israeli state (i.e., this would have been a much easier task if I were to analyse the work of Alan Dershowitz instead). In Said, the dynamic of violent dialogue is indeed missing altogether, but this, I claim, is more reason to undertake an analysis that would be attentive to the dynamic of violent dialogue.

Finally, I wish to make clear that the choices are not driven by political considerations. I did not choose Morris as the separatist voice because I wish to paint the Israeli voice in general as separatist, nor did I choose Said as a conciliatory voice because I wish to paint the Palestinian voice in general as conciliatory. There are, and have been throughout the history of the conflict, numerous Israeli voices for conciliation (e.g., Ilan Pappé), as there are, and have been, Palestinian and Arab separatist voices (e.g., 'Abdel-Wahhab Kayyali', 1978) (see Hochberg, 2007, for an excellent study of Palestinian, Israeli, Palestinian-Israeli, and Arab-Jewish literary works that challenge the separatist imagination). However, Morris and Said simply offer the most fascinating and *complex* formulations of these two sets of voices, and this again is what has driven my choices, and not my wish to constitute either side of the struggle as purely separatist or as purely conciliatory. Indeed, this point should become clear in the following discussion.

I. Morris: Force, Fear, and the State

Morris's work illustrates how the representation of violence mimics the very violence that it seeks only to represent. What is unique is that Morris's mimicry occurs through a method of demystification that challenges and unravels some of the main tenets of the official Israeli state mythology, which, as is the case with other settler-colonial projects (see Coulthard, 2014, pp. 15–17), serve to hide Israel's settler-colonial roots (and indeed, as was discussed with Bourdieu and multiple authors in chapter 1, this is not unique to settler-colonial states, as every state seeks to hide the violence of its founding through founding mythologies). I will illustrate that the demystification works in such a way so as to support and further legitimize what Morris himself calls the colonizing project of Zionism. But in this very mimicry, I argue, the impossibility of Morris's representation – an impossibility he cannot grasp from within the confines of "objective" historiography – becomes visible in the figure of the expelled that reveals a mirroring of Jewish and Palestinian experiences of expulsion. I am not referring here to a reconciliatory potentiality that is found in Morris's text despite himself (akin to the way in which Monk finds a redemptive potentiality in some of the texts that he analyses), but to a hidden dynamic of mirroring that both enables and unsettles Morris's representation – a dynamic that can become visible only if we chase after violence the "thing itself."

These mimetic dynamics are ever present in Morris's classic work *The Birth of the Palestinian Refugee Problem Revisited* (2004) and his voluminous *Righteous Victims* (2001), especially as they pertain to the expulsion of roughly 700,000 Palestinian Arabs from their land and homes during 1947–49 (Morris, 2004, p. 588) (approximately 55 per cent of the Palestinian Arab population).[1] In terms of methodology, Morris asserts that his writing on the history of the Israeli-Palestinian conflict is concerned with (a) the uncovering of historical facts about what happened in specific events and (b) his objective presentation of these facts in a historical-scientific mode of representation. These facts are uncovered primarily in official state documents. His work utilizes, as its core building blocks, recently declassified information. For Morris, these documents constitute the most direct access to any given historical event that the historian wishes to present, study, and analyse, as they make up the archive of "real" historical data.[2] Morris's methodology thus places him in a more or less "classical" or "conventional" historiography[3] that prioritizes and centralizes both internal and external state documents in the analysis (e.g., declassified documents and public speeches, respectively).[4]

In Morris, the eye, ear, and tongue of the state are superior to all others. But what happens when Morris discovers that what declassified information reveals is that this all-knowing state is also a supreme liar? Morris is clearly aware of the discrepancy between state discourse (even after declassification) and the unfolding of historical events.

He is clearly aware that in its representation of historical events, the state will do everything it can to hide its more unpleasant or outright repulsive actions and plans. Yet he remains convinced that state documents remain the historian's best set of clues in uncovering how events "really" unfolded (Morris, 1995, pp. 60–61). Thus Morris's analysis foundationally sides with the state, or more properly with the legitimacy of the state, while at the same time his work questions and challenges state discourse (i.e., discourse that is promulgated by the state for public consumption).

In *The Birth*, Morris demystifies many of the state's official representations of the events that took place around 1948. The most important of these representations involves the so-called exodus[5] of thousands of Palestinians from the land that was to become the Land of Israel. The myths that official Israeli state discourse has promulgated over the years are varied, the most prominent of which are that the land was empty in the first place, there is no such thing as a Palestinian, the Arabs never wanted to negotiate for peace, all of the Israeli actions were carried out in self-defence, and the Israelis never committed egregious war crimes. In the first edition of the book in 1988, Morris argues that there did not exist any master plan or official policy of "transfer" in the Israeli government, despite his "uncovering"[6] of various atrocities committed by the Yishuv's[7] military forces during the war, which in some cases included forceful expulsion.

In the revisited edition, Morris somewhat shifts his position on the issue, and based on his analysis of new declassified information, he asserts that there were indeed many more acts of atrocities and war crimes committed by the Yishuv against Palestinian villagers, and these acts amounted to a pattern in the behaviour of the Jewish forces. Morris is more prepared to argue that even if transfer cannot be said to have been official government policy, it nevertheless was widely discussed among the leadership, and in some cases the army did indeed instruct its soldiers to expel the Palestinian inhabitants out of certain villages. Nonetheless, he maintains that there were also many more instances than previously thought by historians of Arab leaders encouraging the inhabitants to leave their villages well before the Yishuv forces arrived at the scene. Morris concludes from this that the "exodus" cannot be said to have been a direct result of some sort of pillar of Zionist policy that concerned the notion of transfer (Morris, 2004, pp. 5–7).

In Morris, the Zionist leadership was *undecided* on the question of transfer, but nonetheless the expulsion rendered itself a *necessity* in the unfolding of war. So even in challenging the image that the Israeli Defense Forces (IDF) had of itself as a morally upright and disciplined army, as well as the Israeli state's democratic and benevolent self-image in general, Morris's practice of demystification remains tied to a legitimating politics of the political, social, cultural, and religious order (i.e., the Israeli state) that emerged from the violences preceding and up to 1948, and the state's continuing violences beyond 1948. By presenting the expulsion as an *(undecided)necessity* – which is how (not)knowing manifests in this case, providing the first clue as to the avenue through which violence escapes Morris's representation – Morris manages to legitimize the Israeli state through texts that hide the battles of the past, not by building new myths around them, but rather by placing these battles firmly in our view, demystified and naturalized, objectified and fixed. His insistence on the legitimacy of the outcome of the conflict as a brute fact never wavers. All of Morris's representations of the 1948 atrocities and beyond, however graphic and however detailed, are ultimately representations that conceal and fix the violence in question within the rigidly bordered frame of "brute facts." To "free" the concept of violence and to speak with violence, I reiterate, have nothing to do with the presentation of gruesome details (and neither does hiding them). Rather, it is to break down the rigid boundaries around the concept of violence in order to examine what it is that violence can tell us about Morris's representation.

Anyone who is vaguely familiar with Zionism understands that land and demography are of crucial importance to the movement – the goal of Zionism is a Jewish majority inhabiting a Jewish land forming a Jewish state. Morris is much more than vaguely familiar with Zionism, and he fully understands the importance of the idea of a Jewish land for a Jewish majority to the most prominent Zionist leader arguably in history and certainly during the 1930s–1940s – David Ben-Gurion. In the beginning of his analysis, Morris writes,

> Ben-Gurion, a pragmatist, from 1937 on, was willing (at least outwardly) to accept partition and the establishment of a Jewish state in only part of the country. In effect, he remained committed to a vision of Jewish sovereignty over all of Palestine as the ultimate goal of Zionism, to be attained by stages. But in the course of 1947–1948, he resigned himself to the inevitability of Jewish sovereignty over only part of Palestine. (2004, p. 15)[8]

Morris understands that (a) Ben-Gurion's political, ideological, and ultimately military goal was to establish a Jewish state in all of Palestine, which meant that (b) there must be a Jewish majority inhabiting all of the land that is to become Jewish, which meant that (c) the native

Palestinian inhabitants must be transferred out of this land to make room for the Jewish majority. He also understands that (d) Ben-Gurion understood fully well the impossibility of full Jewish sovereignty over all of Palestine at that moment in 1947–48 (i.e., the impracticality of a full policy or program of transfer) because of a variety of international pressures, some internal differences within the Yishuv (I will come back to the conciliatory voices within the Yishuv later), and the resistance posed by the Palestinians and the surrounding Arab states. Seemingly, Morris grasps here the kind of "attain our ultimate goal through various stages and phases" approach of the Ben-Gurion government. He should seemingly have garnered the importance official state discourse assigned to remaining publicly silent on the matter of transfer because of its highly volatile effects (Masalha critiques Morris on these points as well; 2003, pp. 52–63). But this does not turn out to be the case in Morris's representation.

In the chapter that is dedicated to the question of transfer, Morris presents various quotes from a variety of Zionist leaders pre-1948 and shows the prevalence of "transfer thinking" throughout the Zionist movement. He cites how the Zionist leaders were wary of an outright expression of this thinking for a variety of political, strategic, and, for some on the left, moral reasons. However, he refuses to connect this explicitly stated intent toward secrecy on the issue of transfer with his inability to find policy documents that explicitly state a policy of transfer.[9] He thus concludes the chapter as such:

> My feeling is that the transfer thinking and near-consensus that emerged in the 1930s and early 1940s was not tantamount to pre-planning and did not issue in the production of a policy or master-plan of expulsion; the Yishuv and its military forces did not enter the 1948 War, *which was initiated by the Arab side*, with a policy or plan of expulsion. But transfer was inevitable and inbuilt into Zionism.... The transfer thinking that preceded the war contributed to the denouement by conditioning the Jewish population, political parties, military organisations and military and civilian leaderships for what transpired. Thinking about the possibilities of transfer in the 1930s and 1940s had prepared and conditioned hearts and minds for its implementation in the course of 1948 so that, as it occurred, few voiced protest or doubt; it was accepted as inevitable and natural by the bulk of the Jewish population. (2004, p. 60; emphasis added)

And in those necessary, inevitable, and natural respects, Morris accepts transfer as well.[10]

Morris argues that the "exodus" took place in four waves, each unique in its unfolding. For example, in the first wave, during the fighting between the Yishuv and the local Palestinian inhabitants from December 1947 until March 1948, much of the "flight" of the Arabs of Jerusalem (while not pre-planned, Morris affirms over and over again) was the result of "Jewish military attacks and fears of attack" (Morris, 2004, p. 125). Although inter-Palestinian conflict also contributed to the flight, the general state of fear created by Jewish attacks was the deciding factor. But for Morris such a factor is distinguished entirely from a policy of expulsion. He points out a few cases where military initiatives acted on their own in expelling certain villagers, but these, he argues, were indeed rare cases, and most of the refugees fled because of *fear* of attacks (Morris, 2004, pp. 138–139). Such actions, for Morris, are all too natural in the events of war and violence, and he urges us to distinguish them from intentional military and political policies.

I need not delve into Morris's discussion of all four waves, but the same pattern in Morris's representation can be discerned in all four. It is most glaringly revealed when he discusses the now widely known "Plan D" of the second wave (surrounding the Arab–Israeli war of April–June 1948). Morris writes:

> Plan D was not a political blueprint for the expulsion of Palestine's Arabs: It was governed by military considerations and geared to achieving military ends. But, given the nature of the war and the admixture of populations, securing the interior of the Jewish State and its borders in practice meant the depopulation and destruction of the villages that hosted the hostile militias and irregulars. (2004, p. 164)

Morris continuously distinguishes between official policy and the nature of war that required, for all intents and purposes, the expulsion of the Palestinians who in many cases Morris shows were not at all hostile militias and irregulars.[11] Morris then goes on to focus on the strong element of fear[12] as the major precipitator of Arab flight, as seen, for example, in the effects of the atrocious massacre that took place in the Arab village near Jerusalem, Deir Yassin (2004, pp. 237–240, 264–265; Morris, 2005). Morris's account of this massacre is quite telling of his mode of representation, and so worth a closer examination.

Morris situates the attack on Deir Yassin in the context of the period in which "Operation Nahshon" was launched by Ben-Gurion and the Haganah[13] (December 1947–March 1948), where there occurred a shift in the Jewish forces from a defensive police-like posture to a more offensive military posture (2004, p. 233). The operation was meant to secure the Tel Aviv–Jerusalem road by "taking control" of abandoned Arab villages and "intimidating" inhabited Arab villages that stood in the way of the so-called Jerusalem corridor (Morris, 2004, p. 234). Thus, "operation Nahshon was a strategic watershed, characterized by an intention and effort to clear a whole area, permanently, of hostile or potentially hostile villages" (Morris, 2004, p. 236). In the implementation of this operation, the distinction between uninhabited and empty villages did not truly exist, and "in practice, the Plan D provision to leave intact non-resisting villages was superceded by the decision to destroy villages in strategic areas or along crucial routes regardless of whether or not they were resisting" (Morris, 2004, p. 236). This operation opened the door for many like it to follow in April and May 1948 – for example, operations conducted by Palmah units (which were "fulltime 'shock companies' … established with British help in 1941" and were considered the elite part of the Haganah forces) (Morris, 2004, p. 16) continued on the track of occupying and demolishing villages (sometimes only partially demolishing them).

The climax of these operations came when a joint Irgun Zvai Leumi (IZL) and Lohamei Herut Yisrael (LHI) operation was launched in Deir Yassin.[14] This operation was "undertaken with the reluctant, qualified consent of the Haganah," which involved providing support with "Haganah machine-gunners from nearby Givat Shaul and two Palmah armoured car squads" (Morris, 2004, p. 237). It is important to also note that Deir Yassin "had signed a non-belligerency pact with its Jewish neighbours and repeatedly had barred entry to foreign irregulars. The operation loosely meshed with the Nahshon objective of securing the western approaches to Jerusalem" (Morris, 2004, p. 237).

Morris does not hold back in presenting the Deir Yassin atrocities. He presents testimonies from witnesses and perpetrators (but rarely from the victims or relatives of the victims) that describe in detail the gruesome nature of these atrocities.[15] So, for example, he cites Meir Pa'il, a Palmah intelligence officer:

In the quarry near Givat Shaul I saw the five Arabs they had paraded in the streets of the city. They had been murdered and were lying one on top of the other … I saw with my own eyes several families [that had been][16] murdered with their women, children and old people, their corpses were lying on top of each other.… Each dissident [IZL-LHI][17] walked about the village dirty with blood and proud of the number of persons he had killed. Their lack of education and intelligence as compared to our soldiers [i.e., the Haganah][18] was apparent. (Morris, 2004, p. 238)

Even more telling of Morris's insistent siding with the legitimacy of the state is that he is much more willing to engage in moral indignation and political delegitimization of the IZL and LHI operations – groups that he earlier labels as organizations guided by a mantle of "anti-British Jewish terrorism" (Morris, 2004, p. 12). Thus he presents, as I quoted him earlier, the Haganah support, which involved "machine-gunners" and Palmah "armoured car squads," as somehow constituting only "reluctant, qualified consent." Moreover, Morris outlines how these events (along with other atrocities) proved most beneficial for Ben-Gurion and the Haganah, as they "meshed with the Nahshon objective" and, more crucially, created a panic among the Arab population that led to the fleeing of many villagers even before the Haganah approached them (Morris, 2004, pp. 239–265). So in Morris, the Haganah and the Ben-Gurion government, who stood to benefit the most from these atrocities, are represented as involved only in the role of reluctant observers who "consented" by sending machine-gunners and armoured squad cars alongside "uneducated" and "unintelligent" right-wing extremists to massacre non-belligerent villagers. The fact that an entire village of nearly six hundred people that signed a non-belligerency pact with its Jewish neighbours was destroyed and a large number of its inhabitants massacred is represented in Morris, as it predominantly was in official state discourse, as simply an unfortunate part of the natural unfolding of war. But the transfer, Morris and official discourse insist, was not planned; it was left undecided.

So Morris reiterates in his conclusions on the second wave that "from the foregoing, it emerges that the main, second wave of the exodus, resulting in 250,000–300,000 refugees, was not the result of a general, predetermined Yishuv policy" (2004, p. 262). And even though "there is no evidence that the Arab states and the AHC [Arab Higher Committee][19] wanted a mass exodus or issued blanket orders or appeals to flee," Morris maintains that "the AHC and the Arab states often encouraged villagers (and, in some places, townspeople) to send women, children and old people out of harm's way," that "local political and military leaders also ordered some villages to evacuate in order to forestall their (treacherous) acceptance of Jewish rule," and that "in certain areas (around Jerusalem, and along the Syrian border), the Arab states ordered villages to uproot for strategic reasons" (Morris, 2004, p. 263). In Morris, such actions are not seen as efforts to protect civilians during a horrific war where many unarmed civilians had been killed, and he does not examine how the Arab leadership never viewed these evacuations as permanent. He barely even acknowledges that the Arab leadership was fractured and diffuse, that many villages were so isolated that they did not even have a radio through which to receive orders, and that a plan for mass evacuation would have been impossible to articulate let alone implement (Sayigh, 2007 [1979], pp. 62–64); in short, he never examines or considers seriously that what caused the Palestinian mass flight, as Rosemary Sayigh puts it, "was the fact that they found themselves attacked by organized violence on a scale far beyond their means to resist" (2007, p. 97). Instead, Morris includes the Arab states' and the AHC's behaviour as factors leading to the "exodus" and not as reactions against Jewish aggression. But even then, Morris has to conclude,

> Undoubtedly, as was understood by IDF intelligence, the most important single factor in the exodus of April-June was Jewish attack. This is demonstrated clearly by the fact that each exodus occurred during or in the immediate wake of military assault. No town was abandoned by the bulk of its population before the main Haganah\IZL assault. In the countryside, while many of the villages were abandoned during Haganah\IZL attacks and because of them, other villages were evacuated as a result of Jewish attacks on neighbouring villages or towns; they feared that they would be next. In general, Haganah operational orders for attacks on towns did not call for the expulsion or eviction of the civilian population. But from early April, operational orders for attacks on villages and clusters of villages more often than not called for the destruction of villages and, implicitly or explicitly, expulsion. (2004, p. 265)

We can see here how Morris wants to distinguish between the treatment of villages and the treatment of towns. And while it is apparent that such a distinction was operative in the thinking of the Yishuv leadership for mostly military reasons, this is not the main point I am concerned with. The main point here is that in making horrific representations, Morris is more interested in making the reader familiar with the fear of war than he is in presenting an account of the hidden dark side of Israel's emergence or a fully "objective" account of the war. Morris, once again, wants to assert that it was the "'atrocity factor' [that] played a major role in precipitating flight" (2004, p. 491). This is also evident in how Morris speaks of the refugee problem as the "main expression" of Arab defeat in the 1948 war (2004, p. 35). He constantly refers to the fact that the Arabs had lost the war (and various others to Israel) and that the refugee problem cannot be divorced from the fate of the vanquished in war (Morris, 2001, pp. 252–258). In other words, the side that loses in war naturally suffers the humiliation of the vanquished, which includes expulsion of populations and various atrocities of murder, rape, pillaging of public and private property, and so on; and this is all that his uncovered historical facts can tell us. These "facts" can never be challenged outside of Morris's "objective" and "scientific" mode of representation, since any such challenge, as far as Morris is concerned, constitutes an ideological attempt to alleviate the humiliation of defeat. Any counter-argument that may speak of injustice, for example, is for Morris mere propaganda that is driven by ideological intentions, as opposed to the cold hard facts of historical truth that Morris is solely preoccupied with in his role as a historian (Morris, 1991, pp. 98–104; also see Morris's debate with Joseph Massad in Massad, 2002, pp. 155–156, 162–165).

Morris simply cannot allow for a counter-argument to his thesis that would argue that the Israeli state did indeed engage in morally reprehensible actions such as transfer of populations, because such a counter-argument would be for Morris, first and foremost, an attempt to undercut the legitimacy of the state. But this legitimacy, as far as Morris is concerned, has been affirmed once and for all by virtue of the Yishuv's victory in the 1948 war. In emphasizing and naturalizing the elements of the will to life, force, fear, and sovereignty, Morris advances his form of legitimating politics.

The underlying theme in Morris's work postulates a contract that has been established on the basis of a relationship of sovereignty. It is a contract that is characterized by the series of "will, fear, and sovereignty," as Foucault so succinctly captures it under the contract-oppression schema of power discussed in chapter 1. Morris believes that the legitimacy of the Israeli state was established by (a) the forceful assertion of the state's existence (i.e., the Israeli state proved in war, in the relations of force, that it is a state); (b) the fear it inspired in its enemies, who ultimately chose life over death by fleeing rather than to stand firm and fight; and (c) the inability, through this choice, of these enemies to challenge the legitimacy of the state that granted them their wish for life and that on that account can be held accountable to them only to the extent that it does not oppress them, not to the extent that it ceases its rule over them, whether directly, as in the case of Israeli Arabs or Palestinians under occupation, or indirectly, as in the case of the refugees.

In Morris, then, violence is delimited within this space of war. In his representation, war is explained as an instrument that serves specific geopolitical purposes, plans, and goals; and, for him, the violences of the various atrocities and massacres cannot tell us anything about the nature of the interaction between the sides and/or about the sides themselves: these violences cannot even tell us anything about the geopolitical and ideological plans. These violences come to constitute in his representation simply the necessary outcome of a trend and sequence of events that emerged out of specific historical events and necessities. Morris shatters many of the long-held Yishuv and Israeli myths, but he must continuously conclude in accordance with the conclusion of the Israeli mythology itself: that war had bequeathed the Israeli state with a legitimacy to rule that cannot be challenged. Similar to Bernstein's critique of Schmittian appeals to hard "realism" against soft "idealist" notions of justice and my critique of such attempts to delimit violence, we find in this particular case that despite his claim of "objectivity," despite his focus on the legitimacy of the Israeli state that was "won" in war, despite his claim to represent violence beyond the scope of justice, what indeed holds Morris's account together is his conviction in the just cause of Zionism, in the idea that Zionism is the one and only redress and guardian for the righteous victim of history.

Whereas *The Birth* is concerned specifically with the refugee problem, Morris's (2001) *Righteous Victims* is more concerned with the supposed origins and continuations of the conflict in general, providing a window into the notion of justice that underpins Morris's historiography. In this book, it becomes clear how Morris's very writing repeats the violent mimetic structure that he studies. The following analysis shows how this mimetic structure of violence seeps into Morris's representation and is repeated in his work through (a) the manner in which Morris blurs the victim-persecutor distinction, at the same time that (b) Morris posits the Palestinian Arab, while a victim in many respects, as the force that sets in motion cycles of violence, thus (c) illustrating, by going back to Morris's (undecided)necessity, how violence escapes Morris's representation of violence and in the process reveals the operation of a dynamic of violent dialogue in Morris's very representation, which forges his representation in communion with its "other."

In two of the earlier chapters of *Righteous Victims*, detailing the events that took place in Palestine before, during, and after War World I, Morris discusses the different dimensions of Arab–Zionist relations. Though Morris points out that there were elements in each camp that were conciliatory in their approach toward the other side, he paints the overall and general positions of each side as antagonistic toward one another. So, for example, he cites the words of the Jerusalem Muslim dignitary Yusuf Diya al-Khalidi, who, in a letter to chief rabbi of France Zadok Kahn in 1899, expressed sympathy and support for the Jewish cause against European anti-Semitism and the pogroms, as well as the rights of the Jews in Palestine, at the same time that al-Khalidi made it clear in the letter that he did not approve of a Zionist entity that would displace and rule over the Arab inhabitants of the land (Morris,

2001, p. 37). Morris highlights the element of fear again and argues, "The fear of territorial displacement and dispossession was to be the chief motor of Arab antagonism to Zionism down to 1948 (and indeed after 1967 as well)" (2001, p. 37). So despite some of the more conciliatory voices, Morris asserts that this fear always played the major role in Arab views, attitudes, and actions toward the Zionists (for another example, see Morris, 2001, p. 62). Even those Arabs who argued for an alliance between the two sides against Ottoman rule were marginalized, and the fear of losing the land overcame any such efforts at creating a common goal or any real alliance between the two sides (Morris, 2001, p. 65). On the side of the Zionists, Morris discusses, for example, a lecture by Yitzhak Epstein – a Palestinian Jew – who in 1896 argued against a separatist Zionism that ignored the "Arab question" in its efforts to establish a Zionist state that would not include the Arab population and would indeed be in direct conflict with the Arab population (Morris, 2001, p. 57). Morris also highlights the marginality of voices such as Epstein's and discusses the contemptuous view that new Jewish settlers held toward the local Arab inhabitants. He even likens this view to the one European colonists held toward colonized native populations across the world (Morris, 2001, pp. 42–45, 58–59, 61). Regardless of these attitudes, Morris asserts that the chief cause of violence was always the two sides' goal of establishing their respective homelands on the very same land:

> But the major cause of tension and violence throughout the period 1882–1914 was not accidents, misunderstandings, or the attitudes and behaviors of either side, but objective historical conditions and the conflicting interests and goals of the two populations. The Arabs sought instinctively to retain the Arab and Muslim character of the region and to maintain their position as its rightful inhabitants; the Zionists sought radically to change the status quo, buy as much land as possible, settle on it, and eventually turn an Arab-populated country into a Jewish homeland. For decades the Zionists tried to camouflage their real aspirations, for fear of angering the authorities and the Arabs. They were, however, certain of their aims and of the means needed to achieve them. (2001, p. 49)[20]

After World War I, this conflict over land became ever clearer with the expansion of Jewish settlements, neighbourhoods, land purchases, and the advancement of ideas and practices of "Hebrew labour" (to name some of the more prominent factors), and consequently conciliatory voices began to be replaced with violent voices. At this point, Morris begins to describe the course of events that marks for him the "first

Palestinian troubles" (2001, p. 88). While Morris begins this section by highlighting "anti-Zionist activism [that] stopped short of violence" (2001, p. 90), and while he mentions the Zionist leadership's framing of the Jewish–Arab relations as a zero-sum game (2001, p. 91), and finally, while he discusses the eruption of a few violent events in the North (the Galilee Panhandle) (2001, pp. 92–93), for Morris, "the focus of Arab violence against the Jews in 1920 was to be Jerusalem" (2001, p. 94). The actions of the Arab "mob" in Jerusalem in 1920 become for Morris the "first" trouble, even though he showed earlier in the book that this is not literally or empirically the case (e.g., 2001, pp. 50–66). Nevertheless, Morris has located his "origin" in the violent actions of the "mob," which spanned three days of "rioting" in Jerusalem.[21]

He describes these riots beginning with how the orthodox Muslims of Hebron as well as Arabs from other towns and villages surrounding Jerusalem (which included among them some Christians as well) poured into the Old City of Jerusalem, chanted "We will drink the blood of the Jews," clubbed a British military personnel to death, destroyed and vandalized Jewish shops, property, and synagogues, killed six Jews, raped a number of Jews, and injured more than two hundred Jews (Morris, 2001, pp. 95–97). Morris adds, "Several Arabs were also killed and dozens injured by British troops and police and by Jewish defenders" (2001, p. 96). In passing, he also mentions how some Arabs defended and protected their Jewish neighbours (Morris, 2001, 96). But these last two points are downplayed in Morris's account since they do not fit into his legitimating discourse of the Israeli state, and instead he emphasizes what he understands as these incidents' basic political lessons. In this respect, Morris's representation follows the figuration of violence as a "pogrom" and falls into the repetition of the conflict over the name of violence critiqued by Monk (2002).

Morris asserts that these violent events in Jerusalem signalled a few important turning points in the history of the conflict, namely (a) the solidification in the minds of Palestinian Arabs the idea of a Palestinian nation that would not be simply a southern province of Syria, but a nation in its own right that must be defended from the Zionist enterprise, and (b) the confirmation in the minds of the Yishuv of the native Arabs' hostile disposition toward the Zionist enterprise, and thus the necessity of strengthening the defence of Zionism as Jewish control over the land advanced into the ultimate goal of Jewish statehood. Accordingly, when Morris ends this section, he mentions how this second point dealt a blow to the idea that Zionism would be welcomed by the Arab inhabitants of Palestine by virtue of the "civilization" and "prosperity" it would bring to the Arabs, as the confirmation of native

Arab hostility challenged the notion that the violence was being orchestrated by a few "criminals" or a few envious effendis (notables) who were not benefitting from Jewish capital. Rather, it became clear that the majority within the Zionist leadership was right all along in that the violence very much emerged from the poor and difficult political and social conditions that were widespread among the Arab population – conditions that were a direct result of massive Jewish immigration.

Yet Morris discusses how some Zionists fought for the idea of a benevolent Zionism to the bitter end, and he specifically points out Chaim Margaliut Kalvaryski, who continued his "conciliatory" work (which mainly involved providing capital) at the "grassroots" level, "which included a mixed Jewish-Arab school ... and bribes to editors and writers to plant pro-Zionist articles in the Arab press" (Morris, 2001, p. 105). Kalvaryski's efforts, however, came up short, as Arab membership in his clubs and associations never fully materialized. I will quote at length what Morris concludes from this:

> The consistent failure of dialogue and rapprochement had a variety of causes. One problem was that the Zionist officials involved usually regarded their own activities with ambivalence, seeing links with Arabs both as attempts at conciliation and as the cultivation of sources of information.... Kalvaryski embodied this ambivalence: The main advocate of dialogue and accommodation, he was also a key Yishuv intelligence officer.... A more important obstacle to peacemaking was the reluctance of the Zionist establishment to back it. Most leaders felt that there were more important things to do with their time and resources, such as organizing immigration, establishing settlements, and buying land. *But without doubt the main obstacle was the reluctance of the Arab leadership to join in sincere and open, or even covert, dialogue.* None of the peace contacts during the 1920s appears to have been initiated by Arabs. All or nearly all Arabs sought not coexistence but the Yishuv's disappearance. (2001, p. 106; emphasis added)

And without any sense of irony or a moment of reflection, Morris moves into his next section for the period 1921–29 with this quote: "Given the absence of 'troubles,' [in this period] the Yishuv could simply ignore the Arabs and the threat they posed" (2001, p. 106). There is no effort here on the part of Morris to question the Yishuv's intent to conciliate with the Arabs. That is, Morris never interrogates the idea that if the Yishuv could continue their economic, political, and social development separately and exclusive of Arabs, then that would be their first option and indeed primary goal. Only when there were "troubles" did the Yishuv "reach out" to the Arabs in a "conciliatory" approach that Morris has showed was "ambivalent" at the very best. I find it hard to accept that "ambivalence" is the appropriate word to use in this case, since a key intelligence officer undertook the work of "conciliation." Kalvaryski certainly does not sound conciliatory at all when counterposed with Epstein.

Most importantly, despite all of the documents he uncovers, despite his honest presentation of his findings in the sense of not cleansing their repulsive language or their accounts of repulsive behaviour, Morris must always place the ultimate blame on the Arabs, and he thus continuously concludes in accordance with the conclusion of the Israeli mythology itself. If he does not, then he risks the dilution of the distinction between the "illegitimate" and "destructive" violence of "terrorists" that sets in motion cycles of violence and the "legitimate" and "productive" violence of the state. And any such dilution would put into question the legitimacy of that which emerged out of the distinction itself (i.e., the Israeli state).

Morris's demystification is fundamentally accomplished with a blurring of the line between victim and persecutor and then the consequent reaffirmation of that line by the concept of the *righteous* victim. In other words, Morris's "objective history" is based on an ideal of righteousness. He first presents a narrative of a victim (the Jew in anti-Semitic Europe) turned persecutor who is sometimes victimized and sometimes persecutes a persecutor (the Arab, who resembled the European anti-Semite for the first Jewish settlers; e.g., see Morris, 2001, pp. 25–26) who turned victim: throughout the narrative, the terms "victim" and "persecutor" turn into floating signifiers that can be applied in different ways to different sides and sometimes to all sides simultaneously. This can be seen in the following quote regarding the conditions post-1967 and the Israeli occupation of the Palestinian territories:

> Until 1987 Israel proved easily able to control the Palestinian population of the West Bank and Gaza. But it could not staunch either their nationalism or international pressures to alleviate their plight. At the same time, controlling the territories subverted Israel's democratic and legal norms and increasingly fissured society along bitter fault lines. An even more militant, annexationist, racist right wing came to the fore and increasingly determined government policy and behavior. Ultimately, the thrust of Israeli policy and the weight of the occupier's boot were to give rise among the conquered population to powerful fundamentalist Muslim currents – in various ways mirroring developments among Israel's Jews – which were subsequently to mount serious challenges to moderate opinions and

parties. To some degree, the growth of Palestinian guerrilla and terrorist activity against Israel was a response not just to the occupation, which involved daily humiliation of the population by the occupiers, but also to the annexationist spirit that had laid hold of the Israeli polity. (2001, p. 386)

Here we find Israeli Jews who have transformed from victim to persecutor at the same time that they have victimized themselves in the process (i.e., through the bitter fault lines that fissured Israeli society) and victimized Palestinians who are in the process of transforming themselves from victim to persecutor (i.e., "terrorists"), which returns the Israeli Jews back to the status of victim and/or potential victim, and so on. Indeed, in reading *Righteous Victims*, one is left wondering who the "righteous victim" is, since both Palestinians and Jews occupy the place of the victim at different points. However, Morris leaves little room for manoeuvre on the question of who sets in motion cycles of violence. In his concluding chapter, Morris begins by presenting Ben-Gurion's famous quote:

In 1938, against the backdrop of the Arab rebellion against the Mandate, David Ben-Gurion told the Political Committee of Mapai [later to become Israel's Labor Party]: "When we say that the Arabs are the aggressors and we defend ourselves – that is only half the truth. As regards our security and life we defend ourselves.... But the fighting is only one aspect of the conflict, which is in its essence a political one. And politically we are the aggressors and they defend themselves." (2001, p. 676)

Morris agrees with Ben-Gurion's assessment and asserts, "Zionism was a colonizing and expansionist ideology and movement" (Morris, 2001, p. 676). Morris also believes that the language of force, or "the successive displays of persuasive force," often used throughout the history of the conflict by all sides (whether Yishuv or later Israel, whether Arab states or the Palestinians), has "made both peoples sit up and contemplate a future of coexistence without violence" (2001, p. 693). But ultimately, Morris argues that the Zionist story is one of miraculous success and that the Israeli state is the historical and physical emergence and manifestation of a seemingly improbable idea that was born in the midst of the anti-Semitism and pogroms of Europe (particularly Eastern Europe). And the decisive success of this manifestation has yet to be secured because there is something called a "Palestinian" that has stood in its way from the moment of this idea's inception. The very last sentence of the book reads as follows: "If there is one thing that the past teaches, it is this: That *Palestinian violence has repeatedly helped trigger full-scale Israeli-Arab wars*; and that the region is prone to slide into these wars despite the wishes of its states' leaders" (2001, p. 694; emphasis added).

In Morris, despite the fact that both Palestinian and Jew can be called victims in relation to different times and spaces, there can be only one "righteous victim," and in the end, because the Palestinian sets in motion cycles of violence, this "righteous victim" can be only the Israeli Jew. The expelled Palestinian, even though a victim, must therefore be continuously expelled so as to ensure the existence of the righteous victim. The Israeli Jew's attempt to continuously expel the Palestinian, however, ultimately fails since the figure of the expelled Palestinian cannot but linger behind, and indeed comes to form the possibility and impossibility of Morris's representation.

When Morris posits the "atrocity factor" as the major precipitator of flight and claims that the flight was not pre-planned and orchestrated, he fails to grasp all of what he knows in knowing that the expulsion was necessary at the same that it was undecided: that is, in knowing, (not) knowing – in knowing (undecided)necessity in this case. To reiterate, in Morris, the expulsion was necessary because the ultimate goal of the Zionist movement could be realized only with a Jewish majority inhabiting an already inhabited land, thus pitting the two sides against one another in a zero-sum game: destroy in order to gain the land *and* the demographic majority in it, or be destroyed. It was undecided because the Zionist leadership (as far as the documents available are concerned) never drew up a master plan for expulsion, even if it was understood from the time of Herzl (and even prior to Herzl) that such an expulsion was part and parcel of the necessity for a Zionist victory and the realization of the Zionist dream (Morris, 2001, pp. 49–50). It is helpful to see how Morris views these two points in the following exchange with the Israeli journalist Ari Shavit:

> SHAVIT: You went through an interesting process. You went to research Ben-Gurion and the Zionist establishment critically, but in the end you actually identify with them. You are as tough in your words as they were in their deeds.
>
> MORRIS: You may be right. Because I investigated the conflict in depth, I was forced to cope with the in-depth questions that those people coped with. I understood the problematic character of the situation they faced and maybe I adopted part of their universes of concepts. But I do not identify with Ben-Gurion. I think he made a serious historical mistake in 1948. Even though he understood the demographic issue and the need

to establish a Jewish state without a large Arab minority, he got cold feet during the war. In the end, he faltered.

SHAVIT: I'm not sure I understand. Are you saying that Ben-Gurion erred in expelling too few Arabs?

MORRIS: If he was already engaged in expulsion, maybe he should have done a complete job…. My feeling is that this place would be quieter and know less suffering if the matter had been resolved once and for all…. If he had carried out a full expulsion – rather than a partial one – he would have stabilized the State of Israel for generations.

SHAVIT: In his place, would you have expelled them all? All the Arabs in the country?

MORRIS: But I am not a statesman. I do not put myself in his place. But as an historian, I assert that a mistake was made here. Yes. The non-completion of the transfer was a mistake.

SHAVIT: And today? Do you advocate a transfer today?

MORRIS: If you are asking me whether I support the transfer and expulsion of the Arabs from the West Bank, Gaza and perhaps even from Galilee and the Triangle, I say not at this moment. I am not willing to be a partner to that act. In the present circumstances it is neither moral nor realistic…. But I am ready to tell you that in other circumstances, apocalyptic ones, which are liable to be realized in five or ten years, I can see expulsions…. They may even be essential. (Shavit, 2004)

In this exchange between Morris and Shavit, along with the textual materials already presented, we can see how violence escapes his signification of the 1948 war and its waves of expulsions. Violence is "over-there" in the past beyond us at the same time that it is what binds Morris to the very conditions in which he finds himself today as an Israeli Jew: i.e., this is where Morris posits the (undecided)necessity of the expulsion as (a) final or complete in the sense that Morris believes the Palestinian right of return is out of the question, and as (b) at least satisfactorily protective of the Israeli state in the sense that a partial expulsion, while not fully sufficient, is still a better source of security than no expulsion. Violence "is-not" in so far as it is unthinkable for Morris to take part in or to even witness an expulsion in the present (barring an apocalyptic event – an unknowable and unthinkable event in its own right, even if perceived as "predictable" [i.e., Morris estimates its arrival in five to ten years]): that is, this is where Morris posits the (undecided)necessity of the expulsion as (c) hidden from view and covered over in the sense that there is no explicit state document that directly states the expulsion as official policy, and as (d) hyperpoliticized in the sense that the Palestinian articulation of the expulsion is delegitimized in Morris as mere "propaganda." In all of these depictions, violence escapes Morris's very representation via his refusal to authenticate the Palestinian experience of all of these circumstances, and in the process violence, the thing copied, transforms Morris's representation, showing a dynamic of violent dialogue.

The transformation on a political level can be seen and garnered from the exchange above, most notably in Morris's disposition toward the Ben-Gurion government: Morris is at first critical of Ben-Gurion's government for ensconcing the 1948 war in myth; he then begins to identify with the reasons behind various atrocities committed during the war and with the justifications for hiding these atrocities from the public; and finally Morris becomes once again critical of Ben-Gurion's government but this time for not finishing or completing the task of transfer. This transformation toward a violent view is very telling indeed, but the transformation I am speaking about is most interestingly and most significantly seen in the violent dialogue that Morris adopts from the documents he studies.

In his interview with Shavit cited above, Morris talks about the unfinished task of transfer, the rigid identities of each side that will never coexist, the naturalness of war and war crimes, the inevitability of conflict, the indomitable power of the state, the effectiveness and necessity of the language of force when the "civilized" European Jews are faced with the "barbarian" Arabs and their "very sick society," and the neutral observer who objectively reports on events that cannot be challenged by a force that is outside of the state (Shavit, 2004). Although to be fair to Morris, he does not always refer to Palestinians as "barbarians." He does at one point state that Palestinians are like "a wild animal … that has to be locked up in one way or another," preferably in "something like a cage [which] has to be built for them" (Shavit, 2004).

Morris cannot see the Palestinian experience of the expulsion because his communion with the "other" as an enemy prevents him from authenticating the "other" story. His representation reaches its limits at the shouting match between the participants – this is precisely where violent dialogue substitutes for the (un)knowability of violence, and where Morris begins to speak of things such as an unfinished task of transfer, the barbarians, etcetera, but it is also and more importantly the point where Morris forges his very representation in communion with its "other": the very same "other" who Morris tells us has no historians, no oral histories, no legitimacy, no authenticity, but only propagandists, constitutes, in Morris's writing, the possibility (via their expulsion) and the impossibility (via their actual and potential "treachery," "terrorism," and "murderous revenge") of the Israeli state that Morris wants to defend and uphold. His call for more violence indeed forges an Israeli state with its "other": an Israeli state that is simultaneously made possible and impossible with its Palestinian "other" (e.g., impossible because of the Palestinian who cannot be completely eradicated and possible because the Palestinian can be at least partially expelled). This is precisely the transformation I am exploring, and it comes in the form of a communion that paradoxically occurs in violence and in representations that repeat the mimetic structure of violence, even if (and perhaps, *especially* if) this violence is represented as a zero-sum game. So what does this communion look like in Morris?

Morris's representation wants to expel the other in order to secure itself.[22] That is why he must delegitimize the Palestinian experience and cast it as propaganda and/or "unscientific." But when Morris refuses to authenticate the Palestinian experience of the expulsion, he does not secure an absolute separation from the expelled, but instead reveals an indivisible relationship, a communion, with the expelled. The figure of the expelled cannot but remain ever present in Morris's discourse as a barbarian (the anti-civilization figure), terrorist (the figure of destructive violence that sets in motion cycles of violence), and victim (of Israeli productive violence that ends cycles of violence). In all of these respects, the figure of the expelled makes intelligible Morris's historiography on three levels. This figure makes possible Morris's understanding of (1) Zionism since it is understood primarily as the negation of Palestinians (the *necessary* zero-sum battle against the barbarian/terrorist), and of (2) the Israeli state, which is constructed as the only guard against Palestinian violence (the legislative and executive body that is *undecided* on how to deal with the violence of its victim/terrorist). These two levels, then, constitute Morris's mimicry of colonial violence in its desire to expel and continue expelling the Palestinian "other."

The third level is the most complex, as it reveals how the figure of the expelled Palestinian also simultaneously becomes the very impossibility of Morris's representation and of the Israeli state in his representation. The expelled remains within Morris's discourse as that which mirrors the Jewish experience of expulsion (and vice versa). This Jewish experience constantly asks the question of justice in Morris – that is, it brings to the fore the righteous victim that ultimately justifies and establishes the legitimacy of the Zionist project. And likewise, so can and does – to ask the question of justice – the mirror of the Palestinian experience of expulsion. The Palestinian experience of the expulsion, in its continuous challenge to the expellers' actions/programs/narratives, constantly demands justice, which threatens to unmask the veneer of objectivity and thus break open the rigid boundaries that

Morris's representation erects around the violences of 1948. Despite all his efforts to separate, once and for all, the expeller from the expelled, the figure of the expelled remains since it is what makes the historiography intelligible on those three levels and can thus constantly threaten to unravel the historiography from within. This is why the mirroring does not constitute a potentiality within his text but rather a hidden dynamic that is operative in his representation.

Critical in this third level is the complete absence of the massacred people in Morris's understanding of the expulsion.[23] The absence of the voice of the dead bodies "lying on top of each other" in the events themselves is replicated and repeated in Morris's account. Far from "objective," his representation simply repeats the crux of the official representation, which is to silence the unwanted body by death, to try to keep the voices of the dead forever silent, and to delegitimatize all of the voices emanating from the survivors and from the descendants of the dead. But these voices cannot be so simply ignored or brushed aside, as I argued in chapter 1, since they can always be discerned in Morris's representation, particularly in what it cannot grasp from within the confines of its historiography: that is, the mirroring of Jewish and Palestinian experiences of expulsion. Four elements constitute this mirroring: (1) the expulsion can never be final or complete, (2) it can never guard the expellers from the expelled once and for all, (3) it can never allow the expellers to hide the expulsion from themselves, and finally (4) the expulsion can never ensure that the expelled will cease to remember the expulsion.

Crucially, all of these elements are already found in Morris's discourse, as he is fully aware of them in his understanding of the Zionist project and the Jewish experience of the expulsion as it relates to both Palestinian and Jewish communities. From within the Zionist perspective, Morris knows the impossibility of a final and complete expulsion – this can be seen when he talks about the "connection between the Jews of today and the Jews who lived in the land of Israel 2,000 years ago," from which they were expelled and to which they now "return" (Morris in Massad, 2002, p. 164); Morris knows the impossibility of an expulsion that would guard the expellers from the expelled once and for all – this can be seen when he talks about the effects of the expulsion of Palestinians on Israeli society, particularly in how "controlling the territories subverted Israel's democratic and legal norms and increasingly fissured society along bitter fault lines" (Morris, 2001, p. 386); Morris knows the impossibility of hiding the expulsion from the expellers – this can be seen in Morris's own practice of demystification; and finally, Morris knows the impossibility of forcing the expelled to forget the expulsion – this can be seen when Morris talks about the effects of European anti-Semitism and the pogroms in Eastern Europe on the thinking and actions of early Zionist leaders.

Moreover, Morris even grasps these elements in terms of how the Zionist leadership misjudged them. For example, he presents us with various international forces that placed a number of limitations on the Zionist leadership's ability to exercise a complete transfer. He is well aware of the various implications and consequences of the expulsion for Israeli society and of the continued resistance of the expelled and how both of these elements were never properly addressed by the Zionist leadership. And finally, Morris understands that in an "open" society, government secrets cannot remain completely hidden from the public forever. So Morris fully understands all of these shortcomings of the Zionist leadership and their inability to grasp all of these different elements of the (undecided)necessity of the expulsion. Yet he cannot grasp that his representation mimics these very same limitations, particularly when it comes to his position toward the Palestinian experience of the expulsion.

All of the elements above are in fact very visible and ever present in the Palestinian experience of the expulsion: the expulsion was never final or complete. Even as they have faced and continue to face tremendous obstacles and powerful forces, there remain significant numbers of Palestinians throughout the "Promised Land"; the expulsion never stopped the expelled from forming political organizations and even paramilitaries, and continuing its political resistance against the expeller (e.g., through the Palestine Liberation Organization); Palestinian historians (e.g., Walid Khalidi, 1984, 1992; Rashid Khalidi, 1997; and Nur Masalha, 2003), oral histories and museums (e.g., the Association for the Defense of the Rights of the Internally Displaced [ADRID] – see Boqa'i, 2005) have never ceased their challenge of the cover-up created by the expeller; and the continuation of such a challenge in the various forms of resistance and protest – political organization, art, summer camps that visit the demolished villages, and the famous handing down of keys of demolished homes from one generation to the next – all of these elements and more have not only kept the memory of the expulsion visible and permanent in the hearts and minds of the refugees and exiles in particular and Palestinians in general, and more generally still in various discourses within the international community, but also ensured that the expulsion would be deeply embedded into the heart of the Palestinian struggle.

So what prevents Morris from incorporating all of these elements on the Palestinian side into his representation of the conflict and of colonial violence? Why, when faced with these elements, does Morris simply proclaim "propaganda"? I do not believe that one can attribute the reason solely to Morris's xenophobia or racism (or use any other type of ad hominem argument); I believe that the answer is much more complex. My contention is that if Morris knows and understands these significant features of Zionist ideology and of the Zionist project, as well as its shortcomings and limitations, then it is not due to his understanding and study of a purely Jewish experience of expulsion and exile that is autonomously constructed from and independent of the Palestinian Arab experience of expulsion and exile. Morris's understanding of the ancient Jewish experience of expulsion is perhaps possible only because the expulsion of Palestinians, in both the history he has studied and the context in which he presently lives as an Israeli Jew, has made certain features of expulsion abundantly clear for him. It does not much matter which came first, chronologically speaking. If anything, one could strongly argue, I think, that the expulsion of Palestinians, not that of the ancient Jewish community, in the sense of the lived experience of the historian, is the primary anchor point, the primary referential point through which Morris understands and does not understand expulsion. Regardless, the mirroring of both experiences in the four elements that I have outlined is all that is significant. It is precisely the mirroring of Palestinian and Jewish experiences that makes Morris's representation possible at the same time that it constitutes the impossibility of his representation, since his representation rests on the expulsion and exclusion of Palestinian experiences and voices.

Morris cannot see the Palestinian experience of the expulsion because his communion with the other as an enemy prevents him from authenticating the other story and drives him to expel the Palestinian from his representation. What constitutes this drive, which is an important part of what I am attempting to add to scholarly analysis in addition to the important type of analysis provided by Monk, are postures of incommensurability that were forged in acts of violence – a process that is too complex for this limited analysis to venture into. But to all too briefly begin to outline one of these postures is to point out how mirroring comes to be constituted in Morris: mirroring itself becomes dangerous in this case since the mirror promises to reveal an uncomfortable and indeed devastating image – a mirror that would shatter not just the self-image of the one who holds it up but the mirror itself. Part of the posture of incommensurability in this case is to halt the pulling up of that mirror in the first place – to eradicate any attempt that would force one to pull up the mirror and face the shattering of the self and the mirror.

A brief example can illustrate how this posture operates in the indivisible relationship with the figure of the expelled. In the epigraph, Morris, after quoting from Ben-Gurion's diary, states how Ben-Gurion "literally arrived in the Promised Land on the back of an Arab." Ben-Gurion is disgusted by the clambering Arabs at the same time that they were the only possibility available for him to reach the Promised Land. But this is not simply a case of Ben-Gurion viewing the Arabs in purely utilitarian terms; rather, we can see, in Morris's representation of this incident, a communion of self-other who are and are-not with one another: we see a Ben-Gurion that cannot become possible without his condition of impossibility. His possibility as a free and sovereign Jew rests on his arrival to the Promised Land, his "return" there, even though he had never been there before; but this arrival is possible only because his condition of impossibility carries him there, because he could climb on the back of the Arab who has come from the Promised Land, where he lives, the very same land that Ben-Gurion must expel him from if Ben-Gurion is to announce his arrival in the full sense of the "return" as this concept was developed within Zionist ideology. What is most interesting here is not that Ben-Gurion is projecting onto the Arab what he wants to leave behind in Europe (a supposedly "weak" and "wandering" diasporic existence) or what he wants the Arab to be (uncivilized and disgusting natives; or the new anti-Semites); rather, the posture of incommensurability in this case prevents Ben-Gurion from seeing that the back of the Arab is literally carrying onto itself the burden that Ben-Gurion had come to be constituted as in the racist and anti-Semitic climate of Europe: it prevents Ben-Gurion from seeing that *the Jewish question was being transformed into the Palestinian question* (see Massad, 2006, 2013, for a deep/critical analysis of this transformation). This posture, which could very well have been forged in the violence of the pogroms (and hence why such an analysis is too large for this book) – this posture that prevents such a mirror from appearing is part of what then continuously produces and reproduces violent positions against the Arab.

II. Said: Violence and the Question of Justice

To reiterate, violent dialogue encompasses its participants within a communion that emerges from the participants' chase after the elusive subject matter of violence. This communion is marked by a complex interaction between mimesis and alterity in violent acts and in representations of violence that (trans)forms the participants. In violent dialogue is constituted a certain "other" as an enemy-sibling: that is, an enemy that comes to constitute the possibility and the impossibility of the "self." In other words, we are talking here about a communion with a certain "other" as an "enemy." I am not trying to turn the word "communion" on its head here and simply rebrand separation or irreconcilability with the word "communion"; rather, I am referring to the full depth of the word's meaning in the Gadamerian sense I discussed earlier, which indeed does not necessarily have to do with harmony and/or sameness. That is, I am speaking of a fusion of horizons around the subject matter of violence that joins two enemies in communion as enemy-siblings.

Said's mode of representation places the question of justice at the very forefront of its analysis – he very much wants to pull up that mirror – and this I argue further reveals how the notion of enemy-siblings comes to constitute the violent communion of self-other. In the introduction to *The Politics of Dispossession*, there is a quote that is very telling of Said's disposition as a writer. Referring to his general experience of writing about the plight of the Palestinian people in the United States in particular and the West in general, Said writes:

> I had to keep saying that Palestinians were not only the opponents and victims of Zionism, they also represented an alternative: This was what they embodied in fighting for the idea of Palestine, a non-exclusivist, secular, democratic, tolerant, and generally progressive ideology, not about colonizing and dispossessing people but about liberating them. I was always trying to abide by universalist principles and yet be concrete and critical at the same time. (Said, 1995, p. xix)

There are two points to highlight here. First, since this book draws heavily on Derrida's theory, it is worth noting that Derrida failed to present a comprehensive or penetrating critique of Zionism's exclusivist ethno-nationalism (Wise, 2009, pp. 45–74, 128). While Derrida's work can and does easily connect with the goals of a "non-exclusivist" and "democratic" ideology against colonization and displacement, his writing on the Israeli–Palestinian conflict fails to live up to such ideals (also see Massad, 2013). Regardless, as Wise himself puts it, this does not mean that we should not engage with Derrida's "many contributions to contemporary critical thought" (Wise, 2009, p. 188; also see Falk, 2013, for an analysis that uses some of Derrida's concepts to critically think about the Palestinian–Israeli struggle). Derrida's failings in this specific regard can be addressed if we turn to Said's sharper critical eye when it comes to the Israeli–Palestinian struggle, which brings up the second and more important point. Not only does Said's work bring to the forefront the victim's perspective, but he also views this perspective in the positive sense of what it offers: an alternative to the persecutor's perspective. Said understands fully well the potential for persecution within any text, including his own. In contrast to Girard's absolutist distinction between the texts of the victim and the texts of the persecutor, Said remains open to the possibility that we can all be victims and that we can all be persecutors at different times and sometimes simultaneously, and only our admission of this possibility can bind us together in a continuous collective battle against persecution and injustice. In other words, we find in Said a formulation of the victim-persecutor perspectives, not as a distinction between two absolutes separated by an abyss, but rather as an intertwinement of different perspectives. We can see in Said that it is as possible for the persecutor to turn victim as it is possible for the victim to turn persecutor. And this applies not only to the historical actors that are represented in the texts but also, as Said shows us, to the text itself (a historical actor in certain respects). The text itself can also be turned into a persecutor, even when it is avowedly written to account for the victim, or written for the sake of the victim, or even written by the victim. The worlds of victim and persecutor are not far apart but are indeed interwoven, and can be (and are indeed) traversed within one given text.

In this sense, the alternative world being offered is (a) not revealed by a non-human (or partially non-human) Word that keeps sending its message throughout history even when it is constantly being misinterpreted, (b) not pre-made and prepared for humans to simply walk into when they finally see the true path revealed by the Word, and (c) not absolute or final if and when it comes. This can be seen in how Said ends the above-mentioned introduction:

> My hope is that this book will be useful, first, in providing a record of twenty-five years [1969–94] of a Palestinian struggle that will continue for some time to come and, second, in reminding readers that the struggle over Palestine contains within it the elements of reconciliation between Jews and Palestinians. Both peoples have to feel that they can and must live together as equals – equals in rights, equals in history and suffering – before a real community between the two peoples will emerge. My ambition is not to stop working or trying to realize that dream but to press the case for reconciliation and equality in such a way as to reengage people again, to raise questions and provide answers, to keep principles and values in a very prominent place before us. (Said, 1995, p. xlviii)

There are a number of important elements in this quote, and they can be seen throughout the collection of essays that follow this introduction in part 1 (titled "Palestine and Palestinians") of the book: the rigorous author who does not cease their search for voices outside of the discourses of empire or discourses of liberation movements that hide or downplay the experiences of the victims (e.g., Said, 1995, pp. 38–42, 72, 84–86, 100–106, 171); the eye that never ceases its gaze toward justice despite the magnitude of the challenge posed by the powers and forces of oppression (e.g., Said, 1995, pp. 76–77); the importance of placing suffering and injustice at the forefront of the analysis (e.g., Said, 1995, pp. 68, 126–127, 174); the two peoples locked together in a conflict that makes it virtually impossible to separate them (e.g., Said, 1995, pp. 48–51, 123–124, 199); and the difficult yet necessary task of transformation from the state of one's being and into a state of becoming something other (i.e., the alternative to the world of violence and domination) (e.g., Said, 1995, pp. 4–23).

These elements can help explain Said's constant marginality and incessant questioning of not only the discourses of empire, but also discourses of liberation, including his own. Perhaps this incessant movement in Said can be best described in his own words that describe what he admired the most about Foucault's writing: "There is no such thing as being at home in his writing, neither for reader nor for writer" (Said, 2002a, p. 191). The force that sets this constant exilic movement in motion is a sense of justice that began to form early in Said's life and that was directly related to the onset of his exilic life in December 1947 with his family's "departure" from Jerusalem (Ayyash, 2010b).

Said is the first to admit that his life history does not compare to those of the thousands of Palestinian refugees and exiles. He comes from a wealthy family that sheltered him from the hardships and impossible conditions in which many Palestinian refugees found themselves, and in which many still find themselves today. Briefly, Said's family, like other wealthy families at the time, left Palestine with the impending 1948 war approaching. While such an experience was certainly not as harrowing – if that is the right word – as other experiences of exile, forced departure, and cases of expulsion (see Masalha, 1997; Morris, 2004; Pappé, 2007), these wealthy families suffered much in this ordeal. I am not trying to quantify or hierarchize suffering in this statement (and neither is Said), but like many Palestinians in the past and many Palestinians today, Said felt the need to drive this point across when discussing his own life history of exile (e.g., Said, 2002a, pp. 175–176).

His experience of this injustice continuously guides his representation of violence, a representation in which the dynamic of violent dialogue is missing, the main reason being that Said's fundamental disposition toward the violences of the 1948 war is one of caution and humility: or, Said is cautious of modes of representation that claim to know and understand this violence (whether this is done by historians, states, or liberation movements), and relatedly he is careful to articulate but not necessarily represent the voices of the expelled and the oppressed (Said, 2002a, p. 526). In both of these senses, Said accepts the evasiveness of violence without at the same time ignoring or avoiding it. Precisely because Said constitutes a conciliatory voice, precisely because he understands the difficulties of conceptualizing and writing violence, Said can point out that a communion between the two sides already exists (i.e., the two peoples locked together), *but he does not fully speak to what type of a communion this is*, which his very writing is a part of.

In other words, because we cannot find a dynamic of violent dialogue in his writing, Said's mode of representation misses the extent to which the constitution of the two sides as enemy-siblings forms through a communion around the subject matter of violence. Said's writing is opposed to the use of violence, but if we take into account the dynamic of violent dialogue, we consequently see that what Said's writing misses is that conciliatory voices are both outside *and* within the dynamic of violent dialogue.

In an interview with the Israeli journalist Ari Shavit, Said talks about himself as a "Jewish-Palestinian," the affinities he feels toward Jewish intellectuals (e.g., Theodor Adorno) who shared the exilic purview that Said found so fruitful, the injustice done to the victim, the similarities between Jewish and Palestinian experiences of victimhood and exile, the corruption of Palestinian leadership, the crimes of the Israeli state, the devoid notions of an unquestioned neutrality and objectivity, the prospects of coexistence, an end to hostility and violent conflict, a disposition toward the past that never forgets, and justice for all of the region's victims (Said, 2002b, pp. 443–458).

In this interview, Said disrupts our conventional understandings of the history of the conflict. He highlights the victims' perspective and the victims' role in the emergence of the Israeli state, as well the victims' continued repression in the emergence of a Palestinian Authority (PA) through the Oslo Accords, which never addressed the injustice done to the victims and were thus doomed to failure from the beginning. This interview is a succinct example of how Said constantly aims to establish something new in a manner that is attentive to the question of justice.

This is also in stark contrast to the work of Morris, who is all too willing to make what is demystified seem natural, inevitable, and as such legitimate. Morris constantly naturalizes what he finds – in his very austere, formal, and detached form of presentation, Morris makes it seem as if what he is presenting is in-itself detached, formal, and austere. That is, he presents socio-political historical "reality" as if it is really natural, as if it is really indifferent to the suffering of a child whose head is being broken by a stick, for example, and as if all a scholar can do is present this "reality" in a demystified form. Or, the demystified in Morris is equated with a reality that does not care for the suffering of people but is a reality that is simply natural (in the same sense that an earthquake is indifferent to the human suffering it leaves behind).

Said, on the other hand, denaturalizes "reality." For him, what took place in the past, what takes place in the present, and what may take place in the future are the product of a complex intertwinement of human intentions, will, and actions. For instance, in demystifying the power of the Israeli state, which so many commentators treat as a "natural" or brute fact, Said emphasizes the role of intention in early Zionist thinkers and ideological creators such as Herzl, the role of the will in early Zionist leaders such as Ben-Gurion, who never allowed certain unfavourable circumstances and conditions to slow down his advancement of Zionist goals, and the role of action in the various policies and manoeuvres, from town and city planning to vast agricultural developments, that early Zionist leaders undertook to realize the Zionist dream; the upshot for Said here is that Palestinians, Israelis, and activists from around the world who are yearning for peaceful coexistence cannot simply wait for a Messiah or for a miraculous Leader to come and save them, but must rather undertake an effort that matches that of the Zionists in order to achieve their goals and make their own history (e.g., see Said, 2001, pp. 193–199, 244–248).

In Said, then, the point is not simply to highlight that our world is human-made. The constructed nature of our world is not a discovery in and of itself but rather the beginning of a task toward gaining different kinds of knowledge, and the exploration of the possibilities of new and different intertwinements that may produce something new, something just. The point, in other words, concerns what we do with the knowledge we have of, on, about our shared world. The point is to continuously ask oneself the question of one's place in the ongoing history of this world: to be able to understand the world at the same time that we search for something new. To imagine the impossible with one foot firmly planted in the possible; or to understand the movement in human history from domination to domination, but at the same time to strive for something that may break this movement and begin a new kind of movement. This new kind of movement – this contrapuntal movement – would never stand still or rest at a final destination, for it is the movement itself that matters and not some final destination: "there is no home" in Said.

My claim here is that Said positions this new kind movement on the (un)knowability of the violences of the conflict, particularly the expulsion of the Palestinians in the 1948 war. The violences of the expulsion are "over-there" in the sense of beyond us at the same time that such violences *bind us to ourselves and to others*, and "are-not" in the sense that they are unrepresentable violences that mark the very injustice that prevents enemy-siblings from transforming themselves. The new kind of movement in Said, then, must directly face the injustices and build a new kind of partnership, which would take as its guide the cause of justice.

The expulsions in this case take a different form than they did in Morris: the (un)knowability of this violence is what makes the realization of the Israeli state possible (like in Morris, via the expulsion), at the same time that this (un)knowability (in that it is impossible to control and conceal this violence) constitutes the impossibility of the Israeli state *and* of any form of a Palestinian state that would not be attentive to the question of justice. This slight difference from Morris (which is in fact very large) makes the condition of impossibility productive in the sense that it can possibly lead to a new beginning of coexistence, as opposed to Morris's zero-sum game (whereby if Israel is impossible, then it is only because of the murderous revenge of the Palestinian state that desires to take its place).

Having said that, Said focuses on the positive productivity of the condition of impossibility (coexistence in one democratic state) at the expense of the negative productivity of the condition of impossibility (coexistence as enemy-siblings). As discussed in chapter 3, Said understands (alongside many historians and thinkers, of course) that violence has, throughout human history, brought different people together, and he thus constantly advocates a search for a new, just, and peaceful way of bringing people together in our contemporary world. What is missing, however, is a deeper understanding of exactly how people become locked together in violence and in what form. In the manner of this interlocking together in violence is found the main set of obstacles that stand in the way of a peaceful interlocking, whatever that may look like.

Gil Anidjar's (2003) *The Jew, the Arab: A History of the Enemy* moves closer to this latter point. In this work, Anidjar's most central challenge is to our understanding of "the possibility of hidden links and explicit associations" between Jews and Arabs, Europe and Arabs, and Europe and Jews (Anidjar, 2003, p. xvii). He unsettles the supposed dissociation in these different pairings and examines how the history of the enemy – which is an unwritten history and perhaps a history that cannot be written but whose absence can be pointed out in its effects by analyses like Anidjar's – constitutes a certain kind of difference and differentiation between the three elements of Europe, Jew, and Arab whereby the intertwinement of the elements cannot be detected in a straightforward, clear, or explicit fashion. Thus, Anidjar must foreground the ultimate difficulty of asking the question of "What is the enemy?" since the tendency of the concept of the "enemy" is to constantly draw away in the texts that he analyses and deconstructs (2003, pp. xxiii–xxiv). Anidjar points out that the identification of Europe on the basis of this withdrawal is always hidden, and in this process is found the naturalization of both Europe and its enemies, as well as the naturalization of their distance. Europe, in other words, *in and for* its very constitution, has rendered the history of the enemy an impossible one – a history that it hides from itself (thus hiding itself from itself) (2003, pp. xviii, xxii). Furthermore, Anidjar argues that at the basis of this constitution of Europe is a certain political theology: one that distinguishes between politics and religion and then reconfigures these distinct elements together in particular ways (2003, p. 53).

Anidjar outlines the constitutive elements of this political theology in his penetrating and rigorous reading of a variety of philosophical, political, and religious texts (from Augustine to Schmitt to Derrida, to name just a few). Anidjar maintains that the self-identification of Europe operates on a double figure of the enemy – or more precisely, an enemy that is double, whose two halves are distinct from one another in a specific way: "The Jew is the theological (and internal) enemy, whereas the Muslim is the political (and external) enemy" (Anidjar, 2003, p. 38). Much like the conventional Christian readings of the biblical texts, where the two sons of Abraham (Ishmael and Isaac) (and indeed the being-together of Abraham and Lot) cannot be brought together as a fraternity and symbiosis, Anidjar argues that the two poles of Europe's enemies must remain distinct and separate: "Two brothers – and between them war, the political and the theologico-political – two brothers thus provide the poles of an oscillation that never quite gathers as the 'Jew, the Arab,' the Arab Jew" (2003, p. 60). War and violence occupy the space in-between the enemies. Violence creates the distance between them, and in this distance it allows for the annulment of their brotherhood. Anidjar explores how this distance is maintained in the theologico-political, whereby even the potentiality of the brother's symbiosis (the Arab Jew) becomes an unbearable idea since it would threaten the self (Europe) with obliteration. I find Anidjar's argument convincing on the level of the theologico-political, where the distance is maintained and kept, but he leaves unexplored the following question: Does violence merely concern acts of war that create a distance that is in-between supposed enemies?

Anidjar begins his book with the following formulation concerning the question of violence and enmity: "Beyond a horridly all too familiar and inescapable 'cycle of violence,' what is it that maintains the distance and kindles the enmity between the Arab and the Jew?" (Anidjar, 2003, p. xiii). While Anidjar's direction of analysis is insightful and important, I do not wish to shelter the analysis under the notion of cyclical violence, which would prevent an examination of how enemy-siblings are formed together and in difference through violent dialogue. Such an examination essentially challenges the idea that distance and irreconcilability are the only marks of violence. Thus, like Anidjar, one of my goals is to ultimately denaturalize the idea of "natural enemies"; but unlike Anidjar, I do not view the space that is posited in-between them as a space that hides itself from itself behind acts of violence that predominantly separate, but rather focus on four-dimensional violence, whereby the intertwinement of the "sides" marks the operation of a violent dialogue that forms a violent communion between enemy-siblings out in the open, as it were – not at all hiding and not at all "in-between" – an intertwinement that is difficult to see because violence the "thing itself" is always difficult to see, difficult to represent, always possible and impossible at the same time. The reason that the concept of the "enemy" draws away is not a peculiarity within that concept per se, not the difficulty of naming the enemy and naming oneself; rather, it draws away because it belongs to a space of enemy-siblings, a space that is forged in violence, where violence the "thing itself," not the enemy, continuously and consistently draws away. There is no "in-between," not even in acts of violence, because there are no distinct "sides" in violence. Acts of violence create a dash between the "distinct" sides, rendering talk of their irreconcilability and absolute separation off the mark.

Whether in Said or Anidjar, in representations of violence where an attempt is made to move beyond the vortex of reciprocal violence, even when the dynamic of violent dialogue is missing in the writing itself, we can still see how the question of violence is intertwined with the kind of communion that forms around violent acts. When Said proclaims himself a "Jewish-Palestinian," he is to a certain extent moving beyond the vortex of violence (a conciliatory voice operating outside violent dialogue), but he is also doing so from a position that has already been formed and transformed in violent dialogue that joins enemy-siblings together, combining them with a seemingly simple dash, but a dash that is made possible in violence and whose impossibility is the very dynamic of violence that made it possible (conciliatory voices being within violent dialogue). Thus, conciliatory voices are always already situated within violent dialogue even as they simultaneously oppose and challenge it from a position that is, or at least strives to be, outside of the vortex of violence.

It is more important to examine how different voices in the struggle relate and/or do not relate to the dynamic of violent dialogue, as opposed to an analysis that wants to locate and verify an originary violence that is then posited as responsible for the continuation of violence (and this is why I would not present an argument against Morris where I place the originary violence in Zionist/Israeli hands). So, for instance, if indeed the conciliatory voices discussed in Morris, and exemplified in Said's very writing, were minor and inauthentic as Morris claims, they are far from insignificant because they ultimately reveal a mimetic function that is simultaneously operative outside *and* within the dynamic of violent dialogue. So instead of positing these voices as inauthentic dead ends that are in reality geared toward the goal of dominating the other participant, I argue that these voices are indeed engaged *with* the violent dialogue between the sides (as opposed to in or through the violent dialogue). They do not constitute a dialogue born of violent acts in the sense I earlier described, but they do reveal the mimetic function that was already forming around violent acts between the sides, without necessarily being able to speak to the type of communion that is formed between them.

This communion is marked by postures of incommensurability, which this analysis, again, cannot fully pursue. In this chapter, I argued that one such posture concerns the prevention of a mirroring of Jewish and Palestinian experiences of expulsion. In his representation, Morris prevents the mirror from appearing in the first place. Such a measure, I argued, ensures the (re)production of violent positions against the Palestinian experience and perspective in his writing. In contrast, Said pulls up such a mirror in his effort to counter separatist and violent representations. His representation attempts to move beyond violent dialogue at the same time that it remains situated within that dynamic in that Said's position has already been formed and transformed in a violent dialogue that joins the sides as enemy-siblings. Said's representation reveals the extent to which violence has irrevocably interlocked the sides. He highlights the interlocking and then emphasizes the suffering that both sides share for the sake of an alternative and progressive politics. In his opposition to violent dialogue, then, Said's writing reveals the depth of its mimetic operation. Utilizing the insights generated from writings such as Said's can allow analysts to garner the manner of the interlocking (in this case, the mirroring) and how that can help us understand not just a fruitful direction of just and peaceful praxis (the positive productivity of the condition of impossibility, as I referred to it earlier), but better comprehend how all of that which the sides share was/is/continues to be forged in violence and hence can also lead to the propagation of violence (the negative productivity of the condition of impossibility).

The mirroring posture is but one that is operative in the struggle, and I believe that other postures can be found only in detailed analysis of violent acts themselves. I do not believe that they can be found in an analysis of representations of violence alone. Such a task remains for a future project, as it would involve a continuous back-and-forth movement across acts and representations, detailing the ways in which postures of incommensurability form, manifesting themselves in both acts and representations across spatial and temporal points. And when we gain a fuller understanding of what these postures are and how they operate, then a potentiality opens up before us for countering and replacing them.

Conclusion

The dialogical analytic sets for itself the task of continuously engaging in a never-ending dialogue with the participants and commentators of violence. This dialogue has to be attentive to both the recurring themes and conceptions in the conversation over violence as well as the slight, subtle, and sometimes radical or extreme transformations in this conversation. The fact that this task is a continuous one makes it very difficult to present definitive or final conclusions. Having said that, key implications of the book's arguments can be summarized around five themes: (1) violence and extremism; (2) enemy-siblings; (3) power relations and the mystification of violence; (4) defining violence; (5) utilizing the dialogical analytic.

1. On violence and extremism: in its emphasis on the propagation of violence, the preceding analysis suggests that the unfolding of violent dialogue always moves the participants to an increasingly extreme position *and holds them there*. Social scientists often believe that societies living within a violent conflict for extended periods of time undergo a transformation toward more extremist views and actions, and this can certainly be the case. However, it is also important to keep in view the crucial point that the ebb and flow of this transformation is not the only point of analysis, certainly not the most important point. That is, it is not enough to simply point out the extremist elements in any given violent context, reduce the entire problem to those elements' beliefs/actions, and then assert that challenging/removing the extremists would resolve the problem of violence. It is crucial instead to examine this transformation toward extremism qua transformation. We are not dealing here with a modification of attitudes that can be combated and brought back to a middle-of-the-road normalcy, or back to a moderate position. Rather, we are confronted with a dynamic of violent dialogue that holds the participants within the extreme – on the edge of

violence – on a more fundamental level. Extremist views and attitudes can even seemingly disappear within this dynamic, but as long as the fundamental postures remain unchallenged, this seeming disappearance remains an illusion at best.

Violent dialogue can involve extreme positions, views, and actions, but these can vary in degree of extremism without necessarily signalling the end of violent dialogue. Moreover, analysts need not find a constant trend or movement toward more extremism in order to confirm the operation of violent dialogue. Such trends and patterns are important to study, analyse, and oppose, but they are not the key to resolving a violent communion, but simply one of the manifestations of violent dialogue. It is far too simple, and indeed inaccurate, to argue that extremists are the primary source of trouble in contexts of violence and that simply removing them would dissolve the violent communion.

2. On enemy-siblings: even if the protagonists claim that they are separated by an abyss, even if they claim that they will not negotiate with the other side, even if they claim that they are in a zero-sum battle to the death, what they cannot do is outrightly reject the other side from their midst, since violent dialogue has already created a certain kind of communion between them that makes it virtually impossible for them to claim that whatever conceptions they have of themselves or within themselves (e.g., of gender relations, ethnicity, race), of others (e.g., of cross-cultural relations), or of things (e.g., of cities, governments, nations) have not been shaped and transformed by their fight with each other. They are enemy-siblings – more than enemies and less than siblings, they are enemy-siblings that constitute the possibility and impossibility of one another. A dash is formed across the identities, but precisely how (or even whether) the dash between the conflicting terms is to be replaced or transformed or removed remains an open question. I have theorized that the dash itself has been and continues to be forged in violence – without understanding the extent to which this is the case, a different kind of dash, or no dash at all, will continue to be just out of reach. Regardless, the idea of an outright separation, of securing the identities as being exclusive of one another, is out of the question. It is out of the question since you can sooner convince enemy-siblings to briefly drop their weapons than you are likely to see them drop their conceptions of one another as "one" that makes and does not make the "other."

3. On power relations and the mystification of violence: this book does not deny that elites, governments, multi- and transnational corporations, and other powerful actors who are invested in the maintenance and expansion of status-quo power structures mystify violence

for their own benefit and narrow self-interest. They most certainly do. Multinational corporations, for example, will often intentionally call the devastating violence of resource extraction and labour exploitation in poor nations "job creation" or "development." Governments, for example, will intentionally call torture "information gathering," or deny their participation in the violent overthrow of a democratically elected regime, or deny their committing of war crimes, and so on. If they did not, historians would not so eagerly await the release of classified information! That such mystifications take place, and that they do occur with an intention to mystify behind the mystification, is I think a valid position to take, though I will stay out of the contentious question of how often the element of intentionality is present. Suffice it to say, social scientists must be alert to the possibility of such occurrences. But even in such cases, violence will always still evade the ability of the powerful actors to fully control it. Therefore, if evidence exists for an intention to mystify violence for the sake of maintaining/advancing/expanding/gaining power, analysts ought to detail that evidence along with an analysis of how violence still escapes those significations, and how that escape can reveal the ways in which violence transforms such elite and powerful actors *and their intentions* in ways they could not control or foresee. This is one of the points that I wanted to take from my earlier discussion of Bourdieu/Gadamer regarding the question of the misrecognition of the agents versus the evasiveness of the subject matter.

4. On defining violence: a definition of violence may be necessary, but it must always be viewed as provisional. I do not deny that a definition is needed at the outset of a study of violence, but it's a matter of how we approach the defining process itself. The definition ought not guide the analysis, but must rather be viewed as a provisional ground or starting point for the analysis, allowing the analyst to better situate their case of study and partially limiting it. But as the analysis proceeds, the analyst must remain open and fluid in terms of how they understand the violence under study. The definition shifts and moves in the case itself, so it must accordingly shift and move in the analysis and in the analytical process. For example, the building of roads, bridges, and walls can fall just as much under the definition of military violence as does the use of firearms, gunships, and tanks. Moreover, the former actions can occur just as much in the "cold" or "inactive" periods of a confrontation as they would during the "hot" or "active" periods of military campaigns.

Should the definition of violence be constructed as conclusive from the beginning and remain unchanged throughout, then the four-dimensional operation of violence will likely, though not necessarily, remain concealed. The reason that I leave room here for the possibility of a somewhat conclusive and unchanging definition is the potential of small, focused microanalyses of violence to explain the operation of four-dimensional violence while remaining within the confines of a very specific definition of violence. That is, focused analyses of one specific event of violence can be approached in such a way as to allow the analyst to extrapolate four-dimensional violence. There must remain fluidity in such cases, but here fluidity could be found in the very definition of violence used from the outset (i.e., an expansive definition that combines multiple aspects, such as "physical force," "language," "the use of architecture," "cultural genocide," and so on), or in how the analyst follows the elusiveness of violence in the definition provided. So long as the emphasis and attention of the analysis is placed on the elusiveness of violence, then a definition of violence will neither hold back the analysis from reaching for four-dimensional violence nor debilitate the analysis with an ever-expansive area of study.

5. On utilizing the dialogical analytic: in the study of specific cases of violent interactions, the dialogical analytic operates on two basic principles. The first is to always begin with the ways in which participants understand and conceive of their own violence. This concerns the protagonists' own understanding of the following, not at all unfamiliar or new, elements: (a) the political/social/cultural/economic landscape in which they find themselves (e.g., how protagonists situate themselves and formulate their strategic interests within a local/national/global landscape that either oppresses them, colonizes them, allows them to colonize others, marginalizes them, justifies their superiority over others, and so on); (b) the nature of their battle against the enemy (e.g., whether they conceive of the battle as strategic, existential, incidental, accidental); (c) the role of violence in achieving their instrumental goals (e.g., in guerilla-style warfare, small targeted attacks, large military campaigns, proxy wars, targeting the body of the enemy, targeting the soul of the enemy); and (d) the ideals upon which they draw to justify their use of violence (e.g., freedom, liberty, existence, democracy, anti-imperialism, communism, capitalism).

The second basic principle is to interpret further what escapes the protagonists' understanding of their own violence. This should not be accomplished from a Weberian-style distanced position, whereby the analyst declares a judgment on the protagonists' tactics, strategies, worldviews, ideals, and/or strategic interests from a supposedly neutral and rationalist perspective. The latter approach often adopts the stance of the "rational consultant" who seeks to offer a better way forward for either one of the protagonists to achieve their self-interest or strategic goals, or for both sides to reach a peaceful and mutually beneficial agreement. While such attempts, particularly the latter, are often laudable (especially in the literature of peace studies), this approach fails to capture the four-dimensional view of violence and the complexity of its operation. Instead, analysts ought to follow the evasiveness of violence and formulate how violence's escape from the protagonists' significations of violence comes to shape and mould some of their fundamental conceptions of themselves, the world, their position, and their very interaction with the supposedly separate and external enemy.

Both of these premises are captured in the modus operandi of the dialogical analytic, which is to follow violence whereby a perpetrator of violence acts without knowing what one knows in knowing, (not) knowing. The protagonists always provide the best set of clues as to where the analyst ought to follow violence, which is why understanding their actions from their own point of view is a crucial first step. It is only after that is understood that analysts can then determine how to interpret the violent acts themselves (suicide attacks, drone attacks, sexual violence, air campaigns, trench warfare, guerilla attacks, targeted assassinations, labour conditions, cultural genocide, oppressive/repressive legal structures, slavery, murderous ethnic cleansing, military occupation, cultural erasures of lived histories, etc.). In violent acts, analysts can begin to trace the four-dimensional operation of violence in terms of how instrumental goals are achieved and limited; in terms of the dispersal of violence across the social/political spectrum, where its containment becomes impossible; in terms of the operation of a violent dialogue that joins the protagonists together in communion as enemy-siblings; and in terms of how violence the "thing itself" evades all attempts at significations, wherein postures of incommensurability are forged in such a way as to demand the release of violence across temporal and spatial points.

Taken together, these analyses reveal that when postures of incommensurability are formed, violence becomes extremely difficult to oppose because it begins to shape fundamental conceptions such as, for quick and rather vague examples, time (e.g., time as always harkening back to a past injustice that requires redress) and space (e.g., space as an object to be violently captured/held/contained/owned). When postures of incommensurability take hold, they not only underpin the continuous appearance of incommensurable positions across spatial and temporal standpoints, but they indeed begin to underpin diplomatic and grassroots efforts at peace since they come to shape how the protagonists and the analysts come to understand the terms of the violence. And when the struggle for peace and justice is launched from such underpinnings, then it is lost before or as it begins. These postures must first be countered and deconstructed, understood and replaced, before we can have a legitimate chance to achieve something called peace and justice, the conceptions of which must come not necessarily with the intent of opposing violence qua violence, *but with the replacement of our conceptions of what the violences have come to constitute as "real."*

And these are perhaps the only somewhat conclusive set of statements that can be made by this book's analysis. The book certainly cannot answer some of the more common questions that seem to captivate various public intellectuals and commentators. I cannot conclusively state whether contemporary society and politics are moving toward more or less violence; I cannot conclusively state what violence makes of social and political actors qua actors; I cannot provide a step-by-step handbook for defeating, halting, or countering violence; and I most certainly cannot answer the most common question of why violence is sometimes resorted to in the "first" place. The fact that I cannot present conclusive statements on these questions and more is a consequence of one of the goals I set out to achieve, which was to propose an analytic that can account, in its very structure, for the flux or movement inherent to violence. My hope from the beginning was that the dialogical analytic's chase after four-dimensional violence would sufficiently introduce a movement that would always remain inherent to the analysis. At the same time, the analytic and that which it reveals – four-dimensional violence – become embedded within one another, and in the process violence is limited by the analytic to which it was always the guide.

Notes

Introduction

1 Following postcolonial scholars such as Gurminder K. Bhambra (2007),
   it is important to emphasize that colonialism and settler-colonialism,
   as systems and relations of conquest, domination, expulsion, and
   enslavement of peoples and forms of life, are part and parcel of modernity.
   In contrast to modernization theory, postmodern theory, and multiple
   modernities theories, Bhambra's analytic of "connected histories" posits
   that modernity is not to be viewed as being purely "European" but is
   rather to be "placed in a frame of interconnections, or networks, of peoples
   and places that transcend the boundaries established within the dominant
   approaches" (Bhambra, 2007, p. 152). Colonialism and settler-colonialism
   are here examined not as the so-called dark side of modernity, but as a
   historical experience that is integral to and constitutive of modernity.
   Thus I use the term "co-constitutive" in the sense that the social and
   political theories examined in this book are not a development of and for a
   "pure" Europe (away from the colony, as it were), but are always already
   interconnected with the (post)colony, decolonial resistance, revolutionary
   ideas, and practices of the colonized.

1. Instrumental Violence

1 Some of the materials in chapter 1, namely on Arendt, Fanon, Foucault,
   and Deleuze and Guattari, have appeared elsewhere (Ayyash, 2013).
2 In Arendt, "neither violence nor power is a natural phenomenon, that is,
   a manifestation of the life process; they belong to the political realm of
   human affairs whose essentially human quality is guaranteed by man's
   faculty of action, the ability to begin something new" (Arendt, 1969, p. 82).
   But having said that, "power is indeed of the essence of all government,

but violence is not" (Arendt, 1969, p. 51). This is why Arendt finds it crucial to say that power and violence are opposites and not simply different.

3 For a comprehensive overview of Arendt's qualifications on her instrumental view of violence, see Finlay (2009, pp. 29–30). Despite these qualifications, and despite the fact that Arendt is certainly not an instrumentalist thinker per se, her (re)conceptualization of violence, at least after the 1940s (see Birmingham, 2011, p. 12), remains instrumental.

4 As is the case with Arendt, Fanon's conceptualization of violence rests on some of his earlier works regarding the devastating effects of violence (Fanon, 1967 [1952]). While Fanon's sophisticated argument on the master–slave dialectic deserves closer analysis than can be allowed in this book (e.g., see Tamdgidi, 2007, for fruitful roads of inquiry that illuminate and draw on Fanon's multidimensional and complex view of human liberation), I maintain that Fanon's work does not adequately address the question of exactly how the violence of decolonization can be contained and its destructiveness avoided.

5 It should be noted that this mechanism also operates in Fanon's discussion on the cathartic or purifying role of violence (or the existential role of violence) in restoring the humanity of the colonized individual. I would not pose Fanon's existential view of violence as opposed to, or even as different from, the instrumental view of violence (e.g., see Kaempf, 2009). Kaempf rightly points out the importance of the existential dimension in Fanon, but I maintain that Fanon posits this as an existential *role* for violence that serves the purpose of catharsis or purification, and this would take place in Fanon within a productive-destructive distinction of violence.

6 For a similar argument, also see Mbembe (2003, p. 29). For an analysis of how the racialized and gendered modern colonial landscape, among other things, promotes instrumental conceptions of violence and as a result perpetuates structural and relational violences, see Philipose (2007).

7 Christopher Finlay (2009) makes a similar point, although his article focuses more so on the manner in which Arendt's thought is closer to Sorel's thought on violence, power, and politics than she would have us believe in *On Violence*. This, of course, does not mean that the different ways in which Arendt, Sorel, and Fanon theorize violence in instrumentalist terms are not important – Finlay clearly shows that they are (also see Wieviorka, 2009, pp. 23–24); however, my interest lies outside of the instrumentalist perspective altogether, and hence why I focus more so on the element of commonality and continuity as opposed to the differences.

8 I have argued this point in relation to Karl Von Clausewitz's *On War* in previous work (Ayyash, 2007, pp. 623–627).

9 Having said that, the classical social theorist Durkheim did fear that modern individualism and the complex division of labour in modern societies could lead to an upsurge in violence (Wieviorka, 2009, p. 16).

10 Björn Wittrock offers a similar attempt, but it too fails to convince. Wittrock advocates an approach that would view "war as a social phenomenon" that can challenge and breach "key assumptions of modernity," thus playing an important role in modernity's varied and multiple formations (Wittrock, 2001, pp. 64, 67–68). It, however, remains unclear how one can avoid positing violence and war as the basis of all social and political formations and relations, particularly when he advocates its inclusion in our understanding of modernity for the same reason as Joas (i.e., modernity is imbued with violence). There seems to be an element of blind faith in what Wittrock calls "the promissory notes" of modernity (defined as "conceptual origins of modernity … that have come to serve a constitutive role for institutional practices"; 2001, p. 67), which (even though they are being and can be breached by war and violence) can somehow serve to subordinate war and violence. He fails to address the connection between these promissory notes and violence. The following passage seems telling of how Wittrock views this: after discussing the increased spread of low-technology means of destruction around the poorer regions of the world, he concludes that "effectively this entails the emergence of forms of polity that fall outside the cultural programs of modernity and are neither nation-states nor democratic republics but much more reminiscent of forms of political order of an earlier age but of course with access to the communicative and destructive capabilities of modern technology" (2001, p. 66). This conclusion attempts to align violence with only the "backward" polities that lie outside of modernity's promissory notes, and it ignores the connections between modernity (as manifested in "established democratic polities") and the violence that played a role in bringing about democratic polities, as well as these polities' persistent and continued use of violence.

11 Lawrence provides the following illustrations of this: a modern culture that, through an aesthetic frame of reference, controls feelings of shame or guilt by hiding the atrocities being committed by the "righteous side" in war (1997, pp. 36, 171); a modern society that masks society's oppressive structures through the ideals of a liberal-democratic polity (1997, pp. 49, 53); and finally, a modern mind that attempts to control the future through scientific models, calculations, and predictions (1997, pp. 13, 89–118).

12 Allen Feldman argues that the aestheticizing of violence not only awes us by the power of domination through distance, but just as importantly, works to "prescribe modes of seeing and visual objects, and … proscribe or render untenable other modes and objects of perception" (Feldman, 2000, p. 49). Feldman refers to this as a "scopic regime," which is "an ensemble of practices and discourses that establish the truth claims, typicality, and credibility of visual acts and objects and politically correct modes of seeing" (2000, p. 49). This constitutes a different approach to the study of violence, as it, among other things, stresses and analyses the far reaches of violence in a different way than Lawrence does. I will have more to say about this approach to the study of violence through the work of Das, and even later through Michael Taussig's discussion of optics.

13 Wieviorka briefly alludes to state violence or state terrorism (2009, p. 142), but only in so far as to say that this is not the subject of his book – that is, state violence maintains a certain distance in Wieviorka from the metapolitical, incomprehensible, cruel violence of political Islam.

14 One, of course, has to question whether this friend/enemy distinction is indeed possible. Derrida argues that one's hate for an enemy necessarily brings to the equation the name of friendship, since "the enemy can hate or wage war on me in the name of friendship, *for Friendships sake*, out of friendship for friendship" (Derrida, 2005 [1994], p. 72; original emphasis). This connection under friendship (whether posed as a truer friendship, a sublime friendship, an unconscious friendship, etc.) suggests that the "two concepts (friend/enemy) consequently intersect and ceaselessly change places" (Derrida, 2005, p. 72).

15 Schmitt is largely referring to political groups here. In Schmitt, the state is the "decisive entity" and this because of its authoritative political character that draws the decisive distinctions between friend/enemy (1996, p. 44). Having said that, Schmitt still argues that should a social group/association make such a decisive distinction (theoretically speaking – Schmitt paints this as an unlikely occurrence; 1996, p. 43), it could also reach the heights of the political attained by the state.

16 I say this with slight reservation. At one point, Schmitt speaks of the possibility (albeit an unlikely one) that a depoliticized world emerges. He argues that should all distinctions become impossible across the entire globe, then "what remains is neither politics nor state, but culture, civilization, economics, morality, law, art, entertainment, etc." (1996, p. 53). These latter remnants of the political world suggest that a depoliticized world may indeed be worthy of mention, but one still gets the sense that Schmitt views such a development with a certain ambivalence that would yearn for the political. This is a point that Derrida uses to deconstruct Schmitt's work and blur the distinctions it operates upon. The outline of

Derrida's questioning roughly looks like this: Schmitt proposes that (1) a rare state of exception (e.g., war) reveals the truth of the political (sharpens the friend/enemy distinction). This suggests that (2) the more rare the state of exception (the less war there is), the more intense this revelation (the more hostility there is), which, in turn, suggests that (3) the higher the degree of de-politicization, the more politicization is revealed, (4) the more politicization and absolute hostility spreads through de-politicization itself, and (5) the more we begin to see that Schmitt's concept of de-politicization introduces an over-politicization (i.e., the less politics there is, the more there is) that challenges proposition 1 and unravels his discourse (Derrida, 2005, pp. 128–133).

17 Bernstein argues that there is a gap in Schmitt's theory, which cannot properly speak to the relation between individual enmity and public enmity. Though Schmitt seeks to keep the two separated, he nevertheless cannot escape their relation (as a result of his failure to properly account for the emergence of public enmity), and thus despite his efforts, Schmitt ends up relying on certain assumptions about human nature as basically driven toward enmity (Bernstein, 2013, pp. 23–25).

18 Hardt and Negri claim that modern thought neatly separated war from internal politics, including civil conflict (whether potential or actual). So in their reading of Schmitt, they understand the state of exception to concern only an enemy of the state that, in their understanding of the friend/ enemy distinction, was in most cases another state and not a force within the state (Hardt & Negri, 2004, p. 6). This is then contrasted to their notion of a postmodern state of exception, which includes at its core the state's attempt to put an end to civil conflict through, among other things, the "war on terror."

19 That this violence for change becomes difficult to control is found in many studies. For example, Karl von Holdt argues that subaltern violence in apartheid and post-apartheid South Africa has delivered concrete results, such as cleaner water and higher wages, but yet it also had a corrosive and dark side in that such violence often hurt and badly affected a large number of other subalterns (von Holdt, 2012, pp. 124–125).

20 Gramsci is still careful not to make light of the instrument that is political violence, for he posits the following qualification on it: that it ought to be used "in accordance with the nature of the given instrument" (1971, p. 88). He does not explore this nature, but suffice it to say, he was very sensitive to the idea that a leadership cannot ask for "enthusiastic sacrifice" without adhering to, and striving to achieve, a set of aspirations that are felt and sought by the fighting masses (Gramsci, 1971, pp. 88–89).

21 This does not mean that a war of position cannot be won over the hegemonic power if the latter was aware of it; it simply makes it more

difficult. One should also not lose sight of the fact that the hegemonic power is always already engaged in a war of position that maintains its hegemony (1971, p. 235).

22 Gramsci seems to be aware of this point when he says that "political struggle … can be compared to colonial wars.… [where] the defeated army is disarmed and dispersed, but the struggle continues on the terrain of politics and of military 'preparation'" (1971, p. 229). However, he does not seem to take this fully into account when discussing the case of the proletariat – that is, this group seems to be the one that will break this cycle of violence as it fulfils its historical mission.

23 Gramsci largely saw these relations as marked by a state of apathy, and this prevented him from deeply theorizing the violence embedded in the political war of position undertaken by the hegemonic power.

24 Balibar divided this into interrelated "ultraobjective" forms of violence (institutional violences that perpetuate inequality, which could include natural disasters and how they unequally affect different groups, as well as nationalist ideologies and raciologies) and "ultrasubjective" forms of violence (types of subjectivity that limit expressions, politics, identities, and so on) (2015, pp. 13–17).

25 This is a central idea in many of Foucault's writings, and it is perhaps best illuminated in *Discipline and Punish* (1979 [1975]). For an analysis and an overview of Foucault's understanding of violence throughout his most famous works, see Hanssen (2000, pp. 97–157); Frazer and Hutchings (2011, pp. 6–9).

26 Peg Birmingham (2011) contends with Foucault's reading and shows that Hobbes paid as much attention to "glory" as he did to "fear," where the relation between fear and glory constituted the sovereign in Hobbes (Birmingham, 2011, pp. 4–12). While Birmingham is correct in challenging Foucault on this point, especially as it relates to the question of *why* human beings pursue power and sacrifice through political violence (fear, glory, or both?), my interest (and I would argue Foucault's primary interest) lies in Foucault's preoccupation with the *how* question (i.e., how is power exercised?) (Frazer & Hutchings, 2011, pp. 5–6), since I am concerned with how relations of power and relations of domination interconnect in Foucault.

27 This does not mean that a slave can never be in a relationship of power with their master. Hanssen points out that the English translation misses Foucault's point that when the slave is in chains and no possibility of escape exists, then we are talking about a physical relationship of constraint; but when the possibility of a potential escape exists, then we are talking about a relationship of power (Hanssen, 2000, p. 154). Despite the nuance of Foucault's argument here, I believe that Fanon's understanding

of the master–slave dialectic, alluded to above, is more insightful than Foucault's. I cannot delve into this debate here.

28 War, however, seems to be a necessary result of the war machine: the war machine is forced to use war in an attempt to destroy the state form, which will inevitably confront it (Deleuze & Guattari, 1987, p. 417).

29 I have illustrated this point in the American failure to use war as a means toward a political end in their 2003 invasion of Iraq (Ayyash, 2007).

30 Furthermore, some extremists claim that the facts of the Nazi camps are not confirmed. I will not pursue this point, as the questioning of the fact of the extermination itself is baseless, abhorrent, and racist, and does not deserve a retort here.

31 See also Edward Said's critique of Foucault's dismissal or omission of "the determining imprint of individual writers upon the otherwise anonymous collective body of texts constituting a discursive formation" (2003 [1979], p. 23).

32 In exploring Primo Levi's feelings of shame, Agamben argues that "shame is what is produced in the absolute concomitance of subjectification and desubjectification" (2005 [1999], p. 107). Subjectivity in this case has the form of subjectification and de-subjectification in that the subject's ability to speak brings to bear the impossibility to speak – subjectification of the subject as an "I" that writes or speaks on the annihilation of the subject is always accompanied by the de-subjectification of the witness who cannot control, master, or describe the de-subjectification of the subject (Agamben, 2005, pp. 112, 116–117). There is a similar understanding of subjectivity and violence in Das's work, which I explore in more detail in chapter 2. For now, it suffices to point out that subjectivity takes a form that is much more difficult to think about when we examine it in relation to violence.

33 Jenny Edkins illustrates how the state tends to absorb the memory of those who experience and bear witness to violent traumatic events into a "linear time," whereby these experiences are normalized through various nationalist rhetorics (2003, pp. 6–12). Drawing on Lacan and Agamben, Edkins asserts that such state practice must be disrupted by allowing the "testimony" of the witness its radical impossibility (2003, pp. 213–214) – she intends to avoid the normalization and hence the de-politicization of trauma (2003, p. 15). Edkins wants to "encircle" the site of trauma – allow it to mark itself in its impossibility and not attempt to speak from within trauma. This would retain "the trace of another temporality" and unleash a "trauma time" that disrupts the linear time of the state (Edkins, 2003, pp. 15–16). This leads Edkins to suggest that the reformulation of memory is perhaps *the* political act through which we can resist the violence of the state (2003, p. 229).

34 I'm thinking here of Tolstoy's oeuvre, or the writing of Mahmoud Darwish
(specifically, 1995 [1986], 2010 [2006]), but the list is too large to enumerate.
See Miller (2014) for an examination of writers such as Jean Genet and
Samuel Beckett within an Agambean/Foucauldian frame of analysis.

35 Similar to this idea in the discipline of international relations is Anthony
Burke's important intervention (which partly draws on Foucault's work)
in the field of security studies, where he illustrates through a number of
case studies "how the dreams of security, prosperity and freedom hinge,
from their earliest conceptualizations to the contemporary politics of the
national security state, on the insecurity and dying of others" (Burke, 2007,
p. 13). One of the points that Burke emphasizes is how the infliction of
death, pain, and suffering comes to be seen, through grandiose political
ideals such as "freedom," as "regrettable" yet "necessary and productive"
(2007, p. 13). These insights provide further credence to my emphasis on
the message that "violence works," but instead of Burke's reliance on a
socio-political project that is outside of violence to limit and critique that
message (his project relies on rethinking subjectivity around the twin
notions of responsibility and reciprocity; 2007, p. 19), I follow an analytical
path that follows violence to reveal the limiting elements of violence itself.

2. Linguistic Violence

1 Of note here is E. Valentine Daniel's seminal work in *Charred Lullabies*
(1996), which sets the stage for these later developments in the field; Das's
work, in my view, marks the apogee of that development.

2 Since at least Johan Galtung's (1969) famous essay, peace and conflict
studies have always operated on some sort of understanding of objective
or structural violence as distinct yet related to subjective or interpersonal
violence. For a more recent example, see Pilisuk and Rountree (2015).

3 This point is more explicitly and clearly articulated in Žižek than it is in
the aforementioned peace and conflict literatures, which is why I draw on
Žižek instead here.

4 Worthy of mention here is Martin Jay's (2003) similar "refractory"
approach to the study of violence. In his series of essays dealing with
various topics, Jay absorbs the barrage of violent images with which our
world is saturated in order to refract the theme of violence through the
theme of visuality or "ocularcentrism" in the hope of shining a few rays
of light on the problem of violence (Jay, 2003, pp. 2–3). Jay asserts that all
we can hope for is to shine, however dimly, these few rays, as opposed
to the Enlightenment's ideal of placing with complete and clear visibility
the problem of violence (2003, p. 10). Like Žižek's work, Jay's has much to
offer, but I maintain that scholars can indeed directly gaze at violence and

follow its vey elusiveness – we do not have to settle for refractory rays. And this can be accomplished without reverting to the Enlightenment's ideal or project of fixing and capturing the thing called violence *as it is* – this will be developed through Gadamer/Derrida later in the book.

5 One of the more familiar examples of this is the dominant and conventional explanation provided for the emergence of the Nazi regime in Germany. The events of World War II are often marked as one of the most important events in any discussion of contemporary history (e.g., the Frankfurt School is often explained in the context of Nazism and the war, or the global economic order is explained by the conditions of post-war Europe, etc.), but it is also seen as an anomaly in the progress of modernity and the Enlightenment, particularly by modernization theory (see Joas, 2003, pp. 43–54).

6 This is similar to how conventional approaches toward "domestic violence" tend to "incidentalize" cases of violence as a set of separate incidents, which ignores how such violences (physical, emotional, financial, psychological, and other forms) form a continuous pattern of coercive behaviour that exerts power/control in intimate relationships, largely of known men against known women (Hearn, 2013).

7 From early on, Das's fascination with Wittgenstein's work is very much tied to this notion of turning back from the madness of what lies beyond the everyday (a madness that is at bottom nothing) and moving back toward the ordinary by a "gesture of waiting" whereby the anthropologist or the philosopher allows the ordinary to mark their writing (Das, 1998).

8 It is poisonous for abducted women, for example, because recognition of such knowledge would lead to their social death. It can also be poisonous for women who were fortunate enough to escape bodily harm, but witnessed acts of violence whereby the very idea and practice of "being-with-others" is questioned and damaged (Das, 2007, p. 76). Das also explores this feature in how children dealt with the riots, where "the figure of life" itself was put into question, and where children possessed a repository of knowledge that was not quite theirs because it was inexpressible and ill-suited for their growth (2007, pp. 200–203).

9 In this chapter, Das mentions the works of Rabindranath Tagore and Sa'adat Hasan Manto, whose writings relate differently to the question of transcendentalism, madness, and violence, but I need not delve into this here.

10 When confronted with such distortions, it is understandable why Das attempts to overcome the "taint" of official discourse by exploring how these women recovered their lives through the everyday.

11 There is a similar idea to this in Wittgenstein's discussion of "applying a rule." I am not certain why Das shifts to Derrida here and does not

continue to draw on Wittgenstein, but it could be because Derrida's work may be more easily connected to a discussion on state discourse than Wittgenstein's.

12 An example of this would be the lethal power of rumours in inciting violence. Das explores how rumours operate on the basis of a "phenomenal time," whereby events that are physically separated in time can be brought up simultaneously. In such instances, past, present, and future are combined in a manner that serves to enrage a population against a specific enemy, encourage violence against a historical enemy, etcetera (Das, 2007, pp. 97, 119–121). Das does not lay the blame solely on the language of rumour for such lethal outbreaks of violence, but rather highlights their role in it.

13 I would situate Butler's (2004) important work on mourning, violence, and politics within this dimension. In her emphasis on the social dependency, relationality, frailty, and vulnerability of the "subject," Butler attempts to shift American reactions to "terrorist" violence away from the desire to commit and unleash violence on the "other" and toward a form of mourning that opens up toward a politics of non-violence or a non-violent politics (see especially Butler, 2004, pp. 1–49). Thus her work establishes a theoretical ground (espousing certain understandings of the body, power, and critique) that allows for a form of mourning that opens itself up toward healing and away from the continuation of violence. An assessment of her success/failure in this task (which is further developed in Butler, 2010) is beyond the scope of this book.

14 Similarly, and in conversation with Scarry's work, I do not mean to objectify violence in language here, but rather to stretch language in its difficult relationship with violence. So unlike Scarry, I do not posit that "to bring pain into the world by objectifying it in language, is to destroy one of them: either, as in the case of Amnesty International and parallel efforts in other areas, the pain is objectified, articulated, brought into the world in such a way that the pain itself is diminished and destroyed; or alternatively, as in torture and parallel forms of sadism, the pain is at once objectified and falsified, articulated but made to refer to something else and in the process, the world, or some dramatized surrogate of the world, is destroyed" (Scarry, 1985, p. 51). In certain respects, I argue that the instrumentalist perspective (in its "benign" or "peace-oriented" form) is guilty of the first form of objectification, and instrumentalist state discourses that Das counters are guilty of the second (which can be further seen in Scarry's critique of the notion of an absolute or definitive "end" in the use of war, where she argues that the act of injuring makes it only seem as if the outcome of war is final and definitive; see Scarry, 1985, pp. 107–121). I am not advancing an analysis that resorts to either

form of objectification, and by decentring language, by discarding
the notion that language can capture things in-themselves, I maintain
that it is possible to bring violence and language together in the very
space where this relationship is most difficult to conceive without these
forms of objectification. So while Scarry does seek to find a voice of the
fundamentally inexpressible "physical pain," this voice is ultimately
and indeed must be beyond the space of violence – beyond the torture
chamber, for instance; I want to explore the (un)knowability of violence
within the chamber, as it were.

15 Cavell and Wittgenstein more or less fall under the heading of "ordinary
language philosopher," who Cavell, in reference to the Oxford
philosophers (e.g., J.L. Austin) and the later Wittgenstein, identified
as primarily concerned with "reintroducing ideas which have become
tyrannical (e.g., existence … truth …) into the specific contexts in which
they function naturally. This is not a question of cutting big ideas
down to size, but of giving them the exact space in which they can
move without corrupting" (Cavell, 2002a [1958], p. 18). When flown
into transcendentalism, such words can corrupt both the mind of the
philosopher as well as the practice of philosophy itself. Moreover,
ordinary language philosophers are not simply attending to ordinary or
"natural" language, as opposed to the "artificial" language of traditional
philosophy (whether the analytic or continental version), but are interested
in explicating the conditions that make ordinary language possible (i.e.,
there remains a space for philosophy). A philosopher who proceeds from
ordinary language is not interested in describing "how 'other' people
talk, but in determining where and why one wishes, or hesitates, to use
a particular expression oneself" (Cavell, 2002b [1965], p. 99). How this
question is posed and analysed is where ordinary language philosophers
differ, and in many ways Cavell can be seen as pushing further such
questions and thus moving beyond people like Austin and Wittgenstein
(it should be noted that Wittgenstein never ascribed to such a school of
thought, which came after his death). I provide this note to allude to the
historical context of the philosophy and epistemology that underpins
Das's work.

16 One of the main reasons Das wants to follow through with this way of
thinking can be traced back to the dilemma she poses with Kleinman when
discussing the agency-structure debate mentioned in the introduction
to chapter 2. So her sense of a simultaneous process is forged not only
philosophically, but on explicit ethical and political grounds as well.

17 While Wittgenstein repudiates some of the assertions and arguments
he made in this early work of his, I believe that the passage quoted
above is a staple of his later works as well. I think it hasty to completely

separate the late from the early Wittgenstein, as he himself suggests the opposite of such separation in the preface to *Philosophical Investigations*: "It suddenly seemed to me that I should publish those old thoughts [referring to *Tractatus*] and the new ones together: that the latter could be seen in the right light only by contrast with and against the background of my old way of thinking" (Wittgenstein, 1973 [1953], vi). Sadly, such a publication never materialized. I will have more to say about this early-late Wittgenstein connection later in this discussion.

18 On the point of the radical uncertainty of pain and the inability to communicate pain as an inner state, Scarry's position, discussed in chapter 1, is very similar to Wittgenstein (and thus Das).

19 When making this point, a frequent example of Wittgenstein's concerns mathematical calculation: "If you demand a rule from which it follows that there can't have been a miscalculation here [12 x 12 = 144], the answer is that we did not learn this through a rule, but by learning to calculate. We got to know the *nature* of calculating by learning to calculate. But then can't it be described how we satisfy ourselves of the reliability of a calculation? O yes! Yet no rule emerges when we do so. – But the most important thing is: The rule is not needed. Nothing is lacking. We do calculate according to a rule, and that is enough…. Forget this transcendent certainty, which is connected with your concept of spirit" (Wittgenstein, 2006, pp. 8e, sections 44–47; original emphasis).

20 Another example: "The Earth is round" is not an assertion that proves that human beings can say with complete certainty that the external world exists as such – that is, as round; this would be a misfiring philosophical conclusion or hypothesis or discovery. Rather, it is an assertion that commences a language-game that shows "that we belong to a community which is bound together by science and education" (Wittgenstein, 2006, pp. 38e, section 298).

21 Or known by ourselves for that matter (Cavell, 1979, pp. 107–108). As Wittgenstein argues in his posthumous *On Certainty*, one cannot use "I know that …" as proof for the existence of something (e.g., pain); "I know that …" is simply the commencement of a language-game that means "this is how I know that …," which can include compelling grounds for "knowing that" and may even sound convincing for others, but does not on that account prove with certainty (which is a language-game that necessarily implies doubt) the existence of something as it is (Wittgenstein, 2006 [1969], pp. 7e, 32e, ss. 37–41, 243–245). There are of course many other positions one takes in a language-game, and there are instances when language-games change in their structures (Wittgenstein does not want to explain language-games – the concept is left elastic – he simply wants to note a language-game when it is being played; 1973, pp. 167e, ss. 654–55), but I need not deeply delve into this for my purposes.

22 Cavell shares Wittgenstein's somewhat ambiguous stance toward
scepticism. Cavell argues that Wittgenstein affirms the thesis of scepticism
above, but evades the rather preposterous sceptical conclusion that slips
into a form of philosophizing that takes this thesis as a discovery and turns
it into a problem of knowledge – a problem for philosophy to "solve"
by asking "Can we ever know?" (Cavell, 1979, pp. 44–45). Simply put,
affirming such a thesis does not lead to a disappointment concerning the
limit of our language or intellect in Wittgenstein; it rather looks at this
limit in wonderment. I do not wish to enter this long, dense, and difficult
debate anymore than I do in this general observation, since it would take
up a book project on its own. Indeed, this relation to scepticism is much of
what Cavell's book and life's work tackle.

23 The notion of a deficient stock of knowledge is the direction that
traditional philosophy, as opposed to ordinary language philosophy,
moves into. Traditional philosophy claims that persons fail because they
have not mastered a language (its logics, vocabulary, precise meanings,
etc.), hence the necessary vagueness of ordinary language and the
consequent suggestion in traditional philosophy that only a sustained
philosophical effort can succeed in the mastery of language. In ordinary
language philosophy, the notion of mastering a language (via the master
language of philosophy) is done away with, and the emphasis shift toward
the lack of sufficient initiation of persons into the world (Cavell, 1979,
p. 166).

24 For the initiation of children into language, see Das's account of this
Wittgensteinian idea when she explores the notion of a child who, when
learning language, is more properly talked about as a child who has a
"future in language" rather than as an empty vessel to be filled with an
instrumental(ized) language (Das, 1998, pp. 173–180).

25 Ernesto Laclau says something similar to this, and he succinctly and
usefully puts it as such: "The [twentieth] century started with three
illusions of immediacy, of the possibility of an immediate access to the
'things themselves.' These illusions were the referent, the phenomenon,
and the sign, and they were the starting point of the three traditions of
Analytic Philosophy, Phenomenology, and Structuralism. Since then, the
history of these three traditions has been remarkably similar: at some
stage, in all three, the illusion of immediacy disintegrates and gives way
to one or other form of thought in which discursive mediation becomes
primary and constitutive. This is what happens to Analytic Philosophy
after Wittgenstein's *Philosophical Investigations*, to phenomenology
after Heidegger's existential analytic, and to Structuralism after the
poststructuralist critique of the sign. (And, I would argue, to Marxism after
Gramsci.)" (Laclau, 2000, p. 74).

3. Mimetic Violence

1 This dynamic is very different in form and characteristics from the dynamic of violence that is outlined in Randall Collins's micro-sociological approach to the study of violence. Collins seeks a "situational dynamic" that cuts across all the different kinds of violence and that basically consists of an emotional field of tension and fear (Collins, 2008, pp. 7–8). Similar to Collins's dynamic of violence, the dynamic of violent dialogue follows Collins's assertion that violence is like a tunnel: very difficult to enter, but once inside it, the violence of the participants sets in motion a rhythm of its own that is hard to stop. In contrast, however, the dynamic of violent dialogue consists of hidden operations and dimensions that are not reducible to an emotional field. The dynamic of violent dialogue does not reveal itself in an observable emotional field, yet it reveals a depth of effects that far exceeds an emotional field. In that sense, the dynamic of violent dialogue reveals both more and less than Collins's emotional field.

2 There are of course debates over this term and whether the concept of "domestic violence" hides more than it reveals about this phenomenon. I tend to side with Hearn's assertion that there are good pragmatic reasons for adopting this term (namely its political currency in public discourse) over others (Hearn, 2013, p. 158).

3 Jeffrey C. Alexander argues that, thanks to the linguistic turn in twentieth-century philosophy, Clifford Geertz was the first scholar to properly understand Dilthey's hermeneutical method as "collective, structural, and textual," bringing to focus what Geertz and cultural sociologists call "culture structures" (Alexander, 2008, p. 161). In a sense, this interpretation of Dilthey makes his work much closer to Gadamer's philosophical hermeneutics than is perhaps suggested in *Truth and Method*.

4 Gadamer has a long discussion delineating the structure of what he calls the "historically effected consciousness" when making some of the arguments regarding tradition. The main thrust of the concept is to assert the eventfulness of understanding a given text – not the effect a given work has on history (its trace), but the effect of "a consciousness of the work itself" (Gadamer, 2004, p. 336). It is the application of a text in our own time, for our purposes, at the same time that such an application is based on the historicity of the text itself: that is, there is no imposition of something alien to the text in a historically effected consciousness, but what is alien to the text may be produced from our dialogue with it.

5 This also applies to texts, as only a select few occupy the space that we call the "classical." For Gadamer, what makes the classical speak to us is not

its self-significance, but its "timelessness" as its mode of "historical being."
Or, the classical, by its very mode of being of timelessness (which is not
the same thing as saying that its knowledge is timeless), opens itself up to
the future and "overcomes the distance by itself" (Gadamer, 2004, p. 290).
Since not all texts accomplish this, Gadamer can then distinguish between
texts that manage to undertake the above-mentioned commitment while
others fail to do so. I think it is important to add that many texts that
achieve this "timelessness" are sometimes not considered classical or
included in the "canon" for reasons of gender, race, and ethnic inequalities.

6 In the following, Gadamer explains what he means by this more explicitly:
"The dialogical character of language ... leaves behind it any starting point
in the subjectivity of the subject, and especially in the meaning-directed
intentions of the speaker. What we find happening in speaking is not a
mere reification of intended meaning, but an endeavor that continually
modifies itself.... That which becomes a dialogical experience for us
here is not limited to the sphere of arguments and counterarguments
the exchange and unification of which may be the end meaning of every
confrontation. Rather, as the experiences that have been described indicate,
there is something else in this experience, namely a potentiality for
being other ... that lies beyond every coming to agreement about what is
common" (Gadamer, 1989a [1984], p. 26).

7 It is not clear to me if Gadamer has a preferred term for evaluating
different dialogues in *Truth and Method*. There are instances where he calls
this authentic dialogue "real," "true," "proper," or "genuine" dialogue.
However, his affinities to Heidegger's notion of in/authenticity (which at
least for the early Heidegger highlighted the "the intrinsic and indissoluble
interinvolvement" of concealment and un-concealment, or of truth and
error; Gadamer, 1977b [1964], p. 203) suggest that it may be the best term
to understand his distinction between the two forms of dialogue. Clearly,
Gadamer does not assign his distinction this indissoluble interinvolvement
and shifts the question of authenticity to the space that, if properly
undertaken, unleashes the indissoluble interinvolvement of truth and
error. I will delve more deeply into this in the next chapter through Caputo
and Derrida.

8 This model is not limited to two horizons, but I use this example for
simplicity's sake. As Fred Dallmayr has argued, Gadamer's hermeneutics
centre-stage "a mode of dialogue that is open-ended and hospitable to
multiple and expanding horizons" (Dallmayr, 2002, p. 27).

9 To a lesser extent, Dallmayr presents this combination in *Achieving Our
World* (2001), where Dallmayr is much more critical of Derrida and not just
his followers, and where Gadamer is much less central to his argument.

10 For example, see Derrida (1989 [1984]), where Derrida challenges Heidegger's reading of Nietzsche, and as such Gadamer's dismissal or downplaying of the relation between Nietzsche and Heidegger, without ever addressing Gadamer directly.

11 Derrida accuses Gadamer of this as well (Derrida, 1989, p. 54). However, the charge is unsubstantiated, and the three questions directed to Gadamer in this piece are brief and do not reflect Derrida's best efforts. Having said that, this is perhaps due to the limits of the exchange between the two and the brevity imposed on Derrida.

12 In fact, Girard claims that "mimeticism is the original source of all man's troubles, desires, and rivalries, his tragic and grotesque misunderstandings" (1986, p. 165). Although he emphasized the conflictual and bad forms of mimeticism throughout his writings, Girard also admits that there are also vitally important and good forms of mimeticism, without which "there would be no human mind, no education, no transmission of culture" (2007, p. 76). But Girard feels that the bad forms of mimesis have historically been denied or overlooked, and hence why he wanted his work to show that "imitation channels not only knowledge but also violence" (2007, p. 76; also see 2007, pp. 139–141).

13 I am not a Girardian apologist, but let me attempt to rehash how he uses the term "primitive." In addition to Greek tragedy and modern literature, Girard believes that he is undertaking a scientific study of "primitive societies," most of which are no longer in existence (such as Phoenician communities and certain historical Aztec communities). Through this combination of diverse materials, he discovers the mechanism of the surrogate victim that lies behind all distinctions of violence, and as such behind all human cultural orders. In doing this, Girard believes that he is more open to the creativity and richness of such "primitive societies" (and he does often place quotes on the term) than the established disciplines of his time (anthropology, sociology, etc.) (Girard, 2007, pp. 138–139). And to a certain extent, he is correct in this latter claim. He does not hold a contemptuous view of "primitive" society (in fact, he combats such contempt, which is all too prevalent in the Western academy), nor does he, in a limited respect, subscribe to a linear evolutionary model of history, where humanity progresses from "primitive" to "advanced" society. Indeed, he argues that there is little difference between the two since at bottom, they are both sacrificial societies. Having said that, he does argue that Christianity offers us a progression away from "archaic" pagan religions. I will have more to say on his linear thinking in chapter 4.

14 For Girard, "the ritual victim is never substituted for some particular member of the community … *it is always substituted for the surrogate victim*" (1977, p. 101; original emphasis). This is the double substitution that takes

place in sacrificial societies: (1) the original, where the surrogate victim is substituted for all the members of the community, and (2) the ritualistic, which is superimposed on the first, where a specific sacrificial category is substituted for the original substitution (Girard, 1977, p. 102). Or put differently, "ritual is the mimetic repetition of an original mimetic crisis," where the ritual repeats the solution of the surrogate victim that occurred spontaneously in the original mimetic crisis; this leads Girard to conclude that there is "no structural difference between the rite itself and the spontaneous, natural course of the mimetic crisis" (Girard, 1986, p. 139). This is an important claim since it allows for Girard to speak, through the observable rites, about originary events that have not been chronicled and that no one alive today has witnessed.

15 The gap between the victim and the community must be carefully established. The victim cannot be too close to, or too distant from, the community. If this balance is not successfully achieved, the community risks the onset of a sacrificial crisis, where violence becomes unbound again (Girard, 1977, p. 39).

16 In the sacrificial rites, the victim is not and can never be considered innocent. On this point, Girard again distances himself from Freud and stands with Sophocles, who "makes it clear … that the surrogate victim, even when falsely accused, may be as guilty as the others" (Girard, 1977, p. 203). In Girard, collective murder allows guilt and expiation to be distributed across the collective by virtue of the unifying figure of the surrogate victim, whose divinity ensures that violence is alloyed with the religious meanings of the sacrifice (1977, p. 214).

17 Such demystification has often failed in modern, rational thought for the sole reason that modern thought misunderstands what is truly at stake – protecting the community from unbound violence – in mystification. In its attempt to dismiss and expel religious thought from the intellectual landscape, Girard argues that modern thought, in a sense, engages superstitiously and fanatically with religious thought (1977, pp. 266, 317–318).

18 This includes, for Girard, the various modern thinkers who have shaped the intellectual landscape in the last few centuries. From Marx to Freud to Lacan, modern thinking for Girard is very much part and parcel of the sacrificial logic outlined above. They all, first and foremost, engage in the expulsion of a scapegoat, which then paves the way to the erection of their various theories (e.g., for Marx it is the bourgeoisie; for Freud, the father, etc.) (Girard, 1987, pp. 286–287).

19 For Girard, while the history of the "modern" Western world is "marked by the dissolution of differences," and while "the phrase 'modern world' seems almost like a synonym for 'sacrificial crisis,'" the modern legal

system has worked wonders in inducing a cure for this process, thereby averting the disaster that would have been visited upon a "primitive" society undergoing a similar process (1977, p. 188). It is the absence of law that continuously threatens "modern man," and not law itself (Girard, 1977, p. 189). I will engage more with this dimension of Girard's work through the Gospels discussion.

20 This structural difference is what is at stake for Girard, and it does (if accepted) indeed create an abyss between the mythology of the Greeks, for example, and the Gospels. That is, Girard claims that we cannot simply lump together the resurrection of Christ with other tales of resurrection in various other mythologies under the category of "fantasy." The different foundation that the resurrection of Christ is built upon (i.e., the revelation of the surrogate mechanism) far outweighs the similarities that the Gospels share with other mythologies (virgin birth, resurrection, etc.) – and this to the extent that the Gospels are no longer seen in Girard as just another mythology, but rather as the negation of mythology (1986, pp. 147–148, 162–163, 204–205).

21 While it is pivotal for Girard to maintain that the names "Satan" and "Jesus" do indeed refer to a real event and real individuals, he is more interested in what concepts or ideas these names signify when it comes to his interpretation of the Gospels: for example, "Satan" is the false transcendence in its fundamental unity, where the surrogate mechanism originates and conceals itself (disorder and order combined); or in the Gospels, "Satan is the name for the mimetic process seen as a whole" (Girard, 1987, p. 162; for more on the referentiality/non-referentiality of the Bible, see Girard, 2007, pp. 199–211).

22 This quote undoubtedly raises for many the same question that Jean-Michel Oughourlian asks Girard at this point – "Are you not in fact hypostatizing violence by treating it like a kind of subjective agency, which is personally hostile to Jesus Christ?" (Girard, 1987, p. 209) – to which Girard answers that "violence, in every cultural order, is always the true *subject* of every ritual or institutional structure. From the moment when the sacrificial order begins to come apart, this subject can no longer be anything but the *adversary par excellence*, which combats the installation of the Kingdom of God. This is the devil known to us from tradition – Satan himself, of whom some theologians tell us that he is both subject and not subject at once" (Girard, 1987, p. 210; original emphases). The manner in which Girard talks about violence in the quote above, as well as in many other places in his work, is then justifiable – he is simply speaking about it in a manner that is both attentive to and congruent with the texts with which he is working. Ultimately, however, and from a theoretical point of view, I do not find this answer satisfactory, and I will come back to it shortly.

23 Any general term, such as "postcolonial," will be unsatisfactory, as it will inevitably introduce limitations to our understanding/description of what is placed under it. Despite this shortcoming, I have chosen "postcolonial" here because the works that I delve into in this section (as well as the other works that I only make mention of) take seriously the experiences of the colonized/oppressed/racialized margins, and they all seek to trouble and deconstruct the idea of the "sovereignty of a Western self."

24 Said distinguishes between colonialism and imperialism as follows: "'Imperialism' means the practice, the theory, and the attitudes of a dominating metropolitan centre ruling a distant territory; 'colonialism,' which is almost always a consequence of imperialism, is the implanting of settlements on distant territory" (1994, p. 9). According to Said, while direct colonialism has very much receded, or even ended in our recent history, imperialism remains strong and vibrant in our cultural, political, and social practices and beliefs.

25 While all cultures in a sense attempt to control other cultures through representation, what is distinctive about the Western colonial/imperial case in recent history is that it both makes such representations and in fact has controlled and continues to control foreign cultures (Said, 1994, pp. 100, 108–110).

26 Said's masterful analysis of the opera *Aida* in the above-cited pages illustrates this point. For a brief statement that captures how his contrapuntal analysis unfolds, "Kipling's novel *Kim* … occupies a very special place in the development of the English novel and in late Victorian society, but its picture of India exists in a deeply antithetical relationship with the development of the movement for Indian independence. Either the novel or the political movement represented or interpreted without the other misses the crucial discrepancy between the two given to them by the actual experience of empire" (Said, 1994, p. 32). Later in the book, Said examines Kipling in more detail.

27 I am slightly deviating from Said's own framing of these steps here. Said divides, purely for analytical reasons, "decolonizing cultural resistance" along three main related topics: (1) the insistence on the wholeness and integrity of a decolonized community, (2) the establishment of an idea of resistance as an alternative to imperial notions of human history, and (3) conceiving a new vision for human liberty and community (Said, 1994, pp. 215–216). I opted to use the above framing of the steps because it better captures how Said understands resistance culture within the larger scheme of colonial violence (the violent founding of colonies and resistance against them), and because I think that topics 2 and 3 are best articulated together under the third step since the alternative conceptions of human community and liberty are intimately connected to the alternative

conception of human history (i.e., Said's entire argument in this book [1994] suggests that a contrapuntal method of analysis, in its challenge to conventional historical methods of comparative analysis, itself can lead to a new and decolonial worldview – especially well captured on pp. 317–318, 330–336).

28 This is best seen in Gilroy's analysis of "black music" where he outlines two opposing, yet fruitlessly interlocked, perspectives on the question of identity and culture, where we find a conversation between "those who see the music as the primary means to explore critically and reproduce politically the necessary ethnic essence of blackness and those who would dispute the existence of any such unifying, organic phenomenon" (Gilroy, 1993, p. 100). Against this once productive but now stale conversation, Gilroy instead advances the perspective of "black expressive cultures" and "music as a *changing* rather than an unchanging same" (1993, p. 101; original emphasis). The crux of this perspective is to emphasize both the continuous conversation with tradition (same) that takes place in different cultural forms and through varied and heterogeneous identities (changing), thus producing a constant reinterpretation and reinvention of the tradition, producing in the process something new in/of/within the tradition (changing same).

29 In a sense, the first configuration is that of a "primitive" form, the second is that of a "modern" form, and the third is that of a contemporary "postcolonial" form. Taussig writes of a primitive-modern interaction in light of Horkheimer and Adorno's (2002) *Dialectic of Enlightenment*; thus there is not a demarcation between "primitive" and "modern" on geographic, historical, or racial bases, but he is rather more interested in the manner in which the two intermingle in any given setting.

30 In some respects, this is similar to the notion of mimetic violence put forth by Scheper-Hughes and Bourgois – the idea that "violence gives birth to itself" (2004, 1). In addition to explaining the propagation of violence along a continuum where violence begets violence (Scheper-Hughes & Bourgois, 2004, pp. 1–2), mimetic violence in this book opens up an analytical avenue for examining the dialogical dimension of violence. I am not satisfied with making the claim that victims can become perpetrators of violence and vice versa; instead, I want to examine precisely how the dynamic of violent dialogue, which enables such movements across victims-perpetrators, itself unfolds, proceeds, and moves.

4. Transcendental Violence

1 I have no interest in entering a science-versus-religion debate at this point. Needless to say, Girard believes that one can believe in both at the same

time. Simply put, Girard believes that God is the guarantor of reality; God has sent us in scripture all of what we need to know about the foundations of human life; at the same time it is through science (which is ultimately the rationalist demystification that was sent to us by God in scripture) that we may uncover the reality of our world (i.e., its revelation).

2 While one can certainly make the case that Heraclitus associated the Logos with "what is not" in certain respects, it is also indisputable that Heraclitus posited the Logos as Unity, as One, that *is* (e.g., in the following fragment from Heraclitus: "Listening to the Logos and not to me, it is wise to agree that all things are One"; quoted in Geldard, 2000, p. 156). While I cannot delve into the complexities of Heraclitus's fragments here, it suffices to say that these fragments indicate a very complex way of thinking about the relationship between "what is" and "what is not" (as opposed to a simple either/or opposition between them), and thus I certainly do not follow Girard in his assertion that the Logos of Heraclitus belongs or is equivalent to transcendent violence. So while I would agree with Girard that there is a certain affinity between negative theology and the Logos of Heraclitus (which for Girard means that Heraclitus was firmly stationed in "what is not" and thus imprisoned in a sacrificial viewpoint), I tend to follow commentators such as Richard Geldard who argue that Heraclitus sought to negate traditional beliefs and myths while *simultaneously affirming* a new vision that would be aligned with the Logos, which is both beyond us and within us, evasive yet still graspable, whereby "through negation we come to know something positively" (Geldard, 2000, p. 29). Eventually in this chapter, I will draw on Derrida to move beyond Girard and negative theology. Whether this move is undertaken with, through, beyond, and/ or against Heraclitus is an altogether different matter. Suffice it to say, the influence of Heraclitus on thinkers such as Heidegger and Derrida is a much-discussed issue, and is for another book.

3 Girard defines Logos as "the divine, rational and logical principle according to which the world is organized" (1987, p. 263). While, for Girard, there are two distinct types of Logos, this definition suggests that there is only one true Logos and that we can and must choose between the two types.

4 As Richard Kearney argues, Girard can be accused of scapegoating all religions and mythologies by "his claim that only one religious tradition – Judeo-Christian monotheism – can redeem us from the scourge of scapegoating" (Kearney, 2002, p. 26).

5 To my knowledge, Girard does not extensively engage with Islam outside of his reflections on the 9/11 attacks, although a few points could summarize his general view on the religion: (1) it is not a return to archaic religion, (2) it constitutes a reprisal of Christianity and in certain limited

respects improves or builds on it, but ultimately (3) it lacks the cross, and so although it reveals the innocence of the victim, it does so in a "warlike way" (i.e., as opposed to Christianity, Islam is a violent religion that is incapable of unleashing God's true love) (Girard, 2002). Needless to say, there is much to dispute with Girard here, but his position on Islam is rather predictable given his ardent conversion.

6 Concerning this notion of "truth," Caputo describes the Heideggerian project, particularly after *Being and Time*, as follows: "Heidegger is concerned not with the actual metaphysical grid which is spread out in any particular sending of Being but with reading that metaphysics *as* such a spread, with seeing in it a way that Being is sent and articulated within a certain epochal constellation" (1987, p. 114; original emphasis).

7 Heidegger is advocating not a return to the origin as it was, but a reunion with it and its story, whose end has reached us in our time; and thus he hopes to set the stage for a new original beginning which does not end the beginning but rather the beginning's end (i.e., this is a circular view that re-connects beginning with end and end with beginning). Such an accomplishment can be brought about only by human effort – that is, it is not a guaranteed or predictable outcome as teleology might view its beginning-end story, nor is there a specified and absolute distance between beginning and end as teleology would have it. For Derrida, however, such an eschatology, even though radical, is still entrapped in the comforting and reassuring language of metaphysics since it ties radical transformation to the comforting thought that there is reason to the madness (even if there are no guarantees that we will find this reason, the assertion is that it is there). For Caputo's discussion on Heidegger's eschatology, Derrida's critique of it, and the latter's limits, see Caputo (1987, pp. 153–186).

8 It is a structure that is also not a structure – at least not in any sense of structure that the school of structuralism may put forth. Also, the hyper-essential position is akin, in Derrida, to negative theology, which *différance* is not.

9 For different reasons, I also found the notion of a "return" unsatisfactory in Das/Wittgenstein (particularly as it pertains to the debates on ordinary language philosophers discussed earlier) – that is, I want to move away from their tendency to associate transcendence with pure madness or nonsense, thus expelling the notion of transcendence and "returning" to ordinary language.

10 It should be noted that in this essay, "The Thing Itself," which is dedicated to Derrida, Agamben is dealing with Plato's notion of the "thing itself." The connections with Derrida's work can be easily discerned when this essay is read alongside the other essay cited above, *"Pardes"* (1999b).

11 Sean Gaston's (2009) distinction between Agamben and Derrida is akin to
   the previous distinctions I made between Caputo, Derrida, and Heidegger.
   The difference between Agamben and Derrida according to Gaston can
   be summed up as such: Agamben calculates *on* absence (i.e., he finds in a
   space called "absence" a pure potentiality or possibility – a space where
   alterity remains untouched and where the potentiality of the new is, as it
   were, preserved). Derrida, on the other hand, calculates *from* absence (i.e.,
   he relies on a space called "absence" not as an assurance of the existence
   of something pure or ideal but rather as a reminder or a register of the
   constant interplay between presence and absence, of the "more or less"
   that refuses to totalize the present or idealize the absent) (see especially
   part 1 in Gaston, 2009). I find myself in agreement with Gaston here, but
   this distinction is not central to, or even visible in, the two Agamben essays
   cited above. The important point remains, as I asserted earlier, that Derrida
   does not treat the "flux" (to go back to Caputo's terminology) as a space
   that can be visited almost at will in order to shake our foundations, but
   rather attempts to speak according to the flux.

12 In the following quotation, Derrida sums up the view of speech, self-
   presence, God, and writing within the epoch of the "metaphysical closure"
   (i.e., logocentrism) he is deconstructing: "From Descartes to Hegel and in
   spite of all the differences that separate the different places and moments
   in the structure of that epoch, God's infinite understanding is the other
   name for the logos as self-presence. The logos can be infinite and self-
   present, it can be *produced as auto-affection*, only through the *voice*: an order
   of the signifier by which the subject takes from itself into itself, does not
   borrow outside of itself the signifier that it emits and that affects it at
   the same time. Such is at least the experience – or consciousness – of the
   voice: of hearing (understanding)-oneself-speak. That experience lives and
   proclaims itself as the exclusion of writing, that is to say of the invoking of
   an 'exterior,' 'sensible,' 'spatial' signifier interrupting self-presence" (1997a,
   p. 98; original emphases).

13 The two terms "trace" and "arche-writing" may be interchangeable in this
   sense only. "Arche-writing" is more Derrida's "own" term than "trace,"
   which at one point he says was "imposed" on him by the intellectual and
   literary climate of his time (Derrida, 1997a, p. 70). Indeed, arche-writing is
   but *a* trace, rather than "trace," which is more abstract in Derrida and can
   be moved around different contexts more easily than arche-writing (e.g., in
   the discussion on "trace" and "experience" in Derrida's deconstruction of
   Husserl's phenomenology in "The Voice That Keeps Silence"; see Derrida,
   1973, pp. 85–87). It should also be added that "trace" in this abstract sense
   is interchangeable with yet another term that is more Derrida's "own,"

différance (Derrida, 1997a, p. 93), although Derrida also speaks of how *différance* (in a different sense than "trace") imposed itself on him in his essay "Différance" (Derrida, 1973, p. 131).

14 The context behind this quote and Derrida's discussion of violence and naming is Lévi-Strauss's study of the Nambikwara people in South America, where the "proper name" is kept secret and can be revealed only on certain sacred occasions. Derrida does not agree with Lévi-Strauss that the concept of the "proper name" is a simple one that points to the violence of writing and the hiding of what is "proper," but rather shows that in revealing the "proper names" to the anthropologist, the little girls from the Nambikwara community were engaging in a practice that consisted of "tearing the veil hiding a classification and an appurtenance, the inscription within a system of linguistico-social differences" (Derrida, 1997a, p. 111). There has been much debate on Derrida's critique of Lévi-Strauss, but most of it is focused on whether or not (and to what extent) Derrida succeeds in unsettling the hierarchical distinction between the supposedly "advanced" writing of white Europeans and the "primitive" spoken word of the Nambikwara people, and how Derrida may actually be unable to speak to the social-political-economic material effects of the difference between the spoken and written word (Wise, 2009, pp. 7–12). While I do not deny that such material effects are important to study and take into account, and that Derrida may not provide proper analytical tools to understand them, my interest here remains focused on the question of violence and language, which, I agree with Derrida, cannot be divided into a spoken word that is innocent of the violence of representation on the one hand and a written word that embodies such violence on the other.

15 Derrida, Gadamer, and Wittgenstein are not very different on this point; the primary differences reside in how this point is reached and the role it plays in each thinker's work.

16 In the essay cited above, "Violence and Metaphysics," Derrida deconstructs the work of Emmanuel Levinas, mainly *Totality and Infinity*. I leave the details of this essay out of the book for two reasons: (1) Derrida's relation to Levinas's thought seems to me a bit unique and different from Derrida's deconstruction of other thinkers, in that it is especially difficult to discern the points at which Derrida moves from "his" thought to "Levinas's" despite his efforts to outline this movement, meaning that (2) I would necessarily have to bring Levinas into the book if I were to engage with the details of the essay, which would needlessly complicate matters. Thus I present the citations from this essay above with the following caveat: the formulation of the ideas above follows the citations in their overall gesture, but not necessarily in terms of terminology (which is ever shifting in Derrida at any rate) and intention (i.e., some of the points are

not made by Derrida to drive an argument like the one presented above, but rather for the sake of an argument preoccupied with Levinas's polemic against Husserl and Heidegger in particular, and the philosophical relation between "Jewish" and "Greek" thought in general).

17 An example of the shifting or different terminology used in this essay is Derrida's reference here to "transcendental violence" rather than arche-violence, since the former better engages with the work of Levinas.

18 This is where violence the "thing itself" is different from the Lacanian *das Ding*. Slavoj Žižek's (2008) *Violence* is an example of this difference. Briefly, Žižek draws from Lacan's work the impetus to search for what is rendered hidden by violence, which is "the dimension of the Real" that is beyond the immediate "reality" of violence's taking place – an immediate reality that lacks deep meaning in and of itself (Žižek, 2008, pp. 52–53, 76). While I find his work insightful and penetrating, and while there are important similarities between Žižek's and Derrida's understanding of the relationship between violence and language, I am not interested in searching for a "thing itself" that constitutes the "real event" that takes place when violence takes place; I wish to highlight the (un)knowability of violence the "thing itself" as opposed to violence the "thing itself" *as* a knowable (by critical theory) unknowable (hidden reality) – or one of "the 'unknown knowns,' the things we do not know that we know" (Žižek, 2004, p. 9).

19 Having said that, I do not deny that such an effort is fruitless. That scholars (e.g., Stephen M. Feldman, 2000) have attempted to formulate the complementary interdependence of Gadamer's philosophical hermeneutics and Derrida's deconstruction indeed gives more credence to my emphasis on their encounter as a way of thinking through the (un) knowability of violence and the dynamic of violent dialogue.

20 I would argue that this claim is close to a view on the relationship between literature and war that is different than the one Das (along with others) has put forth. As previously discussed, Das associates the language of certain poets with pure madness, since they reach for a language that attempts to speak the abyss of absolute violence. But Sean Gaston has articulated a different view of the relationship between war and literature by drawing on the work of Derrida. For Gaston, naming the unnameable in Derrida, or "naming the without name is a *unity* of chance and rule that cannot be reduced to an assured programme, to a system without a swerve. It is at once the chance of meeting and the risk of not meeting. We are always (not) meeting without name" (Gaston, 2009, pp. 144–145; original emphasis). Meaning, naming the without name is not just at the same time possible and impossible, but also at the same time the risk of a duel and the chance of opening up new and different questions. This,

Gaston concludes, does not mean that in naming the without name, literature can tell us what war cannot, but that literature can tell us what war leaves us with but which, in a sense, war hides. Thus for Gaston, "(not) meeting without name is always the possibility of a violent naming, of a duel or war that ends in a name, in a profound loss of anonymity. But it also ceaselessly announces the edges and borders, the limitations of what can be named.… In times of war, it is in the politics of anonymity, of finding strategic resistances to the sovereign anonymity and the ceaseless sovereign effort to either leave the enemy nameless or to name what cannot be named, that there is a chance for the other of war. In such times, literature confronts us with the voices of the *sans nom* and the injunction to respond to Derrida's question: what are *sans-papiers* lacking?" (2009, p. 157)

21 Another one of these impetuses is certainly Taussig's response to the heavy influence of Geertzian hermeneutics in the discipline of anthropology. I cannot delve into this debate here. Suffice it to say, I am in many ways interested in combining certain elements of Gadamerian hermeneutics (which in different ways have shaped the work of Geertz) with Derridean post-structuralist elements. As previously discussed, these Derridean elements have some roots in the school of phenomenology, and so it is not too far a stretch to come to Taussig at this point and draw on certain aspects of his phenomenology, namely the notion of sensuous welding into the thing copied. To illuminate this latter point further, I discuss a different impetus behind Taussig's manoeuvre above.

22 Many contemporary liberal discourses, which proclaim to counter violences of states or militaries, exhibit this feature, whereby they fall into precisely the type of explanation that contemporary military strategies count on producing: the inexplicability or unrepresentability of violence tends to lead to its acceptance as a brute fact or to its rejection on exclusively moral grounds (banality and melodrama, respectively) (Jabri, 2006, pp. 823–830).

23 I do not wish to enter into the long and dense debate on what constitutes a "liberal politics." Suffice it to say, my interest lies with the manner in which liberal politics (simply understood as the mainstream political left that is often interested in reform as opposed to radical transformations of states and their policies) neatly categorizes violence and approaches it in the manner a physician approaches a disease. Both Taussig and Duffield, more or less, base and expand their critique of liberal politics along these lines.

24 White's discussion here concerns the challenge that Foucault's work posed for structuralism in particular and the human sciences in general. By

freeing the word from the confines of the task of representation, Foucault hopes to free the human sciences from having to claim the status of "scientificity" and thus open up new possibilities for seeing the world.

25 By "philosophy," I think Benjamin refers to the "idea of [violence's] development" (Benjamin, 2004, p. 251).

26 Žižek offers an interesting reading of Benjamin's divine violence, and unlike the majority of social theorists, Žižek insists on naming divine violence even though he readily admits the difficulty of doing so. His most famous example is that of Robespierre (in Robespierre, 2007), but he also offers explanations as to why the looting and destruction of rich supermarkets in Rio de Janeiro by crowds from the favelas constitutes divine violence (Žižek, 2008, pp. 196–205). I think it is important to analyse certain cases as instances of divine violence, and it is important to emphasize that Benjamin never stated that divine violence is a pure concept that can never take place. Having said that, I think that following Derrida's reading that emphasizes the *relation* between mythic and divine violence is more fruitful. In short, instead of separating Danton (mythic violence) from Robespierre (divine violence) (Žižek, 2008, p. 201), it is more analytically valid to study how the two are interrelated.

27 I find Benjamin's conception of violence and sovereignty more convincing than Carl Schmitt's (1996 [1932]). In Schmitt, it is the decision over the friend/enemy distinction that constitutes the sovereign power as sovereign, and violence is delimited within the space of the sovereign. In Benjamin, violence within the space of the sovereign, who is constituted as such in the state of exception, is only one kind of violence (i.e., mythic violence), and it is distinct from the "divine" violence that is itself sovereign. Thus Schmitt's work must delimit violence within a firm space in which it operates but never leaves, while Benjamin is more fluid in his understanding of the flux of violence as it relates to sovereignty. Derrida's deconstruction of Schmitt's friend/enemy distinction is a perfect illustration of this distinction's fragility and the inability of Schmitt's model to sustain the binary opposition of friend-enemy that makes it possible in the first place (Derrida, 2005 [1994], pp. 72, 128–133; also see Wise, 2009, pp. 129–148).

28 Alongside historical examples where "justice" was used to question the legitimacy of an established order of law (Derrida, 2002, p. 249), this is most evident in Derrida's very text. He draws on justice (which cannot be deconstructed because it only founds, but itself can never exist) as an opening wherein a deconstruction of law (which is constructible through justice) may be carried out (2002, p. 243). Edward Said similarly draws on justice in his work.

29 Derrida explains the reasoning behind this point in the following quote: "Since the origin of authority, the founding or grounding, the positing of the law cannot by definition rest on anything but themselves, they are themselves a violence without a ground" (Derrida, 2002, p. 242).

30 *L'avenir* is what is to-come, what cannot be accounted for, that which arrives completely unexpected. This is different in Derrida from the calculable and predictable future.

31 In addition to its challenge of the founding-maintaining distinction of violence, this Derridean unravelling of the distinction between a supposedly purely expiating divine violence and a supposedly ritualized mythic violence is also helpful in unravelling productive-destructive distinctions of violence.

32 Mouffe's non-essentialist and post-structural approach highlights (1) the multiplicity and plurality of the social body without subsuming difference under a common consensus that closes avenues for change, and (2) the power relations that create a certain configuration of hegemonic relations that govern the social body, and in a Gramscian gesture, seeks to (3) establish a counter-hegemonic force that would radically transform the socio-political order toward a more equitable and inclusive progressive politics (Mouffe, 2005, pp. 11, 15–16, 20, 33, 48–49, 90–93, 98–105).

5. Dialogical Analysis of the Representation of Violence

1 There are of course some debates on these numbers. The lower numbers (500,000 and below) that were circulated by official Israeli state discourse and the higher numbers (one million and over) that were circulated by Arab states are disputed in most academic studies. The 700,000 to 750,000 range (which is Rashid Khalidi's number; 2001, p. 12) and the approximate 55 per cent of the total population in Mandatory Palestine (75–80 per cent of the total population in what became Israel) are more or less agreed upon in academic study. The Israeli historian Ilan Pappé puts the number at 800,000 people, which remains roughly 55 per cent of the total population in Mandatory Palestine (Pappé, 2007, p. xiii).

2 Morris argues these points in numerous places. The preface to *Righteous Victims* offers a succinct and concise view of Morris's approach to the study of history (Morris, 2001, pp. xiii–xiv).

3 For a discussion and analysis of Israeli historiography more generally, its relation to Zionism, and the place of the revisionist historians within Israeli historiography, as well as the development of a post-revisionist or post-post-Zionist historiography, see, for example, Nimni (2003) and Likhovski (2010).

4 For a critical examination of Morris's theoretical and analytical framework as well as a critique of Morris's work on the level of his "facts," see, for example, Lockman (1989, pp. 190–195), Finkelstein (1991), and Masalha

(1991). Morris certainly does not pay much attention to (nor does he properly understand) the challenges that have been raised against such a historiography by a variety of different schools of thought such as postcolonialism, the history of the present literature, or ethnographic studies that pay close attention to materials and sources outside of official documentation (e.g., oral histories).

5 The use of the term Palestinian or Arab "exodus" harkens to Judean notions of a lost people who must wonder the desert first before they reach their "true" promised land, which, whatever it may be, is at the very least *not* the land from which the exodus occurred. In other words, these Palestinian refugees are never going back to the land from which their "exodus" occurred. Needless to say, one could write an entire book on the notion of "exodus" in Judean thinking, but this general description of the term seems to correspond with how Morris understands the Palestinian "exodus."

6 Palestinian historians and, just as importantly, Palestinian oral histories knew, spoke, and wrote about these atrocities and constantly recount them.

7 Yishuv, which literally means "settlement," was the name of the Jewish community in the British Mandate of Palestine before the establishment of the state of Israel.

8 For samples of direct quotes from Ben-Gurion that suggest his thinking and position on the matter, see Morris (2004, pp. 47–48, 50, 55, 313–314, 360, 379, 431, 555–561, 597).

9 An example of Morris's explicit understanding of this trend toward secrecy and the strategic separation between what was publicly stated and what was internally understood is found in *Righteous Victims* as well: "For many Zionists, beginning with Herzl, the only realistic solution lay in transfer.... Publicly they all continued to speak of coexistence and to attribute the violence [during the 1920s–1930s] to a small minority of zealots and agitators. But this was merely a public pose, designed to calm the worried inhabitants and the troubled British" (Morris, 2001, pp. 139–140). There are numerous other examples in this book roughly spanning the period 1900–85 (e.g., Morris, 2001, pp. 246–247, 265, 278–279, 311, 338–343, 454–455, 530–531, 540–549).

10 This is evident in a subtle form throughout *The Birth*, but more explicitly in the conclusion (Morris, 2004, pp. 588–601, particularly in some of the statements made on pp. 590, 598–600). I found Morris's views more explicit throughout *Righteous Victims*, particularly in his discussions on more contemporary events. See also Morris's well-known interview with Ari Shavit (2004).

11 Another example of this is found in Morris's discussion on transfer after the 1948 war: "In general ... the political desire to have as few Arabs as

possible in the Jewish State and the need for empty villages to house new immigrants meshed with the strategic desire to achieve 'Arab-clear' frontiers and secure internal lines of communication. It was the IDF that set the policy in motion, with the civil and political authorities often giving approval after the fact" (Morris, 2004, p. 505).

12 In *Righteous Victims*, Morris also highlights the element of fear as "the chief motor of Arab antagonism to Zionism" (2001, pp. 37, 62–65).

13 The name of the organized Jewish forces before the 1948 war. After the establishment of the state of Israel, they became known as the Israeli Defense Forces (IDF).

14 The group names translate to "National Military Organization" (IZL) and to "Freedom Fighters of Israel" (LHI), who are also known as the "Stern Gang." Both of these groups were disbanded with the establishment of the Israeli state in 1948, and their members absorbed into the Israeli Defense Forces, but not without incidents, which I need not delve into here. It is also important to note that many right-wing leaders and parties emerged from these two groups (e.g., the Irgun was the political predecessor to future right-wing parties in Israel such as the Likud; the Israeli prime minister during parts of the 1980s, Yitzhak Shamir, was a prominent leader in LHI).

15 For an example in addition to Deir Yassin, see his representation of the atrocities committed in the village of Dawayima, where, among other things, one soldier spoke of children being killed by having their heads broken with sticks (Morris, 2004, pp. 469–470).

16 Morris's addition.

17 My addition.

18 Morris's addition.

19 AHC was a political organization that acted as the national leadership of the Palestinian Arab community. The AHC was indeed unified at the outset of its formation and was an integral part of the 1936 revolt and general strike against the British Mandate and the Zionist enterprise. Having said that, the organization, which was chaired by the mufti of Jerusalem, Hajj Amin al-Husayni, was by no means a total or unified representative of the community. Divisions between its prominent members from the Husayni and Nashashibi families soon emerged, and the AHC was effectively divided by the British, who successfully brought down the revolt and ended the strike. I cannot delve into the history of the Husayni-Nashashibi rivalry here, but needless to say, there existed some deep divisions within Palestinian society that in many ways were manifested in, and in other ways created through, this political rivalry between the two families. These divisions were exploited with great success by both the British and the Yishuv (see Khalidi, 1997).

20 Morris states in this discussion that the Zionist leadership always understood that armed conflict would be an integral part of the means mentioned in this quote (2001, pp. 49–50).

21 The use of terms such as "mobs" and "riots" in this case – even if unintentional – is not accidental, since it constitutes the Palestinian Arabs as unruly and mindless vandals, criminals, and murderers engaged in illegitimate forms of violence, as opposed to the rule of law, order, and legitimate monopoly on violence that is supposedly found in the state. This is not surprising, and is indeed predictable, given Morris's alignment with the state, as I argued earlier.

22 This feature continues in Morris's (2009) *One State, Two States*, where he argues that the one-state solution is simply another effort by the Palestinians to drive out Jewish claims to the land and make all of the land, more or less, strictly Palestinian. His proposed solution is to create a federalized state in Jordan/West Bank/Gaza that would be jointly run by the Hashemites and the Palestinians, and this would ensure that all of the Palestinian refugees from 1948 and beyond would have ample new spaces in Jordan to move into. Once again, this illustrates Morris's zero-sum viewpoint and how his discourse operates on the expulsion of the other and aims to silence the voices of the expelled.

23 In contrast, when Said talks about Deir Yassin, he is concerned with what the position of the victim tells us, and not with the validating and legitimating discourse of the state (Said, 2001, pp. 156–159).

References

Adams, M. (2006). Hybridizing habitus and reflexivity: Towards an understanding of contemporary identity? *Sociology, 40*(3), 511–528.

Agamben, G. (1999a [1984]). The thing itself. In D. Heller-Roazen (Trans. & Ed.), *Potentialities: Collected essays in philosophy* (pp. 27–47). Stanford, CA: Stanford University Press.

Agamben, G. (1999b [1990]). *Pardes*: The writing of potentiality. In D. Heller-Roazen (Trans. & Ed.), *Potentialities: Collected essays in philosophy* (pp. 205–219). Stanford, CA: Stanford University Press.

Agamben, G. (2005 [1999]). *Remnants of Auschwitz: The witness and the archive* (Trans. D. Heller-Roazen). New York, NY: Zone Books.

Alexander, J. C. (2008). Clifford Geertz and the strong program: The human sciences and cultural sociology. *Cultural Sociology, 2*(2), 157–168.

Alexander, J. C. (2012). *Trauma: A social theory*. Malden, MA: Polity Press.

Anidjar, G. (2003). *The Jew, the Arab: A history of the enemy*. Stanford, CA: Stanford University Press.

Arendt, H. (1969). *On violence*. San Diego and New York, NY: Harcourt Brace & Company.

Arendt, H. (1973 [1951]). *The origins of totalitarianism* (New ed., with added prefaces). New York, NY: A Harvest Book, Harcourt.

Arendt, H. (2006 [1963]). *Eichmann in Jerusalem: A report on the banality of evil* (Penguin Classics ed., with an introduction by A. Elon). New York, NY: Penguin Books.

Ayyash, M. (2007). The appearance of war in discourse: The neoconservatives on Iraq. *Constellations: An International Journal of Critical and Democratic Theory, 14*(4), 613–634.

Ayyash, M. (2010a). Hamas and the Israeli state: A "violent dialogue." *European Journal of International Relations, 16*(1), 103–123.

Ayyash, M. (2010b). Edward Said: Writing in exile. *Comparative Studies of South Asia, Africa and the Middle East, 30*(1), 107–118.

Ayyash, M. (2013). The paradox of political violence. *European Journal of Social Theory, 16*(3), 342–356.

Balibar, É. (2015). *Violence and civility: On the limits of political philosophy* (Trans. G. M. Goshgarian). New York, NY: Columbia University Press.

Baudrillard, J. (2003). *The spirit of terrorism and other essays* (Trans. C. Turner). New York, NY: Verso.

Bauman, Z. (1989). *Modernity and the Holocaust.* Cambridge: Polity Press.

Benjamin, W. (2004 [1921]). Critique of violence (Trans. E. Jephcott). In M. Bullock & M. W. Jennings (Eds.), *Walter Benjamin: Selected writings, 1913–1926* (Vol. 1, pp. 236–252). Cambridge, MA: The Belknap Press of Harvard University Press.

Bernstein, R. J. (2013). *Violence: Thinking without banisters.* Malden, MA: Polity Press.

Bhabha, H. K. (1994). *The location of culture.* New York, NY: Routledge.

Bhambra, G. K. (2007). *Rethinking modernity: Postcolonialism and the sociological imagination.* New York, NY: Palgrave Macmillan.

Bhambra, G. K. (2014). *Connected sociologies.* New York, NY: Bloomsbury.

Birmingham, P. (2011). Arendt and Hobbes: Glory, sacrificial violence, and the political imagination. *Research in Phenomenology, 41*(1), 1–22.

Blasim, H. (2009). *The madman of freedom square* (Trans. J. Wright). Great Britain: Comma Press.

Bloom, M. (2005). *Dying to kill: The allure of suicide terror.* New York, NY: Columbia University Press.

Boqa'i, N. (2005). Patterns of internal displacement, social adjustment and the challenge of return. In N. Masalha (Ed.), *Catastrophe remembered: Palestine, Israel and the internal refugees* (pp. 73–112). New York, NY: Zed Books.

Bourdieu, P. (1990). *The logic of practice.* Stanford, CA: Stanford University Press.

Bourdieu, P. (1998). *Practical reason: On the theory of action.* Stanford, CA: Stanford University Press.

Bourdieu, P. (2000). Symbolic violence and political struggles. In *Pascalian Meditations* (Trans. R. Nice, pp. 164–182). Stanford, CA: Stanford University Press.

Bufacchi, V. (2007). *Violence and social justice.* New York, NY: Palgrave Macmillan.

Burke, A. (2007). *Beyond security, ethics and violence: War against the other.* New York, NY: Routledge.

Butler, J. (2004). *Precarious life: The powers of mourning and violence.* New York, NY: Verso.

Butler, J. (2010). *Frames of war: When is life grievable?* New York, NY: Verso.

Caputo, J. D. (1987). *Radical hermeneutics: Repetition, deconstruction, and the hermeneutic project.* Indianapolis: Indiana University Press.

Caputo, J. D. (1997). Khôra: Being serious with Plato. In J. D. Caputo (Ed.), *Deconstruction in a nutshell* (pp. 71–105). New York, NY: Fordham University Press.

Cavell, S. (1979). *The claim of reason: Wittgenstein, skepticism, morality, and tragedy.* New York, NY: Oxford University Press.

Cavell, S. (2002a [1958]). Must we mean what we say? In *Must we mean what we say? A book of essays* (Updated ed., pp. 1–43). Cambridge, UK: Cambridge University Press.

Cavell, S. (2002b [1965]). Austin at criticism. In *Must we mean what we say? A book of essays* (Updated ed., pp. 97–114). Cambridge, UK: Cambridge University Press.

Cockburn, C. (2004 [1999]). The continuum of violence: A gender perspective on war and peace. In W. Giles & J. Hyndman (Eds.), *Sites of violence: Gender and conflict zones* (pp. 24–44). Berkeley: University of California Press.

Cockburn, C. (2012). *Anti-militarism: Political and gender dynamics of peace movements.* New York, NY: Palgrave Macmillan.

Collins, R. (2008). *Violence: A micro-sociological theory.* Princeton: Princeton University Press.

Coulthard, G. (2014). *Red skin, white masks: Rejecting the colonial politics of recognition.* Minneapolis: University of Minnesota Press.

Critchley, S. (1999). *The ethics of deconstruction: Derrida and Levinas* (2nd ed.). West Lafayette, IN: Purdue University Press.

Croce, M. (2015). The *habitus* and the critique of the present: A Wittgensteinian reading of Bourdieu's social theory. *Sociological Theory, 33*(4), 327–346.

Dallmayr, F. (1989). Hermeneutics and deconstruction: Gadamer and Derrida in dialogue. In D. Michelfelder & R. Palmer (Eds.), *Dialogue and deconstruction: The Gadamer-Derrida encounter* (pp. 75–92). New York, NY: State University of New York Press.

Dallmayr, F. (2001). *Achieving our world: Toward a global and plural democracy.* Lanham, MD: Rowman & Littlefield.

Dallmayr, F. (2002). *Dialogue among civilizations: Some exemplary voices.* New York, NY: Palgrave Macmillan.

Daniel, E. V. (1996). *Charred lullabies: Chapters in an anthropology of violence.* Princeton: Princeton University Press.

Darwish, M. (1995 [1986]). *Memory for forgetfulness* (Trans. I. Muhawi). Berkeley, CA: California University Press.

Darwish, M. (2010 [2006]). *Absent presence* (Trans. M. Shaheen). London: Hesperus Press.

Das, V. (1998). Wittgenstein and anthropology. *Annual Review of Anthropology, 27,* 171–195.

Das, V. (2007). *Life and words: Violence and the descent into the ordinary.* Berkeley: University of California Press.

Das, V., & Kleinman, A. (2000). Introduction. In V. Das, A. Kleinman, M. Ramphele, & P. Reynolds (Eds.), *Violence and subjectivity* (pp. 1–18). Berkeley: University of California Press.

Das, V., Kleinman, A., Ramphele, M., & Reynolds, P. (Eds.). (2000). *Violence and subjectivity.* Berkeley: University of California Press.

Davidson, B. (1978). *Africa in modern history: The search for a new society.* London: Allen Lane.

Deleuze, G., & Guattari, F. (1987). Treatise on nomadology: The war machine. In *A thousand plateaus: Capitalism and schizophrenia* (Trans. B. Massumi, pp. 351–423). Minneapolis: University of Minnesota Press.

Derrida, J. (1973 [1967]). *Speech and phenomena: And other essays on Husserl's theory of signs* (Trans. D. B. Allison, preface by N. Garver). Evanston, IL: Northwestern University Press.

Derrida, J. (1978 [1964]). Violence and metaphysics: An essay on the thought of Emmanuel Levinas. In *Writing and difference* (Trans. A. Bass, pp. 79–153). Chicago: University of Chicago Press.

Derrida, J. (1988 [1972]). Signature event context (Trans. S. Weber & J. Mehlman). In G. Graff (Ed.), *Limited Inc* (pp. 1–23). Evanston, IL: Northwestern University Press.

Derrida, J. (1989 [1984]). Three questions to Hans-Georg Gadamer. In D. Michelfelder & R. Palmer (Trans. & Eds.), *Dialogue and deconstruction: The Gadamer-Derrida encounter* (pp. 52–54). New York, NY: State University of New York Press.

Derrida, J. (1993). *Aporias* (Trans. T. Dutoit). Stanford, CA: Stanford University Press.

Derrida, J. (1997a [1967]). *Of grammatology* (Corrected ed., Trans. G. C. Spivak). Baltimore: Johns Hopkins University Press.

Derrida, J. (1997b). The Villanova roundtable: A conversation with Jacques Derrida. In J. D. Caputo (Ed.), *Deconstruction in a nutshell* (pp. 3–28). New York, NY: Fordham University Press.

Derrida, J. (2002 [1990]). Force of law: The "mystical foundation of authority" (Trans. M. Quaintance). In G. Anidjar (Ed.), *Acts of religion* (pp. 228–298). New York, NY: Routledge.

Derrida, J. (2005 [1994]). *Politics of friendship* (Trans. G. Collins). New York, NY: Verso.

Devji, F. (2005). *Landscapes of the jihad: Militancy, morality, modernity.* New York, NY: Cornell University Press.

Duffield, M. (2001). *Global governance and the new wars: The merging of development and security.* New York, NY: Zed Books.

Edkins, J. (2003). *Trauma and the memory of politics*. Cambridge: Cambridge University Press.

Elias, N. (1982). Civilization and violence: On the state monopoly of physical violence and its infringements. *Telos*, (54) (Winter), 134–154.

Elias, N. (2000 [1939]). *The civilizing process: Sociogenetic and psychogenetic investigations* (Revised ed., Trans. J. Jephcott, Eds. E. Dunning, J. Goudsblom, S. Mennell). Malden, MA: Blackwell Publishing.

Engels, F. (2007 [1878]). Anti-Dühring. In B. Lawrence & A. Karim (Eds.), *On violence* (pp. 40–61). Durham, NC: Duke University Press.

Enloe, C. (2013). *Seriously!: Investigating crashes and crises as if women mattered*. Berkeley: University of California Press.

Enloe, C. (2014). *Bananas, beaches and bases: Making feminist sense of international politics* (2nd ed.). Berkeley: University of California Press.

Euben, R. (2002). Jihad and political violence. *Current History, 101*(658), 365–376.

Falk, R. (2013). How to live together well: Interrogating the Israel/Palestine conflict. In E. Weber (Ed.), *Living together: Jacques Derrida's communities of violence and peace* (pp. 275–292). New York, NY: Fordham University Press.

Fanon, F. (1967 [1952]). *Black skin, white masks* (Trans. C. L. Markmann). New York, NY: Grove Press.

Fanon, F. (2004 [1961]). *The wretched of the earth* (Trans. R. Philcox). New York, NY: Grove Press.

Feldman, A. (2000). Violence and vision: The prosthetics and aesthetics of terror. In V. Das, A. Kleinman, M. Ramphele, & P. Reynolds (Eds.), *Violence and subjectivity* (pp. 46–78). Berkeley: University of California Press.

Feldman, S. M. (2000). Made for each other: The interdependence of deconstruction and philosophical hermeneutics. *Philosophy and Social Criticism, 26*(1), 51–70.

Finkelstein, N. (1991). Myths, old and new. *Journal of Palestine Studies, 21*(1), 66–89.

Finlay, C. J. (2009). Hannah Arendt's critique of violence. *Thesis Eleven, 97*(1), 26–45.

Foucault, M. (1972 [1969]). *The archeology of knowledge and the discourse on language* (Trans. A. M. Sheridan Smith). New York, NY: Pantheon Books.

Foucault, M. (1979 [1975]). *Discipline and punish: The birth of the prison* (Trans. A. Sheridan). New York, NY: Vintage Books.

Foucault, M. (1980). *Power/knowledge: Selected interviews and other writings 1972–1977* (Ed. C. Gordon). New York, NY: Pantheon Books.

Foucault, M. (1983). The subject and power (Trans. L. Sawyer). In H. L. Dreyfus & P. Rabinow (Eds.), *Michel Foucault: Beyond structuralism and hermeneutics* (2nd ed., pp. 208–226). Chicago: University of Chicago Press.

Foucault, M. (2003 [1997]). *Society must be defended: Lectures at the Collège de France 1975–1976* (Eds. M. Bertani & A. Fontana, Trans. D. Macey). New York, NY: Picador.

Frazer, E., & Hutchings, K. (2011). Avowing violence: Foucault and Derrida on politics, discourse and meaning. *Philosophy and Social Criticism, 37*(1), 3–23.

Gadamer, H-G. (1977a [1963]). The phenomenological movement. In D. E. Linge (Trans. & Ed.), *Philosophical hermeneutics* (30th Anniversary ed., pp. 130–181). Berkeley: University of California Press.

Gadamer, H-G. (1977b [1964]). Martin Heidegger and Marburg theology. In D. E. Linge (Trans. & Ed.), *Philosophical hermeneutics* (30th anniversary ed., pp. 198–212). Berkeley: University of California Press.

Gadamer, H-G. (1989a [1984]). Text and interpretation (Trans. D. J. Schmidt & R. Palmer). In D. Michelfelder & R. Palmer (Eds.), *Dialogue and deconstruction: The Gadamer-Derrida encounter* (pp. 21–51). New York, NY: State University of New York Press.

Gadamer, H-G. (1989b [1986]). Destruktion and deconstruction (Trans. G. Waite & R. Palmer). In D. Michelfelder & R. Palmer (Eds.), *Dialogue and deconstruction: The Gadamer-Derrida encounter.* New York, NY: State University of New York Press.

Gadamer, H-G. (2004 [1960]). *Truth and method* (2nd revised ed., Trans. J. Weinsheimer & D. G. Marshall). New York, NY: Continuum.

Gadamer, H-G. (2006 [1970]). Language and understanding (Trans. R. Palmer). *Theory, Culture, & Society, 23*(1), 13–27.

Gallie, W. B. (1978). *Philosophers of peace and war: Kant, Clausewitz, Marx, Engels and Tolstoy.* Cambridge, UK: Cambridge University Press.

Galtung, J. (1969). Violence, peace, and peace research. *Journal of Peace Research, 6*(3), 167–191.

Gaston, S. (2009). *Derrida, literature and war: Absence and the chance of meeting.* New York, NY: Continuum.

Geldard, R. (2000). *Remembering Heraclitus.* Great Barrington, USA: Lindisfarne Books.

Giles, W., & Hyndman, J. (2004). New directions for feminist research and politics. In W. Giles & J. Hyndman (Eds.), *Sites of violence: Gender and conflict zones* (pp. 301–315). Berkeley: University of California Press.

Gilroy, P. (1993). *The black Atlantic: Modernity and double consciousness.* Cambridge, MA: Harvard University Press.

Gilroy, P. (2000). *Against race: Imagining political culture beyond the color line.* Cambridge, MA: Harvard University Press.

Girard, R. (1965 [1961]). *Deceit, desire and the novel: Self and other in literary structure* (Trans. Y. Freccero). Baltimore: Johns Hopkins University Press.

Girard, R. (1977 [1972]). *Violence and the sacred* (Trans. P. Gregory). Baltimore: Johns Hopkins University Press.

Girard, R. (1986 [1982]). *The scapegoat* (Trans. Y. Freccero). Baltimore: Johns Hopkins University Press.

Girard, R. (1987 [1978]). *Things hidden since the foundation of the world* (Trans. S. Bann & M. Metteer); Research undertaken in collaboration with Jean-Michel Oughourlian & Guy Lefort. Stanford, CA: Stanford University Press.

Girard, R. (1992). Origins: A view from the literature. In F. J. Varela & J. P. Dupuy (Eds.), *Understanding origins: Contemporary views on the origin of life, mind and society* (pp. 27–42). Dordrecht, Boston & London: Kluwer Academic Publishers.

Girard, R. (2002). What is happening today is mimetic rivalry on a global scale (Interview conducted by H. Tincq, Trans. T. C. Hilde). *South Central Review, 19*(2–3), 22–27.

Girard, R., Antonello, P., & de Castro Rocha, J. C. (2007). *Evolution and conversion: Dialogues on the origins of culture.* New York, NY: T & T Clark.

Gramsci, A. (1971 [1929–1935]). *Selections from the prison notebooks of Antonio Gramsci* (Trans. & Eds. Q. Hoare & G. N. Smith). New York, NY: International Publishers.

Hanssen, B. (2000). *Critique of violence: Between poststructuralism and critical theory.* London: Routledge.

Hardt, M., & Negri, A. (2004). *Multitude: War and democracy in the age of empire.* New York, NY: Penguin Press.

Hearn, J. (2013). The sociological significance of domestic violence: Tensions, paradoxes and implications. *Current Sociology, 61*(2), 152–170.

Heidegger, M. (1962 [1927]). *Being and time* (Trans. J. Macquarrie & E. Robinson). Cambridge, USA: Blackwell Publishing.

Heidegger, M. (1993 [1961]). On the essence of truth (Trans. J. Sallis). In D. F. Krell (Ed.), *Martin Heidegger: Basic writings* (Revised & expanded ed., pp. 111–138). New York, NY: Harper Collins.

Hochberg, G. Z. (2007). *In spite of partition: Jews, Arabs, and the limits of separatist imagination.* Princeton: Princeton University Press.

Horkheimer, M., & Adorno, T. W. (2002 [1947]). *Dialectic of enlightenment: Philosophical fragments* (Ed. G. S. Noerr, Trans. E. Jephcott). Stanford, CA: Stanford University Press.

Jabri, V. (2006). Shock and Awe: Power and the resistance of art. *Millennium: Journal of International Studies, 34*(3), 819–839.

Jay, M. (2003). *Refractions of violence.* New York, NY: Routledge.

Joas, H. (2003). *War and modernity* (Trans. R. Livingstone). Cambridge, UK: Polity Press; Malden, MA: Blackwell Publishing.

Kaempf, S. (2009). Violence and victory: Guerrilla warfare, "authentic self-affirmation" and the overthrow of the colonial state. *Third World Quarterly, 30*(1), 129–146.

Kafka, F. (2002 [1915]). *Metamorphosis and other stories* (Trans. R. Stokes). London: Hesperus Press.

Kayyali', A-W. (1978). *Palestine: A modern history*. London: Croom Helm.

Kearney, R. (2002). Strangers and others: From deconstruction to hermeneutics. *Critical Horizons, 3*(1), 7–36.

Khalidi, R. (1997). *Palestinian identity: The construction of modern national consciousness*. New York, NY: Columbia University Press.

Khalidi, R. (2001). The Palestinians and 1948: The underlying causes of failure. In E. L. Rogan & A. Shlaim (Eds.), *The war for Palestine: Rewriting the history of 1948* (pp. 12–36). Cambridge: Cambridge University Press.

Khalidi, W. (1984). *Before their diaspora: A photographic history of the Palestinians 1876–1948*. Washington, DC: Institute for Palestine Studies.

Khalidi, W. (Ed.). (1992). *All that remains: The Palestinian villages occupied and depopulated by Israel in 1948*. Washington, DC: Institute for Palestine Studies.

Kögler, H. H. (1999 [1992]). *The power of dialogue: Critical hermeneutics after Gadamer and Foucault* (Trans. P. Hendrickson). Cambridge, MA: The MIT Press.

Krohn-Hansen, C. (1997). The anthropology and ethnography of political violence. *Journal of Peace Research, 34*(2), 233–240.

Kurtz, M. M., & Kurtz, L. R. (Eds.). (2015). *Women, war, and violence: Topography, resistance, and hope* (2 vols.). Santa Barbara, CA: Praeger.

Laclau, E. (2000). Identity and hegemony: The role of universality in the constitution of political logics. In J. Butler, E. Laclau, & S. Žižek (Eds.), *Contingency, hegemony, universality* (pp. 44–89). New York, NY: Verso.

Laurier Decoteau, C. (2013). Hybrid habitus: Toward a post-colonial theory of practice. In J. Go (Ed.), *Postcolonial sociology* (pp. 263–293). Bingley, UK: Emerald.

Lawrence, P. (1997). *Modernity and war: The creed of absolute violence*. New York, NY: St. Martin's Press.

Likhovski, A. (2010). Post-post-Zionist historiography. *Israel Studies, 15*(2), 1–23.

Linge, D. (1977). Editor's introduction. In D. E. Linge (Trans. & Ed.), *Philosophical hermeneutics* (30th anniversary ed., pp. xi–lviii). Berkeley: University of California Press.

Lockman, Z. (1989). Original sin. In Z. Lockman & J. Beinin (Eds.), *Intifada: The Palestinian uprising against Israeli occupation* (pp. 185–203). Toronto: Between the Lines.

Lutz, C. (2001). *Homefront: A military city and the American twentieth century*. Boston: Beacon Press.

Malešević, S. (2013). Forms of brutality: Towards a historical sociology of violence. *European Journal of Social Theory, 16*(3), 273–291.

Malešević, S., & Ryan, K. (2013). The disfigured ontology of figurational sociology: Norbert Elias and the question of violence. *Critical Sociology, 39*(2), 165–181.

Mamdani, M. (1996). *Citizen and subject: Contemporary Africa and the legacy of late colonialism.* Princeton: Princeton University Press.

Mamdani, M. (2001). *When victims become killers: Colonialism, nativism, and the genocide in Rwanda.* Princeton: Princeton University Press.

Mann, M. (2005). *The dark side of democracy: Explaining ethnic cleansing.* New York, NY: Columbia University Press.

Masalha, N. (1991). A critique of Benny Morris. *Journal of Palestine Studies, 21*(1), 90–97.

Masalha, N. (1997). *Land without a people: Israel, transfer, and the Palestinians, 1949–1996.* London: Faber and Faber.

Masalha, N. (2003). *The politics of denial: Israel and the Palestinian refugee problem.* Sterling, VA: Pluto Press.

Massad, J. A. (2002 [2006]). History on the line: Joseph Massad and Benny Morris discuss the Middle East. In *The persistence of the Palestinian question: Essays on Zionism and the Palestinians* (pp. 154–165). New York, NY: Routledge.

Massad, J. A. (2006). *The persistence of the Palestinian question: Essays on Zionism and the Palestinians.* New York, NY: Routledge.

Massad, J. A. (2013). Forget semitism! In E. Weber (Ed.), *Living together: Jacques Derrida's communities of violence and peace* (pp. 59–79). New York, NY: Fordham University Press.

Mbembe, A. (2003). Necropolitics (Trans. L. Meintjes). *Public Culture, 15*(1), 11–40.

McKenna, A. J. (1992a). *Violence and difference: Girard, Derrida, and deconstruction.* Chicago: University of Illinois Press.

McKenna, A. J. (1992b). Supplement to apocalypse: Girard and Derrida. In F. J. Varela & J-P. Dupuy (Eds.), *Understanding origins: Contemporary views on the origin of life, mind and society* (pp. 45–76). Boston: Kluwer Academic Publishers.

Mennell, S. (2017). Norbert Elias's contribution to Andrew Linklater's contribution to international relations. *Review of International Studies, 43*(4), 654–670.

Miller, S. (2014). *War after death: On violence and its limits.* New York, NY: Fordham University Press.

Monk, D. B. (2002). *An aesthetic occupation: The immediacy of architecture and the Palestine conflict.* Durham, NC: Duke University Press.

Morris, B. (1991). Response to Finkelstein and Masalha. *Journal of Palestine Studies, 21*(1), 98–114.

266   References

Morris, B. (1995). Falsifying the record: A fresh look at Zionist documentation of 1948. *Journal of Palestine Studies, 24*(3), 44–62.

Morris, B. (2001). *Righteous victims: A history of the Zionist-Arab conflict, 1881–2001.* New York, NY: Vintage Books.

Morris, B. (2004). *The birth of the Palestinian refugee problem revisited.* Cambridge, UK: Cambridge University Press.

Morris, B. (2005). The historiography of Deir Yassin. *The Journal of Israeli History: Politics, Society, Culture, 24*(1), 79–107.

Morris, B. (2009). *One state, two states: Resolving the Israel/Palestine conflict.* New Haven: Yale University Press.

Mouffe, C. (2005). *The democratic paradox.* New York, NY: Verso.

Mouffe, C. (2013). *Agonistics: Thinking the world politically.* New York, NY: Verso.

Moules, N. J., McCaffrey, G., Field, J. C., & Laing, C. M. (2015). *Conducting hermeneutic research: From philosophy to practice.* New York, NY: Peter Lang.

Nimni, E. (Ed.). (2003). *The challenge of post-Zionism: Alternatives to Israeli fundamentalist politics.* New York, NY: Zed Books.

Oksala, J. (2010). Violence and the biopolitics of modernity. *Foucault Studies, 10,* 23–43.

Pape, R. (2003). The strategic logic of suicide terrorism. *American Political Science Review, 9*(3), 343–361.

Pappé, I. (2007). *The ethnic cleansing of Palestine.* Oxford: Oneworld.

Philipose, L. (2007). The politics of pain and the end of empire. *International Feminist Journal of Politics, 9*(1), 60–81.

Pilisuk, M., & Rountree, J. A. (2015). *The hidden structure of violence: Who benefits from global violence and war.* New York, NY: Monthly Review Press.

Pinker, S. (2011). *The better angels of our nature: The decline of violence and its causes.* New York, NY: Allen and Lane.

Rabinow, P., & Sullivan, W. M. (1987). The interpretive turn: A second look. In P. Rabinow & W. M. Sullivan (Eds.), *Interpretive social science: A second look.* Berkeley: University of California Press.

Ricoeur, P. (1994 [1990]). *Oneself as another* (Trans. K. Balmey). Chicago: University of Chicago Press.

Robespierre, M. (2007). *Virtue and terror* (Introduction by Slavoj Žižek, Text Selected by Jean Ducange, Trans. J. Howe). New York, NY: Verso.

Said, E. (1994). *Culture and imperialism.* New York, NY: Vintage Books.

Said, E. (1995). *The politics of dispossession: The struggle for Palestinian self-determination, 1969–1994.* New York, NY: Vintage Books.

Said, E. (2001). *The end of the peace process: Oslo and after.* New York, NY: Vintage Books.

Said, E. (2002a). *Reflections on exile and other essays.* Cambridge, MA: Harvard University Press.

Said, E. (2002b). *Power, politics, and culture: Interviews with Edward W. Said* (Ed. G. Viswanathan). New York, NY: Vintage Books.

Said, E. (2003 [1979]). *Orientalism*. New York, NY: Vintage Books.

Sayigh, R. (2007 [1979]). *The Palestinians: From peasants to revolutionaries*. New York, NY: Zed Books.

Scarry, E. (1985). *The body in pain: The making and unmaking of the world*. New York, NY: Oxford University Press.

Scheper-Hughes, N., & Bourgois, P. (2004). Introduction: Making sense of violence. In N. Scheper-Hughes & P. Bourgois (Eds.), *Violence in war and peace: An anthology* (pp. 1–31). Malden, MA: Blackwell Publishing.

Schmidt, B. E., & Schröder, I. W. (Eds.). (2001). *Anthropology of violence and conflict*. New York, NY: Routledge.

Schmitt, C. (1996 [1932]). *The concept of the political* (Trans. G. Schwab). Chicago: University of Chicago Press.

Shapiro, M. J. (1997). *Violent cartographies: Mapping cultures of war*. Minnesota: University of Minnesota Press.

Sharoni, S., Welland, J., Steiner, L., & Pedersen, J. (Eds.). (2016). *Handbook on gender and war*. Cheltenham, UK: Edward Elgar Publishing.

Shavit, A. (2004). *Survival of the fittest? An interview with Benny Morris*. Retrieved August 5, 2017, from http://www.logosjournal.com/morris.htm. Originally appeared in *Haaretz*.

Simpson, L. B. (2014). Land as pedagogy: Nishnaabeg intelligence and rebellious transformation. *Decolonization: Indigeneity, Education & Society, 3*(3), 1–25.

Singer, B. (1990). Violence in the French revolution: Forms of ingestion/ forms of expulsion. In F. Fehér (Ed.), *The French revolution and the birth of modernity*. Berkeley: University of California Press.

Smith, D. (1990). *The conceptual practices of power: A feminist sociology of knowledge*. Toronto: University of Toronto Press.

Sorel, G. (1999 [1908]). *Reflections on violence* (Ed. J. Jennings). Cambridge: Cambridge University Press.

Tamdgidi, M. H. (2007). Intersecting autobiography, history, and theory: The subtler global violences of colonialism and racism in Fanon, Said, and Anzaldúa. *Human Architecture, 5*(3), 113–136.

Taussig, M. (1987). *Shamanism, colonialism, and the wild man: A study in terror and healing*. Chicago: University of Chicago Press.

Taussig, M. (1993). *Mimesis and alterity: A particular history of the senses*. New York, NY: Routledge.

Taylor, C. (1985). *Philosophy and the human sciences*. In *Philosophical Papers* (Vol. 2). Cambridge, UK: Cambridge University Press.

Thorpe, C. (2004). Violence and the scientific vocation. *Theory, Culture & Society, 21*(3), 59–84.

Tilly, C. (2003). *The politics of collective violence*. Cambridge, MA: Cambridge University Press.

Van Krieken, R. (1998). *Norbert Elias*. New York, NY: Routledge.

Von Holdt, K. (2012). The violence of order, orders of violence: Between Fanon and Bourdieu. *Current Sociology, 61*(2), 112–131.

Walby, S. (2012). Violence and society: Introduction to an emerging field of sociology. *Current Sociology, 61*(2), 95–111.

Weber, M. (1958a). Politics as a vocation. In H. H. Gerth & C. W. Mills (Trans. & Eds.), *From Max Weber: Essays in sociology* (pp. 77–128). New York, NY: Oxford University Press.

Weber, M. (1958b). Science as a vocation. In H. H. Gerth & C. W. Mills (Trans. & Eds.), *From Max Weber: Essays in sociology* (pp. 129–156). New York, NY: Oxford University Press.

Weheliye, A. G. (2014). *Habeas viscus: Racializing assemblages, biopolitics, and black feminist theories of the human*. Duke, NC: Duke University Press.

Weizman, E. (2006a, March–April). Walking through walls: Soldiers as architects in the Israeli-Palestinian conflict. *Radical Philosophy, 136*, 8–22.

Weizman, E. (2006b). *The art of war: Deleuze, Guattari, Debord and the Israeli defense force*. Retrieved August 5, 2017, from http://www.metamute.org/editorial/articles/art-war-deleuze-guattari-debord-and-israeli-defence-force.

White, H. (1978). *Tropics of discourse: Essays in cultural criticism*. Baltimore: Johns Hopkins University Press.

Wieviorka, M. (2009 [2005]). *Violence: A new approach* (Trans. D. Macey). Los Angeles, CA: Sage.

Wise, C. (2009). *Derrida, Africa, and the Middle East*. New York, NY: Palgrave Macmillan.

Wittgenstein, L. (1973 [1953]). *Philosophical investigations* (The English text of the Third Edition, Trans. G. E. M. Anscombe). New York, NY: Macmillan Publishing.

Wittgenstein, L. (2005 [1921]). *Tractatus logico-philosophicus* (Trans. D. F. Pears & B. F. McGuiness, with an introduction by B. Russell). New York, NY: Routledge.

Wittgenstein, L. (2006 [1969]). *On certainty* (Eds. G. E. M. Anscombe & G. H. von Wright, Trans. D. Paul & G. E. M. Anscombe). Malden, MA: Blackwell Publishing.

Wittrock, B. (2001). History, war and the transcendence of modernity. *European Journal of Social Theory, 4*(1), 53–72.

Young, R. J. C. (1995). *Colonial desire: Hybridity in theory, culture and race*. New York, NY: Routledge.

Yuval-Davis, N. (2004). Gender, the nationalist imagination, war, and peace. In W. Giles & J. Hyndman (Eds.), *Sites of violence: Gender and conflict zones* (pp. 170–189). Berkeley: University of California Press.

Žižek, S. (2004). *Iraq: The borrowed kettle*. London and New York, NY: Verso.

Žižek, S. (2008). *Violence*. New York, NY: Picador.

Index